RAWLS'S *A THEC*

A Theory of Justice, by John Rawls, is widely regarded as the most important twentieth-century work of Anglo-American political philosophy. It transformed the field by offering a compelling alternative to the dominant utilitarian conception of social justice. The argument for this alternative is, however, complicated and often confusing. In this book Jon Mandle carefully reconstructs Rawls's argument, showing that the most common interpretations of it are often mistaken. For example, Rawls does not endorse welfare-state capitalism, and he is not a "luck egalitarian" as is widely believed. Mandle also explores the relationship between *A Theory of Justice* and the developments in Rawls's later work, *Political Liberalism*, as well as discussing some of the most influential criticisms in the secondary literature. His book will be an invaluable guide for anyone seeking to engage with this ground-breaking philosophical work.

JON MANDLE is Associate Professor of Philosophy at the University at Albany (SUNY). His previous publications include *What's Left of Liberalism? An Interpretation and Defense of Justice as Fairness* (2000) and *Global Justice* (2006).

CAMBRIDGE INTRODUCTIONS TO KEY PHILOSOPHICAL TEXTS

This new series offers introductory textbooks on what are considered to be the most important texts of Western philosophy. Each book guides the reader through the main themes and arguments of the work in question, while also paying attention to its historical context and its philosophical legacy. No philosophical background knowledge is assumed, and the books will be well suited to introductory university-level courses.

Titles published in the series:

DESCARTES'S *MEDITATIONS* by Catherine Wilson

WITTGENSTEIN'S *PHILOSOPHICAL INVESTIGATIONS* by David G. Stern

WITTGENSTEIN'S *TRACTATUS* by Alfred Nordmann

ARISTOTLE'S *NICOMACHEAN ETHICS* by Michael Pakaluk

SPINOZA'S *ETHICS* by Steven Nadler

KANT'S *CRITIQUE OF PURE REASON* by Jill Vance Buroker

HEIDEGGER'S *BEING AND TIME* by Paul Gorner

KANT'S *GROUNDWORK OF THE METAPHYSICS OF MORALS* by Sally Sedgwick

HEGEL'S *PHENOMENOLOGY OF SPIRIT* by Larry Krasnoff

NIETZSCHE'S *ON THE GENEALOGY OF MORALITY* by Lawrence J. Hatab

HUME'S *A TREATISE OF HUMAN NATURE* by John P. Wright

RAWLS'S *A THEORY OF JUSTICE* by Jon Mandle

RAWLS'S
A THEORY OF JUSTICE

An Introduction

JON MANDLE

The University of Albany (SUNY)

CAMBRIDGE
UNIVERSITY PRESS

CAMBRIDGE UNIVERSITY PRESS
Cambridge, New York, Melbourne, Madrid, Cape Town, Singapore, São Paulo, Delhi

Cambridge University Press
The Edinburgh Building, Cambridge CB2 8RU, UK

Published in the United States of America by Cambridge University Press, New York

www.cambridge.org
Information on this title: www.cambridge.org/9780521853927

First published 2009

Printed in the United Kingdom at the University Press, Cambridge

A catalogue record for this publication is available from the British Library

Library of Congress Cataloguing in Publication data
Mandle, Jon, 1966–
Rawls's 'A theory of justice' : an introduction / Jon Mandle.
p. cm. – (Cambridge introductions to key philosophical texts)
Includes bibliographical references and index.
ISBN 978-0-521-85392-7
1. Rawls, John, 1921–2002. Theory of justice. 2. Justice. I. Title.
JC578.R383M355 2009
320.01'1 – dc22 2009024643

ISBN 978-0-521-85392-7 Hardback
ISBN 978-0-521-64667-3 Paperback

for Jack

Contents

Preface

I was not fortunate enough to know John Rawls personally. However, the interactions that I did have with him were consistent with what virtually everyone who knew him reports – he was generous, modest, and kind. Since our interactions were mostly professional – he was replying to my questions, commenting on papers and ideas – he was serious and focused and very helpful. I wrote to him for the first time soon after I read *A Theory of Justice* in graduate school. I am still amazed that he took the time to respond – as he did whenever I wrote to him over the subsequent years. He was a wonderful role model for a philosopher. It is to his memory that I dedicate this book.

A Theory of Justice was published in 1971. In early 1975 Rawls revised the text in preparation for the German translation. It was not until 1999, however, that this revised text was published in English. Rawls made no attempt to incorporate developments in his theory that occurred between 1975 and 1999 – in particular, he did not make revisions in light of the publication of *Political Liberalism* in 1993. Still, the revised edition includes some significant changes that Rawls regarded as improvements over the original text. It should be regarded as the authoritative text, and I quote from it accordingly. However, owing to the existence of the enormous secondary literature published before 1999, I have cited passages by giving first the page numbers from the original edition and then from the revised edition. Where the editions differ, I have indicated this in a footnote.

Many people contributed to this project. Some did not know they were doing so while others knew it all too well. Those that I wish to thank include Chris Bertram, Harry Brighouse, Josh Cohen, Sam Freeman, Kristen Hessler, Jay Mandle, Joan Mandle, Rex Martin, Pete Murray, Thomas Pogge, Mardy Rawls, David Reidy, Arthur Ripstein,

Karen Schupack, and Anna Schupack, as well as two reviewers from Cambridge University Press. Hilary Gaskin deserves special mention for her great patience and encouragement as editor. Finally, I thank the Belknap Press of Harvard University Press for permission to quote from *A Theory of Justice* by John Rawls, © 1971, 1999 by the President and Fellows of Harvard College.

Introduction

"The smarter you get, the smarter it gets."
(Hilary Putnam on *A Theory of Justice*)

In 1971 the philosophical world was waiting both literally and metaphorically for *A Theory of Justice*. Many philosophers eagerly anticipated it because John Rawls had already published key elements of his theory in a series of articles, and for several years he had circulated drafts of sections of the book. Just a year after its publication, one author began his review by stating that "Rawls' theory of justice is too well-known to need detailed exposition."[1] Metaphorically, the field of political philosophy was waiting for it because, in the words of Isaiah Berlin in 1964, "no commanding work of political philosophy has appeared in the twentieth century."[2] The field was looking for such a work in order to escape from what was widely believed to be its very poor condition. Perhaps the most dramatic expression of this despondent state was Peter Laslett's declaration, in the introduction to his 1956 collection *Philosophy, Politics and Society*, that "For the moment, anyway, political philosophy is dead."[3] This certainly overstated the case, but his identification of "the culprit" revealed clearly what he thought had gone wrong in the field: "The Logical Positivists did it."[4]

[1] B. Parekh, "Reflections on Rawls's Theory of Justice," *Political Studies*, 20 (1972), p. 478.

[2] Isaiah Berlin, "Does Political Theory Still Exist?" in *Philosophy, Politics and Society* (second series), Peter Laslett and W. G. Runciman, eds. (Blackwell, 1964), p. 1.

[3] Peter Laslett, "Introduction" in *Philosophy, Politics and Society*, Peter Laslett, ed. (Blackwell, 1956), p. vii.

[4] *Ibid.*, p. ix. For a contemporaneous analysis that speculates on the explanation for changes in the emphasis and approach to political theory, see P. H. Partridge, "Politics, Philosophy, Ideology," *Political Studies*, 9 (1961). A useful discussion of the period is Brian Barry, "*Political*

The work of T. D. Weldon was characteristic of this approach. In an article included in Laslett's 1956 collection, Weldon declared that "The purpose of philosophy . . . is to expose and elucidate linguistic muddles; it has done its job when it has revealed the confusions which have occurred and are likely to recur in inquiries into matters of fact because the structure and the use of language are what they are."[5] Its purpose is decidedly not to advocate one set of moral principles over another. Individual philosophers, like anyone else, can promote their favored principles, but such advocacy cannot rise to the level of true philosophy. Indeed, it is "dishonest to misstate the logical character of such pronouncements and to claim special status for them; that is, to pretend that they are like the highest grade of physical principles when they are in fact like the lowest."[6] For the purposes of philosophy properly understood, "any set of principles would do equally well."[7]

Although Rawls was not the first political philosopher to reject this vision of philosophy, *A Theory of Justice* burst open the dam and revealed how narrow it had been. Suddenly, vast new areas of enquiry were available to philosophical investigation. It became respectable for political philosophers to defend substantive and even controversial evaluative principles. Rawls showed that philosophical reflection could offer justifications for specific conceptions of justice. Not all principles "would do equally well." When Rawls wrote that "[t]he analysis of moral concepts and the a priori, however traditionally understood, is too slender a basis" from which to develop a substantive theory of justice (*TJ*, 51/44), the logical positivists would have agreed. From that assumption they drew the conclusion that philosophy had no business engaging in such a project at all. *A Theory of Justice*, however, showed how political philosophy can offer a defense of substantive principles by exploring territory beyond the traditional limits of conceptual analysis.

The immense influence of *A Theory of Justice* on contemporary political philosophy is explained in large part by the fact that it brought philosophical respectability to the project of justifying moral

Argument after Twenty-Five Years: An Introduction to the Reissue" in *Political Argument: A Reissue with a New Introduction* (University of California Press, 1990).

5 T. D. Weldon, "Political Principles" in Laslett, *Philosophy, Politics and Society*, p. 23.

6 *Ibid.*, p. 33. 7 *Ibid.*, p. 34.

principles. Almost as important, however, was the content of the principles that it defended. While there certainly were some dissenters, when the book was published there was a widespread assumption that some form of utilitarianism must be correct. One of Rawls's central tasks was to "offer an alternative systematic account of justice that is superior . . . to the dominant utilitarianism of the tradition." (*TJ*, viii/xviii) By the end of the decade, H. L. A. Hart could write:

> We are currently witnessing, I think, the progress of a transition from a once widely accepted old faith that some form of utilitarianism, if only we could discover the right form, *must* capture the essence of political morality. The new faith is that the truth must lie not with a doctrine that takes the maximization of aggregate or average general welfare for its goal, but with a doctrine of basic human rights, protecting specific basic liberties and interests of individuals, if only we could find some sufficiently firm foundations for such rights to meet some long-familiar objections.[8]

With the publication of *A Theory of Justice*, utilitarianism – which holds that morality requires that we maximize the aggregate or average level of happiness – could no longer be taken for granted.

It would be hard to overstate the importance of *A Theory of Justice* to political and ethical philosophy. It was not unusual for reviewers to compare Rawls's work to that of the giants in the history of philosophy such as John Stuart Mill and Immanuel Kant.[9] Whatever their many disagreements, virtually all contemporary political philosophers recognize the centrality of John Rawls's great 1971 work to their field. Brian Barry calls it "the watershed that divides the past from the present,"[10] and Robert Nozick's assertion remains as true

[8] H. L. A. Hart, "Between Utility and Rights" [1979] in *Essays in Jurisprudence and Philosophy* (Oxford University Press, 1983), p. 198.

[9] See, for example, "The Good of Justice as Fairness," *Times Literary Supplement*, May 5, 1972, p. 505; Marshall Cohen, "Review of *A Theory of Justice*," *New York Times Book Review*, July 16, 1972, p. 18.

[10] Barry, "*Political Argument* after Twenty-Five Years," p. lxix. Reflecting on the intellectual world in which *Political Argument* was first published in 1965, he observes: "The difference can be simply but entirely accurately characterized by saying that *Political Argument* belongs to the pre-Rawlsian world while the world we live in is post-Rawlsian." (p. lxix) Compare Jonathan Wolff: "Contemporary English-language political philosophy began in 1971 with the publication of *A Theory of Justice*, and the announcement of a new journal *Philosophy and Public Affairs*" ("John Rawls: Liberal Democracy Restated" in *Liberal Democracy and its Critics*, April Carter and Geoffrey Stokes, eds. (Polity, 1998), p. 118).

today as it was in 1974: "Political philosophers now must either work within Rawls' theory or explain why not."[11]

BIOGRAPHY

John Bordley Rawls – "Jack" to his friends and acquaintances – was born in Baltimore in 1921.[12] His father was a successful lawyer who had dropped out of high school to work in a law firm, where he taught himself law and soon passed the bar exam. His mother served as president of the Baltimore chapter of the League of Women Voters, and both parents were very interested in politics. After attending schools in Baltimore, he was sent to high school at an Episcopalian school in Kent, Connecticut. Upon graduation in 1939 he enrolled at Princeton. After some uncertainty he wound up majoring in philosophy, where Norman Malcolm was an important influence. His senior thesis, submitted in 1942, was entitled "A Brief Inquiry into the Meaning of Sin and Faith: An Interpretation Based on the Concept of Community,"[13] and Rawls seriously considered going to the Virginia Theological Seminary to prepare for a career as a priest. Instead, after graduating a semester early in January, 1943, he enlisted in the army and was sent to the Pacific for two years. He served in New Guinea, the Philippines, and in occupied Japan. Although he viewed his service as "singularly undistinguished," he was awarded a Bronze Star for work behind enemy lines.

His wartime experience was formative and led to the abandonment of his previous religious faith. Years later, he wrote:

> How could I pray and ask God to help me, or my family, or my country, or any other cherished thing I cared about, when God would not save millions of Jews from Hitler? When Lincoln interprets the Civil War as God's punishment for the sin of slavery, deserved equally by North and South, God is seen as acting justly. But the Holocaust can't be interpreted

[11] Robert Nozick, *Anarchy, State, and Utopia* (Basic Books, 1974), p. 183.

[12] The two best sources of biographical information on Rawls are Thomas Pogge, *John Rawls: His Life and Theory of Justice* (Oxford University Press, 2007), and Samuel Freeman, *Rawls* (Routledge, 2007).

[13] John Rawls, *A Brief Inquiry into the Meaning of Sin and Faith: With "On My Religion,"* Thomas Nagel, ed. (Harvard University Press, 2009). See also the discussion in Eric Gregory, "Before the Original Position: The Neo-Orthodox Theology of the Young John Rawls," *Journal of Religious Ethics*, 35 (2007).

in that way, and all attempts to do so that I have read of are hideous and evil. To interpret history as expressing God's will, God's will must accord with the most basic ideas of justice as we know them. For what else can the most basic justice be? Thus, I soon came to reject the idea of the supremacy of the divine will as also hideous and evil.[14]

In early 1946 Rawls returned to Princeton on the GI Bill to pursue graduate work in philosophy. He spent a year at Cornell, where Malcolm was then a professor, and returned to Princeton to write his dissertation, "A Study in the Grounds of Ethical Knowledge: Considered with Reference to Judgments on the Moral Worth of Character," during the 1948–9 year. Months after he went on a blind date with Margaret Fox ("Mardy"), the two were married in the summer of 1949. Upon receiving his degree Rawls taught as an instructor at Princeton for two more years, during which time he was able to read widely in fields outside of philosophy, especially in economics. He received a Fulbright fellowship to spend the 1952–3 year at Oxford, where he attended a lecture course by H. L. A. Hart and a seminar taught by Isaiah Berlin and Stuart Hampshire. In 1953 he was hired as an assistant professor at Cornell, and he received tenure there in 1956, despite having published only two articles.[15] In 1958 he published "Justice as Fairness,"[16] which was the name of the theory that he would develop and refine for nearly a half-century. The following year he accepted a one-year visiting professorship at Harvard. While he was there, Massachusetts Institute of Technology, which had no independent philosophy department, offered him a tenured position. Two years later, in 1962, he returned to Harvard, where he would remain until his retirement in 1991. Despite a significant stutter, he became an immensely popular undergraduate and graduate lecturer. Over the course of his career he served as advisor to many graduate students (including a striking number of women) who, in turn, have made significant contributions to the field.

A very modest man, Rawls declined numerous awards and honorary degrees over the years. Among those that he accepted was the

[14] "On My Religion" [1997] in *A Brief Inquiry into the Meaning of Sin and Faith*, p. 263.

[15] The two were "Outline of a Decision Procedure for Ethics" [1951] (based on his dissertation) and "Two Concepts of Rules" [1955], both in *Collected Papers*, Samuel Freeman, ed. (Harvard University Press, 1999).

[16] In Freeman, *Collected Papers*.

National Humanities Medal, awarded by President Clinton, in 1999. He also granted very few personal interviews. However, in one interview conducted in 1991 he stated that he "began to collect notes [for what would become *A Theory of Justice*] around the fall of 1950 after I had completed my thesis."[17] During the twenty-year period of its development he published many articles that, subject to various degrees of revision, were incorporated into *A Theory of Justice*. According to his student, friend, and editor, Samuel Freeman, "Rawls often said that he sees these papers as experimental works, opportunities to try out ideas that later may be developed, revised, or abandoned in his books."[18] After *A Theory of Justice* Rawls continued to work on justice as fairness, publishing more articles, revising, extending, and defending the theory. And after another approximately twenty-year period, in 1993 he published his second book, *Political Liberalism*.[19] Two years later, following a conference celebrating the twenty-fifth anniversary of the publication of *A Theory of Justice*, Rawls suffered the first of a series of strokes. In the remaining seven years of his life he continued to work. With the assistance of his wife, friends, and colleagues, he completed a new introduction to *Political Liberalism*, "The Idea of Public Reason Revisited," and *The Law of Peoples*, and participated in the editing of his *Collected Papers* and of three collections of his lectures: *Lectures on the History of Moral Philosophy*, *Justice as Fairness: A Restatement*, and *Lectures on the History of Political Philosophy*.[20] He passed away at his home in Cambridge, Massachusetts, on November 24, 2002.

Nearly fifty years after his wartime experiences Rawls would write that the destruction of Hiroshima and the fire-bombing of Japanese cities "were great evils" that the political leadership of the United States had a duty to avoid.[21] As well as opposing the US war in Vietnam, he also believed that the 2-S deferment, which allowed

[17] "John Rawls: For the Record," *The Harvard Review of Philosophy* (Spring, 1991), p. 39.

[18] Samuel Freeman, editor's preface, *Collected Papers*, p. ix.

[19] John Rawls, *Political Liberalism*, expanded edn. (Columbia University Press, 2005).

[20] See "The Idea of Public Reason Revisited" [1997] in Freeman, *Collected Papers*; *The Law of Peoples* (Harvard University Press, 1999); *Lectures on the History of Moral Philosophy*, Barbara Herman, ed. (Harvard University Press, 2000); *Justice as Fairness: A Restatement*, Erin Kelly, ed. (Harvard University Press, 2001); *Lectures on the History of Political Philosophy*, Samuel Freeman, ed. (Harvard University Press, 2007).

[21] John Rawls, "Fifty Years after Hiroshima" [1995] in Freeman, *Collected Papers*, p. 570.

college students to avoid the military draft, was unfair. He held that if, in fact, circumstances were such that conscription was necessary, this burden should be shared equally, and that the children of the privileged should not be able, in effect, to buy their way out. In addition to the intrinsic unfairness, he thought that a society would be less likely to engage in aggressive and unjust wars if the children of the political elite were among those on the front lines. In 1966 he introduced a resolution to the Harvard faculty condemning the 2-S deferment, despite the fact that Harvard students were among its direct beneficiaries.[22] For the most part *A Theory of Justice* avoids discussing particular policy matters such as these. However, one of the points where Rawls's more practical concerns become clear is in his discussion of conscientious refusal as it relates to a country's foreign policy. Acknowledging that conscription may in principle be defended despite its imposition of hardships, it is morally permissible only when "the risks of suffering from these imposed misfortunes are more or less evenly shared by all members of society over the course of their life, and that there is no avoidable class bias in selecting those who are called for duty." (*TJ*, 381/334) On the other hand, he continues, "the conduct and aims of states in waging war, especially large and powerful ones, are in some circumstances so likely to be unjust that one is forced to conclude that in the foreseeable future one must abjure military service altogether." (*TJ*, 381/335)

NON-ACADEMIC INFLUENCE

Despite the enormous influence of *A Theory of Justice* on academic philosophy and related fields such as political science and jurisprudence, Samuel Freeman comments that outside of academia Rawls's influence has been "nil."[23] This should be qualified somewhat for a few European countries such as Germany, the Netherlands, and the Nordic countries, and perhaps for the Chinese students who are said to have shown copies of *A Theory of Justice* to photographers during

[22] See Robert Samuelson, "Faculty Shelves Draft Resolution after Debating for Hour and Half," *The Harvard Crimson*, January 11, 1967, www.thecrimson.com/article.aspx?ref=270764.

[23] Freeman, *Rawls*, p. 457.

the Tiananmen Square protests in 1989.[24] Still, it is clear that *The New York Times* was wildly optimistic when, in naming *A Theory of Justice* one of the "Five Significant Books of 1972," it asserted that "Rawls's arguments are persuasive; its political implications may change our lives." Rawls himself knew better, however, and commented that he was "pessimistic of philosophy's influence."[25] The practical influence of philosophical work is much more indirect and generally takes a very long time to percolate through a culture.

To take Freeman's examples, consider Locke's influence on the American Revolution a century after he wrote or Marx's on twentieth-century communism.[26] Or consider what Rawls himself says in the introduction to the paperback edition of *Political Liberalism*. He notes that among the questions that political philosophers may consider is "whether a just and well-ordered constitutional democracy is possible and what makes it so." The answer that we give to this question,

> affects our background thoughts and attitudes about the world as a whole. And it affects these thoughts and attitudes before we come to actual politics, and limits or inspires how we take part in it. Debates about general philosophical questions cannot be the daily stuff of politics, but that does not make these questions without significance, since what we think their answers are will shape the underlying attitudes of the public culture and the conduct of politics . . . A cause of the fall of Weimar's constitutional regime was that none of the traditional elites of Germany supported its constitution or were willing to cooperate to make it work. They no longer believed a decent liberal parliamentary regime was possible.[27]

The practical influence of philosophy is gradual and indirect. Anyone who imagines that a philosophical argument could be deployed in the heat of battle to ward off physical attack is delusional. But this does not mean that philosophical arguments cannot have significant effects. As Joshua Cohen observes,

[24] See the various contributions to the "Symposium on the Reception of Rawls in Europe" in the *European Journal of Political Theory*, 1 (2002), and Ronald Dworkin's remarks at Rawls's memorial service, "John Rawls," *The Harvard Review of Philosophy*, 11 (2003), p. 7.

[25] "Rawls is Given Two Awards for Book on Justice Theory," *The Harvard Crimson*, December 7, 1972, www.thecrimson.com/article.aspx?ref=245388.

[26] Freeman, *Rawls*, p. 458.

[27] Rawls, *Political Liberalism*, p. lix.

When the Gestapo arrive, philosophy's time has long passed. To avoid the great horrors of political life, political values need to be a settled part of the public culture . . . [Philosophy can] articulate principles of political morality, defend them from the cynicism of self-styled realists, hope they take hold in the background culture, and show that that hope is reasonable.[28]

Still, some critics disparage political philosophy, and moral theory more generally, for not being effective tools in influencing people's behavior. Richard Posner, for example, argues that "[m]oral intuitions neither do nor should yield to the weak arguments that are all that philosophers can bring to bear on moral issues."[29] He continues:

academic moralism has no prospect of improving human behavior . . . [because] the analytical tools employed in academic moralism . . . are too feeble to override either narrow self-interest or moral intuitions. And academic moralists have neither the rhetorical skills nor the factual knowledge that might enable them to persuade without having good methods of inquiry and analysis.[30]

It appears that the only useful role that Posner can imagine for moral theory is the propagandistic one of convincing otherwise immoral or amoral people to become moral. So conceived it aims to convince others to behave in ways that are already known to be correct. Given this understanding, Posner plausibly concludes that academic philosophy is not especially well suited to bringing about such changes in behavior. Unlike academic moralists, Posner allows that those that he calls "moral entrepreneurs" can effectively propagandize for morality, but they do so primarily through non-rational methods. "If you want to make a person disapprove of torturing babies, show him a picture of a baby being tortured; don't read him an essay on moral theory."[31]

Richard Rorty exhibits a similar attitude when he argues that we should put aside abstract theories of human rights in order to concentrate on the "manipulation of sentiments."[32] For Rorty the best that philosophy can achieve is to tell us what we already know: "the most

[28] Joshua Cohen, "The Importance of Philosophy: Reflections on John Rawls," *South African Journal of Philosophy*, 32 (2004), p. 118.

[29] Richard Posner, *The Problematics of Moral and Legal Theory* (Harvard University Press, 1999), p. ix.

[30] *Ibid.*, p. 7. [31] *Ibid.*, p. 52.

[32] Richard Rorty, "Human Rights, Rationality, and Sentimentality" [1993] in *Truth and Progress: Philosophical Papers*, vol. III (Cambridge University Press, 1998), p. 176.

philosophy can hope to do is to summarize our culturally influenced intuitions about the right thing to do in various situations."[33] As we will see when we discuss Rawls's idea of "reflective equilibrium" in chapters 1 and 5, there is a sense in which this is correct. Moral knowledge cannot come from anywhere but our own reflective consideration. But this does not make it trivial or obvious, and there is an important role for philosophy other than promoting what we already know.

As Rawls conceives it, the task of political philosophy is not one of propaganda in which we attempt to manipulate the sentiments of those who do not already share our moral outlook. Nor is it to establish a firm foundation from which to establish the possibility of moral knowledge. Rather, the goal is to help make progress toward resolving the many uncertainties and tensions within our already rich set of moral principles, beliefs, hunches, and prejudices. If we were as confident about all moral questions as we are about the wrongness of torturing babies there would be little practical need for moral theory, and we could get on with the propagandistic project of manipulating sentiments. But in many areas, especially in matters of public policy, we are far less certain about what justice requires. For example, we may be conflicted and unsure about the moral permissibility of imposing taxes on the wealthy to assist the poor. On the one hand, we may think it is unjust for some to have so much while others lack basic necessities. But on the other hand, we may be pulled by a sense that such taxation would be an unjust restriction on the liberty of the wealthy. Conflicts like this, Rawls believes, show that,

> there is at present no agreement on the way the basic institutions of a constitutional democracy should be arranged if they are to satisfy the fair terms of cooperation between citizens regarded as free and equal. This is shown in the deeply contested ideas about how the values of liberty and equality are best expressed in the basic rights and liberties of citizens so as to answer to the claims of both liberty and equality.[34]

Utilitarianism, in particular, cannot "provide a satisfactory account of the basic rights and liberties of citizens as free and equal persons, a

[33] *Ibid.*, p. 171. [34] Rawls, *Political Liberalism*, p. 4.

requirement of absolutely first importance for an account of democratic institutions."[35] (*TJ*, xii) The main goal of *A Theory of Justice* is to develop a theory that could serve as "the most appropriate moral basis for a democratic society." (*TJ*, viii/xviii) The core idea is that a just society will make its fundamental decisions on the basis of mutual respect among its members. Justice as fairness aims to work out what this reciprocity requires by formulating and defending fundamental principles of social justice.

It cannot be stressed enough that Rawls's project is not an attempt to defeat a moral skeptic. It is not an attempt to manipulate the sentiments of those lacking an adequate sense of justice in order to generate such a motivation. It is, rather, a contribution to a public discussion concerning the most adequate conception of justice to be used by a democratic society when addressing matters of basic social justice. It aims to develop an account of the basic organization of a just society under favorable, but not unrealistic, conditions – what Rawls would later call "a realistic utopia."[36] The idea is to extend "what are ordinarily thought to be the limits of practicable political possibility"[37] and therefore to show what we could be at our best. Showing the possibility of such an achievement does not, of course, establish its likelihood. Still, even showing that a just order is possible can affect our political and social attitudes and therefore have significant practical effects. "By showing how the social world may realize the features of a realistic utopia, political philosophy provides a long-term goal of political endeavor, and in working toward it gives meaning to what we can do today."[38]

BASIC OVERVIEW OF *A THEORY OF JUSTICE*

Although the term "justice" is used in a many different contexts, justice as fairness addresses a fairly narrow topic, although an indisputably important one. It is concerned with what we might call "basic social justice." The theory assumes that members of a society will value many different goals and projects. These different conceptions

[35] This is from the preface for the revised edition.

[36] Rawls, *The Law of Peoples*, pp. 6–7, 11–12; Rawls, *Justice as Fairness*, pp. 4, 13.

[37] Rawls, *The Law of Peoples*, p. 11.

[38] *Ibid.*, p. 128.

of the good may conflict with each other, at least to the extent that they make incompatible demands on social resources. These conflicts are due not only to irrationality or immorality. Perfectly reasonable and morally permissible values and goals may also make incompatible demands. Basic social justice is concerned with resolving these conflicts fairly. This can often be done in a decentralized way, for example, by specifying a scheme of property rights that ensures that each individual controls a fair share of resources to devote to the ends that he or she values. These procedures will be realized in the basic institutions of society – what Rawls calls "the basic structure of society." Justice as fairness asks: which principles should we use when evaluating whether the basic structure is fair?

This means that justice as fairness will have little to say (at least directly) about many topics commonly considered under the broad heading of "justice." For example, in addition to being a virtue of social institutions, justice is also a virtue of individuals and individual conduct. Justice as fairness recognizes this, but only gives an incomplete account of this individual virtue. Its account is limited to the influence that individuals can have on the design of the basic structure and to the relations among individuals when they are mediated by those institutions. But justice makes additional demands on individuals. These are often based on special relationships such as being a family member, a friend, a co-worker, or a member of a religious or professional community. While not denying any of this, justice as fairness does not develop an account of these more role-specific demands. It certainly does not aspire to be a general guide to individual conduct.

Furthermore, justice as fairness is an exercise in "ideal theory." It aims to develop principles for the evaluation of a "well-ordered society." It assumes, that is, that most citizens will have an adequate and shared sense of justice and that the institutions of their society will conform to its demands. This involves two distinct idealizations. First, in any actual society there will be some people who have an inadequate or mistaken sense of justice. All societies need mechanisms to cope with such cases, and the criminal law will be a component of such a response. For the most part, justice as fairness abstracts away from such issues. Notice, however, that it does not abstract away from the need for principles of basic social justice because it assumes that even in an idealized well-ordered society there will be conflicts – such as disagreements over how social resources should be deployed – that need to be resolved fairly. Second, justice as fairness has little to say about the transition from existing social injustices to a more just basic structure. The mechanisms of social change fall outside of its scope. Furthermore, sometimes political realities may force us to accept second-best arrangements. Judgments concerning when such compromises are appropriate also lie beyond the reach of the theory. Still, part of the idea of a realistic utopia is that if we can make progress in developing an account of what a just society would look like under favorable circumstances, we can then go on to face the more concrete problems that we confront in our actual condition.

The most distinctive part of justice as fairness is the defense that Rawls offers for his principles. In order to determine which principles would be just, he proposes a thought experiment in which we imagine the principles being chosen from a fair initial choice situation. The idea is to stipulate the features of this situation so that we can recognize that whatever principles would be chosen there would be just. Because we want the principles to be fair to all citizens, we want to force the parties in this choice situation to select only those principles that they believe could be justified to everyone. We do this by imagining them behind a "veil of ignorance" that denies them knowledge of any identifying or specific information about themselves or their society. The idea is that since they do not know which social position or set of values they will turn out to hold when the veil of ignorance is lifted, they are forced to consider how the choice of principles would affect everyone. Rawls calls this purely hypothetical choice situation "the original position."

Despite its importance, the original position is designed to play a limited and specific role. Obviously, Rawls does not suppose that we ever were or could be in such a position. Although he views justice as fairness as part of the social contract tradition, the principles of justice chosen from the original position do not bind us in the same way that ordinary contracts do. Their binding character does not depend on any voluntary act of the will, such as an affirmative act of consent. The construction of the original position does not show why we should be concerned with the virtue of justice in the first place. It is designed to help clarify the content of the principles of basic social justice. Nor is the original position an appropriate perspective for general moral deliberation. It is limited to the task of constructing first principles of basic social justice. Indeed, as we will see in chapter 2, it is not even an appropriate perspective for applying those principles in concrete circumstances in order to design social institutions. Finally, it is crucial to keep distinct the perspective of you and me and Rawls – theorists interested in developing a conception of justice – and the point of view of the imaginary parties in the original position. We set the features of the choice situation to help us clarify which principles of basic social justice we think would be fair. In order to do this, we choose features that force the parties to consider which principles would be acceptable from every social position. If we can identify the principles that they would find to be most acceptable, then we have good reason to believe that those principles would be fair to everyone, and this is exactly what we want. In this sense, the construction of the original position is artificial. The parties do not represent "who we really are" or our "true selves." We imagine them with certain features and choosing from an imaginary situation in order to help us solve a problem that we face.

The parties in the original position are to make pair-wise comparisons among various historically prominent or compelling conceptions of justice, comparing especially the two principles that Rawls defends and average utilitarianism. Rawls argues that when our fundamental interests are at stake, as they are in the design of the basic structure, the features of the original position force the parties there to be especially concerned with the worst possible outcomes. The people who occupy the least advantaged social positions will be those whose fundamental interests are at the greatest risk. So by forcing the parties in the original position to be especially concerned that they may turn out to occupy one of the least advantaged positions, we ensure that they choose principles that protect everyone's fundamental interests. That is what we want, because only a set of principles that protects everyone's fundamental interests will be acceptable to everyone. This special concern for the least advantaged is reflected in the two principles that Rawls argues would be chosen. The basic idea of the two principles has remained consistent since he formulated them in "Justice as Fairness" in 1958,[39] although, as we will see in chapters 1 and 3, Rawls made some slight changes to the formulation of the first principle. The first principle guarantees an equal scheme of basic liberties to all citizens. These include liberties familiar from existing constitutional democracies, such as the right to vote, the rule of law, and liberty of conscience, among others. The second principle itself has two parts. First, it requires "fair equality of opportunity." Individuals must have a fair chance of obtaining the various social positions in the society. Second, structural inequalities are just (relative to a baseline of equality) only if they work to the advantage of the least advantaged position. In other words, for a structural inequality to be just, all social positions must benefit from it, although they need not all benefit equally, of course. This second part of the second principle is called "the difference principle." While the first principle is implemented primarily in the political institutions of the basic structure, the two parts of the second principle are realized mainly through the social and economic institutions.

A Theory of Justice is divided into three parts: "Theory," "Institutions," and "Ends," each one of which is divided into three chapters. Part I is concerned with the main features of the theory just discussed. Here we find discussions of the basic structure, the two principles of justice, the original position, and (most of) the argument for the choice of the two principles. But the argument for the choice of the principles depends in part on the assumption that the principles could actually be implemented in a feasible institutional structure. Part II is devoted to making that case by considering the application of the first principle, then the second, and then some of the implications for individual conduct. The idea is not that there is only one set of institutions that would satisfy the principles. Which institutions would best satisfy them depends in part on features of the specific society in question. The point, rather, is to provide an example of how they might be implemented and to show that this could plausibly be done. Finally, part III takes up the question of "stability," which also is relevant to the choice of principles in the original position. Assuming that the principles were widely accepted and that the

[39] See "Justice as Fairness" [1958] in Freeman, *Collected Papers*.

basic structure met their demands, would such a well-ordered society remain stably just? This question cannot be answered absolutely, of course. The best we can do is to identify some considerations that would lead citizens to continue to support their just institutions and to compare the strength of these forces with the corresponding forces in societies structured according to rival conceptions of justice. Not surprisingly, Rawls argues that justice as fairness would be at least as stable as its rivals. However, as we will see, it was his dissatisfaction with an element of this argument that gave rise to the developments in *Political Liberalism*.

JUSTIFICATION

The previous section described in very broad terms the general features of justice as fairness. When we press beyond such an overview and look at the details, we find many conflicting interpretations. Despite being somewhat austere, Rawls's writing is very complex and it is easy to lose track of what he aims to establish with the myriad arguments and considerations. One result of this richness is that, as Hilary Putnam told generations of his students, "The smarter you get, the smarter it gets." It repays careful and repeated study.

In describing his teaching of the great figures in the history of political philosophy, Rawls wrote:

> I always took for granted that the writers we were studying were much smarter than I was . . . If I saw a mistake in their argument, I suppose those writers saw it too and must have dealt with it . . . [Although] a kind of reverence [may be appropriate, this] is sharply distinct from adulation or uncritical acceptance of the text or author as authoritative. All true philosophy seeks fair criticism and depends on continuing and reflective public judgment.[40]

I have tried to follow this model in presenting my interpretation of *A Theory of Justice*. My interpretation departs from the orthodoxy in a number of ways, and it is worth drawing attention to these points. In this section I will discuss two issues related to how the principles

[40] John Rawls, "Afterword: A Reminiscence" in *Future Pasts: The Analytic Tradition in Twentieth-Century Philosophy*, Juliet Floyd and Sanford Shieh, eds. (Oxford University Press, 2001), pp. 427–8.

of justice are justified, while in the next two sections I will discuss how the second principle should be understood.

As noted above, justice as fairness does not aim to convince a skeptic to be concerned with justice in the first place. Confusion on this issue derives in part from a misunderstanding of the distinctive ideas of justification that Rawls offers.[41] Justice as fairness presents the principles of justice as those that would be chosen from the hypothetical original position. Because the original position is hypothetical, it is up to us to determine, as best we can, the principles that the parties there would select. The hope is that once we have fully specified their motivations and the circumstances in which they find themselves, it will be clear which set of principles they would rationally choose. "Ideally anyway, I should like to show that their acknowledgment is the only choice consistent with the full description of the original position. The argument aims eventually to be strictly deductive." (*TJ*, 121/104) although Rawls acknowledges that his argument "will fall far short of this, since it is highly intuitive throughout." (*TJ*, 121/105) But if the argument aspires to be "deductive," why does Rawls think that "it is obviously impossible to develop a substantive theory of justice founded solely on truths of logic and definition"? (*TJ*, 51/44) The answer is that while the argument concerning which principles would be chosen from the original position aspires to be deductive, we need some reason to take an interest in that hypothetical choice situation. After all, there are numerous other hypothetical choices that we could consider. Logic and definitions cannot, by themselves, establish the special status of the original position. The reason to take an interest in the original position (if there is one) is because of the contribution it makes to our effort to reach reflective equilibrium. The consideration of the choice from the original position and the idea of reflective equilibrium are not rival conceptions of justification, as is sometimes assumed, but the former is an attempt to help achieve the latter.

Unfortunately, there is a lot of confusion concerning Rawls's argument that the parties in the original position would, in fact, choose the two principles of justice over their main rivals. Jon Elster is not

[41] See, for example, Adina Schwartz, "Moral Neutrality and Primary Goods," *Ethics*, 83 (1973), p. 297.

alone in thinking that the argument in *A Theory of Justice* "is notoriously elliptical or worse."[42] We will examine the details of this argument in chapter 1 (and partially in chapter 2), but here I want to address one common misinterpretation and source of confusion. Because in their choice of principles the parties give special attention to the least advantaged position, Rawls notes that "it is useful as a heuristic device to think of the two principles as the maximin solution to the problem of social justice." (*TJ*, 152/132) The maximin rule requires that we select the option in which the worst outcome is better than the worst outcome of any of the alternatives – it requires that we maximize the minimum outcome. It is sometimes assumed that Rawls simply postulates that the parties would make their selection on the basis of maximin reasoning because he believes that this is an appropriate general standard of choice under uncertainty.[43] This assumption may be reinforced by Rawls's remark that "The theory of justice is a part, perhaps the most significant part, of the theory of rational choice." (*TJ*, 16/15) He later repudiated this formulation since it may misleadingly suggest that the principles of justice could be derived "from the concept of rationality as the sole normative concept."[44]

But even in *A Theory of Justice* it was clear that Rawls did not intend simply to stipulate that the parties would be moved by maximin reasoning or that this was an appropriate general standard for choice under uncertainty. On the contrary: "Clearly the maximin rule is not, in general, a suitable guide for choices under uncertainty." (*TJ*, 153/133) Nor does Rawls simply stipulate that the parties would be moved by "this unusual rule." (*TJ*, 154/134) As he pointed out in a 1974 article, such a stipulation "would indeed have been no argument at all."[45] Instead, we need an argument to establish that it would be rational, given their motivation and the situation that they find themselves in, for the parties to give special attention to the worst-case outcome for each set of principles. As Rawls explains: "What must

[42] Jon Elster, *Local Justice: How Institutions Allocate Scarce Goods and Necessary Burdens* (Russell Sage Foundation, 1992), p. 227.

[43] See, for example, John Harsanyi, "Can the Maximin Principle Serve as a Basis for Morality? A Critique of John Rawls's Theory" [1975] in *Essays on Ethics, Social Behavior, and Scientific Explanation* (D. Reidel, 1976).

[44] Rawls, *Political Liberalism*, p. 53, n. 7.

[45] John Rawls, "Reply to Alexander and Musgrave" [1974] in Freeman, *Collected Papers*, p. 247.

be shown is that given the unique features of this situation, agreeing to these principles rather than the principle of utility is rational for anyone whose aversion to uncertainty in regard to being able to secure their fundamental interests is within the normal range." (*TJ*, 149)[46]

The most important – and most frequently neglected – factor that makes it rational for the parties to choose in this unusual way is the model of the person on which they rely. They are not "bare-persons" but rather have "a determinate character and will, even though the specific nature of their system of ends is unknown" to the parties in the original position.[47] (*TJ*, 152) The parties assume, for example, that they have "fundamental aims and interests" such as a religious interest and an interest in the integrity of the person, although, of course, they do not know the specific content of these aims and interests, and that they "must secure these interests" if it is possible to do so.[48] (*TJ*, 131) While the first principle of justice directly secures these interests, average utilitarianism would do so only indirectly at best and subject to difficult and uncertain calculations. If the parties select the two principles of justice they can be confident that their basic interests will be protected even if they occupy the least advantaged position, while they have much less assurance that they would be protected if they select the principle of maximizing average utility. Therefore, the parties would select the two principles over average utilitarianism based on a comparison of these worst-case scenarios. As Rawls explains in *Justice as Fairness*,

> it is not essential for the parties to use the maximin rule in the original position. It is simply a heuristic device. Focusing on the worst outcomes has the advantage of forcing us to consider what our fundamental interests really are when it comes to the design of the basic structure.[49]

The parties choose as if they were selecting according to maximin reasoning because of the features of the original position (such as the veil of ignorance) and the requirement that they secure their basic interests as best they can.

[46] In the original edition, the corresponding sentence reads: "What must be shown is that choosing as if one had such an aversion is rational given the unique features of that situation irrespective of any special attitudes toward risk." (p. 172)

[47] This passage appears only in the revised edition. Obviously, Rawls came to believe that he had not made this important point clearly enough in the original edition.

[48] These passages appear only in the revised edition.

[49] Rawls, *Justice as Fairness*, p. 99.

There is an obvious similarity between the maximin principle of choice and the difference principle.[50] This similarity may explain the very widely held but mistaken belief that Rawls argues that the parties in the original position would select the difference principle based on maximin reasoning. The argument sketched above, which establishes the superiority of the two principles over average utilitarianism, does not refer to distributive principles at all. It focuses exclusively on our basic interests, which are primarily secured not by the difference principle but by the first principle of justice. This is sufficient to establish the superiority of the two principles over their main rival, average utilitarianism. However, some other conceptions would also provide adequate protection to our fundamental interests. They may do this, for example, by accepting the first principle of justice that secures the basic liberties, but substituting some other principle of distributive justice. Rawls calls these "mixed conceptions." It is only when making such a comparison that we will get an argument for the selection of the difference principle. One might suppose that at this point Rawls would once again appeal to the maximin heuristic. Yet he does not. As he explains in *Justice as Fairness*: "in arguing for the difference principle over other distributive principles (say a restricted principle of (average) utility, which includes a social minimum), there is no appeal at all to the maximin rule for decision under uncertainty."[51] The mixed conception that Rawls mentions parenthetically and discusses in *A Theory of Justice* (see chapter 2 below) secures our fundamental interests. Therefore, the argument for a risk-averse choice cannot establish the superiority of the two principles over this mixed conception. Put more simply:

[50] Rawls himself refers to "the maximin equity criterion" (i.e. the difference principle applied to expected utility) and "the so-called maximin rule for choice under uncertainty." ("Some Reasons for the Maximin Criterion" [1974] in Freeman, *Collected Papers*, p. 225.) In order to avoid confusion, in *Justice as Fairness* he reserves the term "maximin" for the principle of choice, and the term "the difference principle" for the criterion of justice. (Rawls, *Justice as Fairness*, p. 43, n. 3)

[51] Rawls, *Justice as Fairness*, p. 43, n. 3. This slightly understates the power of maximin reasoning in the original position. The mixed conception that Rawls considers would secure our fundamental interests, but not all would since not all guarantee a social minimum. Given a choice between the two principles and a mixed conception that failed to secure a social minimum, the parties would select the former in order to avoid the risk of leaving their basic interests unprotected, that is, as if they were choosing according to the maximin criterion.

Rawls does not use maximin reasoning to argue for the difference principle.[52]

A final aspect of my interpretation of Rawls's account of justification concerns the relationship between *A Theory of Justice* and *Political Liberalism* (discussed below in chapter 4). When Rawls introduced the idea of an "overlapping consensus," some critics thought that it was intended as yet another method of justification. Rather than aiming at principles that can be justified from the original position, some held that he was now primarily concerned with finding a conception of justice that would be likely to receive widespread acceptance in a given society.[53] For these critics it was no surprise that Rawls appeared to back off from his defense of the difference principle, which is far more egalitarian than the current practice of most societies.[54] But the idea of an overlapping consensus is not an alternative method of justifying principles of justice. On the contrary, any effort to select principles directly on the basis of their purported fitness to serve as the focus of an overlapping consensus would make the conception "political in the wrong way."[55] Furthermore, there is no backing away from the difference principle as an element in the most favored conception of justice. What Rawls says is something that he never denied – that some other (liberal) conceptions of justice may also be reasonable, even if not as reasonable as justice as fairness. Policies based on these rivals could, therefore, be legitimate if implemented by a legitimate political mechanism, even if they would not be as fully just as policies consistent with justice as fairness.[56]

On my interpretation, the developments in *Political Liberalism* entail far less dramatic revisions to the arguments of *A Theory of Justice* than is commonly believed. To be sure, there are a few points where Rawls explicitly revises his view, including, for example, the precise formulation of the first principle of justice. And most dramatically, *Political Liberalism* entails a significant revision in our understanding of the "congruence" argument for stability in part III

[52] See Freeman, *Rawls*, pp. 188–9.

[53] See, for example, Chandran Kukathas and Philip Pettit, *Rawls: "A Theory of Justice" and its Critics* (Stanford University Press, 1990), p. 142.

[54] See, for example, Bruce Ackerman, "Political Liberalisms," *The Journal of Philosophy*, 91 (1994), pp. 371, 374; and Bernard Williams, "A Fair State," *London Review of Books*, May 13, 1993, p. 8.

[55] Rawls, *Political Liberalism*, pp. xlv, 39–40, 389.

[56] *Ibid.*, p. xlvi.

of *A Theory of Justice* (see chapters 3 and 4 below). But even here it would be misleading to say that Rawls rejects the argument for the congruence of the right and the good in part III. He came to see that the argument that he presents there depends on premises that not all reasonable people would accept. It depends on a particular "comprehensive doctrine" (or partially comprehensive doctrine) – an account, that is, that includes values that go beyond the value of basic social justice. The problem is that this doctrine would not be shared by all reasonable people. But this does not mean that he came to reject that doctrine or the soundness of the argument. As Samuel Freeman argues,

> Rawls never wavers in his conviction that these philosophical and moral positions set forth in *A Theory of Justice* are all correct and philosophically justifiable . . . just as he never wavers in his conviction that justice as fairness is also true (or "most reasonable" in his parlance). But to say these positions are *philosophically* justifiable and true does not mean that they are *publicly* justifiable to the members of a democratic society.[57]

Furthermore, there is nothing objectionable – nothing that violates the limits of public reason as set forth in *Political Liberalism* – about exploring the implications of a particular comprehensive doctrine, even if they exceed the limits of public reason since not all reasonable citizens would accept them.

Understood in this way, the argument in part III of *A Theory of Justice* establishes that congruence would hold for those who share a certain partially comprehensive doctrine. But Rawls came to see that this argument would not establish congruence for those who reasonably reject this partially comprehensive doctrine. In other words, the goal of establishing the congruence of the right and the good for all (or most) citizens in a well-ordered society of justice as fairness remains elusive. In fact, no general argument can establish this. What is required is an examination of each particular (reasonable) comprehensive doctrine in order to determine whether it can properly affirm the principles of justice consistent with its understanding of other virtues and values. If a sufficient number of citizens affirm a common conception of justice and place sufficient value on their society's public reason, then their society will have achieved an overlapping

[57] Freeman, *Rawls*, p. 325.

consensus and it will be stable. The question that *Political Liberalism* asks is: "how is it possible for there to exist over time a just and stable society of free and equal citizens, who remain profoundly divided by reasonable religious, philosophical, and moral doctrines?"[58] The answer is given by the idea of an overlapping consensus of reasonable comprehensive doctrines.

It is crucial to emphasize that the central question of *Political Liberalism* is merely: "how is it possible?" As Rawls writes in the introduction to the paperback edition,

> *PL* makes no attempt to prove, or to show, that such a consensus would eventually form around a reasonable political conception of justice. The most it does is to present a freestanding liberal political conception that does not oppose comprehensive doctrines on their own ground and does not preclude the possibility of an overlapping consensus for the right reasons.[59]

In other words, *Political Liberalism* aims to show that stability in a pluralistic society requires an overlapping consensus and that one could possibly emerge around justice as fairness. Whether a given comprehensive doctrine would be part of such an overlapping consensus can only be determined from within that comprehensive doctrine. This represents a significant scaling back from the ambitions of part III of *A Theory of Justice*. Instead of an argument that a well-ordered society of justice as fairness would be stable, we get an account of what must happen in order to achieve stability.

So, what is left of the congruence argument from *A Theory of Justice*? Rather than a general argument that a society endorsing justice as fairness would be stable, we should see it as an argument that those citizens who hold a partially comprehensive doctrine (based roughly on the Kantian interpretation of justice as fairness) would be able to achieve congruence. Assuming the argument is successful, this is still a very significant accomplishment. What remains, then, is to offer a comparable argument to establish the relationship between social justice and other values from within each rival reasonable comprehensive doctrine – utilitarianism, liberal Catholicism, rational intuitionism, etc. From the point of view of *Political Liberalism*, we must abandon the aspiration of part III of *A Theory of Justice* to

58 Rawls, *Political Liberalism*, p. 4.

59 *Ibid.*, pp. xlv–xlvi.

give a general argument for the stability of justice as fairness. We need not, however, abandon the specific argument for congruence of those accepting the partially comprehensive doctrine of the Kantian interpretation. In fact, this argument can serve as a model for what must be done from the perspective of other reasonable comprehensive doctrines.

JUSTICE AS FAIRNESS IS NOT A FORM OF LUCK EGALITARIANISM

Probably the most significant way in which my reading differs from standard interpretations concerns Rawls's understanding of distributive justice and the difference principle. According to the dominant interpretation, Rawls holds that justice requires correcting any inequality that is "arbitrary from a moral point of view." As Thomas Nagel presents it, the difference principle "depends on the moral claim that it is unfair if people suffer or benefit differentially because of differences between them that are not their fault."[60] Luck egalitarians are committed to the view that inequalities that are truly arbitrary should be redressed.[61] Distinguishing the inequalities for which people are responsible from those that are arbitrary is a subtle and difficult task, and Rawls is often thought to have a rather crude view of such matters. But I believe that this interpretation of Rawls is mistaken from the start. He does not hold that all inequalities that are arbitrary – those which are nobody's fault – are presumptively unjust. In fact, he is explicit on this point: "The natural distribution [of natural talents] is neither just nor unjust; nor is it unjust that persons are born into society at some particular position. These are simply natural facts. What is just and unjust is the way that institutions deal with these facts." (*TJ*, 102/87) Social institutions allow individuals to transform natural contingencies (some of which are unequal) into shares of social resources, and social justice is concerned with ensuring that that is done fairly. In chapter 5 we will consider some criticisms of Rawls made by luck egalitarians, but here I want to argue in some

[60] Thomas Nagel, "Rawls and Liberalism" in *The Cambridge Companion to Rawls*, Samuel Freeman, ed. (Cambridge University Press, 2003), p. 71.

[61] See the discussion in Elizabeth Anderson, "What is the Point of Equality?" *Ethics*, 109 (1999). Anderson is critical of this approach and rejects this interpretation of Rawls. (p. 290)

detail that he does not share their basic understanding of distributive justice.[62]

The widespread interpretation of Rawls as a luck egalitarian rests on the convergence of several factors. First, insufficient attention is paid to the fact that the principles of distributive justice, including the difference principle, are not to be applied directly to individual shares of social goods such as income and property. Rather, in justice as fairness they are to be applied to the background institutions within which individuals interact. In a just society individuals acquire shares of social resources by following the procedures that their society specifies. For example, there will be laws about inheritance, legal property transfer, taxes, the hiring and firing of employees, the extraction of natural resources, and much, much else. The principles of justice are designed to evaluate this system of public rules that forms part of the basic structure of society. The principles are not appropriate standards for directly evaluating the conduct of individuals within this scheme of just institutions. Furthermore, "A distribution cannot be judged in isolation from the system of which it is the outcome or from what individuals have done in good faith in the light of established expectations." (*TJ*, 88/76) In Rawls's jargon individual entitlements are a matter of "pure procedural justice." Individuals come to acquire their shares by interacting with others against a just institutional background and system of procedures. It is largely unpredictable what specific shares of resources an individual will eventually have because this depends not only on his or her own actual behavior but also on the actions of numerous others.

A further factor that contributes to the interpretation of Rawls as a luck egalitarian is the fact that commentators (and to some extent Rawls himself) give insufficient attention to the distinction between the principles of justice and the process by which they are justified. The principles themselves do "not require society to try to even out handicaps as if all were expected to compete on a fair basis in the same race." (*TJ*, 101/86) Rawls explicitly rejects the principle of redress which holds that "undeserved inequalities call for redress; and since

[62] See also Samuel Scheffler, "What is Egalitarianism?" *Philosophy and Public Affairs* 31 (2003) and Samuel Freeman, "Rawls and Luck Egalitarianism" in *Justice and the Social Contract: Essays on Rawlsian Political Philosophy* (Oxford University Press, 2007).

inequalities of birth and natural endowment are undeserved, these inequalities are to be somehow compensated for." (*TJ*, 100/86) It is true that the principle of redress and the difference principle may recommend some similar policies, especially when compared to an exclusive concern with economic efficiency or utility maximization. But the difference principle, unlike the principle of redress, does not hold that all contingent inequalities are unjust.

On the other hand, the original position, the hypothetical situation from which we imagine the principles being chosen, does eliminate arbitrary contingencies. That is, it prevents factors that are morally arbitrary from influencing the choice of principles. The fact that one person has greater natural mental or physical gifts than another should provide no grounds for selecting one set of principles of justice over another. It is appropriate, therefore, to eliminate the influence of such contingencies from the hypothetical choice situation itself. But this must not be confused with what would be required in a just society – a society that satisfies the principles that would be chosen from the original position. Here is one of Rawls's statements that is often cited as a basis for the luck egalitarian interpretation:

> Once we decide to look for a conception of justice that prevents the use of accidents of natural endowment and the contingencies of social circumstances as counters in a quest for political and economic advantage, we are led to these principles. They express the result of leaving aside those aspects of the social world that seem arbitrary from a moral point of view. (*TJ*, 15/14)

Taken in isolation, it may not be clear whether Rawls means that the principles themselves force us to "leave aside" what is "arbitrary from a moral point of view" or whether they are the result of doing so. The former interpretation amounts to an acceptance of the principle of redress which, as we have already seen, Rawls rejects. But the latter interpretation fits, since the principles themselves are the result of the choice from the original position, in which such contingencies are left aside. Other statements lend further support to this interpretation. For example: "The arbitrariness of the world must be corrected for by adjusting the circumstances of the initial contractual situation."[63]

[63] Cf. *TJ*, 136/118; and Rawls, *Justice as Fairness*, p. 16.

(*TJ*, 141/122) The original position leaves aside the arbitrary contingencies that are irrelevant for the justification of a conception of justice, but the principles chosen there do not aim at redressing all arbitrary inequalities.

A further factor that leads many to suppose that Rawls is a luck egalitarian concerns the way he introduces his second principle of justice. Before offering the argument that the second principle would be chosen from the original position, he attempts to explain its content in a way that makes it seem more intuitively appealing so that it "will not strike the reader as extreme."[64] (*TJ*, 65) This presentation is not intended to be the official argument for the second principle of justice (*TJ*, 54/47; cf. 75/65), and it is significant, although not by itself decisive, that this way of presenting the principles is not found in his published lectures on justice as fairness.[65] The second principle itself has two parts – fair equality of opportunity and the difference principle – and Rawls contrasts each of these elements with a less demanding alternative. In contrast to "fair equality of opportunity," he considers "careers open to talents." This limited, more formal interpretation of equal opportunity ensures only that the procedures by which individuals come to occupy social positions are free from overt discrimination. Employers, for example, would be prohibited from discriminating on the basis of race or other factors that were irrelevant to one's qualifications. This limited conception does not prevent inequalities from accumulating from generation to generation and influencing one's prospects. The social class into which one is born can have a decisive influence over one's prospects without there being any formal discrimination. Justice as fairness endorses the more demanding standard of fair equality of opportunity, according to which "those who are at the same level of talent and ability, and have the same willingness to use them, should have the same prospects of success regardless of their initial place in the social system." (*TJ*,

[64] In the first edition of *TJ*, instead of "extreme," Rawls says "too eccentric or bizarre." (p. 75)

[65] When he does refer to "contingencies," it is to point out their inevitability even in a just society:

> Even in a well-ordered society, then, our prospects over life are deeply affected by social, natural, and fortuitous contingencies, and by the way the basic structure, by setting up inequalities, uses those contingencies to meet certain social purposes. (Rawls, *Justice as Fairness*, p. 55)

73/63) Consistent with respecting the basic liberties, a just society will seek to eliminate inequalities that can be traced to class background and the wealth of one's parents. The less demanding "careers open to talents" implies that any outcome of a formally free market procedure – one that is free from overt discrimination – would be just. Justice as fairness rejects this and places additional requirements in order for market outcomes to be just.

When he turns to introduce the difference principle, Rawls continues to stress how his conception of justice places additional constraints on more libertarian conceptions. The outcomes that market mechanisms are likely to generate will depend on how schemes of property rights and taxes are specified. Many of these outcomes will be "efficient" in the technical sense to be discussed in chapter 1. Now, we might be tempted to leave it at that and to say that any scheme likely to generate an efficient outcome would be just. Alternatively, we might look for additional criteria in order to select from among efficient procedures the ones that would also be just. The difference principle tells us to select the institutional scheme in which the share of resources likely to go to the least advantaged social position is as large as possible. As we will see in chapter 1, assuming that certain technical conditions are met the difference principle will select the mechanism that will generate the most egalitarian among the efficient outcomes. By choosing the most egalitarian scheme, it will limit – although not necessarily eliminate – the influence of the factors that would generate even larger inequalities under other institutional schemes.

Rawls calls attention to how the two parts of the second principle require that we select institutional mechanisms that limit the influence of factors that could generate larger inequalities under other institutional schemes: "For once we are troubled by the influence of either social contingencies or natural chance on the determination of distributive shares, we are bound, on reflection, to be bothered by the influence of the other. From a moral standpoint the two seem equally arbitrary." (*TJ*, 74–5/64–5) The common reading of this passage assumes that when we are "troubled" by something that is arbitrary from a moral point of view, justice requires that we eliminate it. But Rawls does not say that, and, to repeat once again, the difference principle is not the principle of redress. The point of this passage, I believe, is to emphasize that a libertarian conception of distributive justice is inadequate. There is no "natural" or obvious mechanism for transforming social or natural inequalities into unequal shares of social resources. This can only be done by social institutions, and different institutional schemes will do this in different ways. When we are troubled by the influence of arbitrary contingencies, we must decide for ourselves when and to what extent social and natural inequalities ought to be able to be transformed into unequal shares of social resources. Both social and natural inequalities are arbitrary in an important sense, but justice as fairness treats them differently. Fair equality of opportunity prohibits social inequalities (such as different class backgrounds) from being transformed into unequal shares of social resources, but the difference principle allows natural inequalities in talent and ability to influence shares of social resources when doing so works to the advantage of the least advantaged position.

DESERT AND RESPONSIBILITY

The interpretation of Rawls as a luck egalitarian is closely related to an even more widely held misunderstanding concerning the role of individual responsibility in justice as fairness. Consider, first, Rawls's so-called "rejection of desert." According to an influential reconstruction, we cannot base justice on desert because, in the words of one critic, Rawls holds that "no one can strictly speaking be said to deserve anything."[66] This is allegedly because of his belief that "We do not deserve our place in the distribution of native endowments" or even "the superior character that enables us to make the effort to cultivate out abilities."[67] (*TJ*, 89) (It is also based on a misreading of his claim about representing the "distribution of natural talents" as "a common asset" (*TJ*, 101–2/87) – a passage we will discuss in chapter 1.) If we do not deserve our character, how can we be said to deserve anything

[66] Michael Sandel, *Liberalism and the Limits of Justice*, second edn. (Cambridge University Press, 1998), p. 139. The origin of this interpretation seems to be Nozick, *Anarchy, State, and Utopia*, pp. 224–5. See the discussion in my "Justice, Desert, and Ideal Theory," *Social Theory and Practice*, 23 (1997).

[67] In the original edition, the corresponding sentence reads: "It seems to be one of the fixed points of our considered judgments that no one deserves his place in the distribution of native endowments, any more than one deserves one's initial starting place in society." (p. 104)

at all? For that matter, how can we be properly held responsible for anything at all? Although this interpretation is widespread, it is a radical distortion of justice as fairness.

What Rawls says, famously, is this:

> There is a tendency for common sense to suppose that income and wealth, and the good things in life generally, should be distributed according to moral desert. Justice is happiness according to virtue . . . Now justice as fairness rejects this conception. (*TJ*, 310/273)

The key to understanding his position is to notice that Rawls assumes that distributing goods according to desert is the same as distributing them according to moral virtue. He is using the term "desert" in a narrow and technical sense when compared to common usage. Once this is recognized, it becomes obvious that we do not deserve (in his technical sense) our "native endowments."[68] They are products of the "natural lottery" and not a reflection of moral virtue. Similarly, we do not deserve our ability to "make the effort to cultivate our abilities" since this reflects not our moral virtue but "depends in good part upon fortunate family and social circumstances in early life for which we can claim no credit."[69] (*TJ*, 89) The point is not that we cannot be held responsible for our character. It is simply that our perseverance is a reflection of many factors other than our degree of moral virtue.

However, Rawls also thinks that it is obvious that "the more advantaged have a right to their natural assets, as does everyone else."[70] (*TJ*, 89) The point is that this right is not grounded in the absurd belief that the more talented are of greater moral virtue than everyone else. Similarly, individuals come to be entitled to – they come to have rights to – specific shares of social resources in ways independent of their moral virtue. They acquire these rights by acting in ways specified by the procedures of a just basic structure. For example, when I buy something from you in accordance with a just system of rules, the property rights that are exchanged do not reflect any assessment

68 See Rawls, *Justice as Fairness*, p. 74.

69 In the original edition, the corresponding passage is presented in the third person and reads: "depends in large part upon fortunate family and social circumstances for which he can claim no credit." (p. 104)

70 Rawls added this passage to the revised edition, apparently in response to the misinterpretation of the "common asset" passage (*TJ*, 101–2/87), which he also revised. See the discussion in chapter 1.

of the moral virtue of either of us. Because the social resources that individuals come to acquire by following these procedures do not reflect moral virtue, they are not a matter of desert in the narrow sense that Rawls is using. The question that justice as fairness aims to answer is: against what background institutional scheme should we acquire our shares of social resources and pursue our goals?

Still, it may be hard to see what role there is for individual responsibility in the acquisition of entitlements. It is often thought, for example, that by focusing exclusively on the least advantaged, justice as fairness is insensitive to different levels of work or social contribution. We might think that, other things being equal, people who work hard deserve (in a colloquial sense of "should be entitled to") greater reward than those who do not. William Galston, for example, argues that:

> [J]ustice as fairness was a systematic effort to discard, as morally arbitrary or irrelevant, precisely those features of human life on which the claims, and the self-respect, of the working class rested. Rawls severed the connection between the willingness to produce and the right to consume; he replaced claims based on achievement with those based on bare existence.[71]

Often this is put in terms of a contrast between the "deserving" and the "undeserving" poor. The thought is that justice should come to the aid of the former but not the latter. There are many conflicting ways in which one might determine who is deserving and who is not. Galston himself appears not to notice the difference between "willingness to produce" and "achievement." But to illustrate how this common interpretation distorts justice as fairness, let us begin with a relatively simple case. Consider a society that is committed to satisfying the difference principle, and imagine a member of that society who has an average or above-average share of wealth. Suppose now that he foolishly gambles it all away and finds himself destitute – below the level of the least advantaged representative person in the society. Must the society raise him to the level of the least advantaged? For that matter, must it continue to replenish his resources fully each time he gambles and loses until he finally wins? If the difference principle had this implication, it would be absurd.

[71] William Galston, *Liberal Purposes: Goods, Virtues, and Diversity in the Liberal State* (Cambridge University Press, 1991), p. 162.

As we have seen, the difference principle is designed not to evaluate individual shares of resources but institutional schemes. It evaluates these schemes based on the structural inequalities that they are likely to generate. As Rawls explains, "when [the] principles mention persons, or require that everyone gain from an inequality, the reference is to representative persons holding the various social positions, or offices established by the basic structure."[72] (*TJ*, 56) It is obvious that there is no change to the basic structure of society when an individual squanders his resources. Because there is no structural change – there is no change among the representative persons – the difference principle is not violated. Furthermore, the difference principle refers to the shares of social resources that representative individuals can reasonably expect over a complete life. It is concerned with "their life prospects as viewed from their social station." (*TJ*, 64/56) The fact that some individual falls below these expectations, whether due to bad luck or due to actions for which he or she is responsible, does not show that the difference principle is violated.[73]

This is not to say, however, that the principles of justice taken together are not concerned with individuals. On the contrary, the first principle requires that each individual be guaranteed an equal scheme of basic liberties. And as we have seen, the first part of the second principle requires that each individual have fair equality of opportunity. But the difference principle is structural. "Since it applies to institutional forms, the second principle (*or rather the first part of it* [i.e. the difference principle]) refers to the expectations of representative individuals." (*TJ*, 64/56, my emphasis) So the difference principle does not require that we maximize the share of resources repeatedly for the gambler who continually squanders his resources. This does not mean that society should allow individuals who have foolishly dissipated their resources literally to starve to death. Presumably, a just society will provide emergency medical care to those in great need, but this requirement is not based on the demands of the difference principle.

Now consider more directly the treatment of those who work hard – say, those who work longer hours than others. Fair equality

[72] In the original edition, Rawls adds "or whatever" after "offices." (p. 64)

[73] See the discussion in Walter Schaller, "Rawls, the Difference Principle, and Economic Inequality," *Pacific Philosophical Quarterly*, 79 (1998).

of opportunity ensures that "there should be roughly equal prospects of culture and achievement for everyone similarly motivated and endowed." (*TJ*, 73/63) The clear implication is that those who are not similarly motivated or endowed will (typically) not receive equal shares of social resources, such as income. Once fair equality of opportunity is ensured, we allow allocations of shares of resources to particular individuals to be a matter of pure procedural justice. "The role of the principle of fair opportunity is to insure that the system of cooperation is one of pure procedural justice. Unless it is satisfied, distributive justice could not be left to take care of itself, even within a restricted range."[74] (*TJ*, 76) The question, as we have seen, is what the procedures should be. The difference principle answers that they should be those in which the prospective shares of the least advantaged position are as large as possible. Given reasonable assumptions, a basic structure satisfying the difference principle will be likely to provide greater rewards, other things equal, to those who work longer hours. Those who choose to work fewer hours than is typical do not thereby decrease their prospective shares any more than the gambler does in the case above. It is also likely that a just basic structure will provide greater rewards to those who have rare and valuable natural talents, at least in some cases. It will provide these additional rewards when doing so leads to a greater aggregate product in the society and on the condition that the increase benefits the least advantaged representative person.

Although justice as fairness will often provide a premium to those who work additional hours and to those who have certain unusual talents, this bonus may be less than that provided under some other institutional arrangements. For example, it is likely to be less than that provided under a scheme that aims to maximize the value of the aggregate social product. Therefore, it seems unlikely that a well-ordered society of justice as fairness would maximize the value of its aggregate social product. Thus, we face a choice between an economic scheme that aims to maximize the value of its aggregate product and a scheme that aims to maximize the share going to the least advantaged structural position. It may not be obvious which scheme would be more just. Justice as fairness is committed to the claim that the

74 In the original edition, the first quoted sentence begins: "It is evident that." (p. 87)

difference principle – together with the prior commitments to an equal scheme of basic liberties and to fair equality of opportunity – is the most appropriate standard, and it aims to establish this by considering the choice from the original position.

The most common interpretation of justice as fairness misinterprets several passages from *A Theory of Justice* and stitches them together to construct an argument that Rawls does not make for a position that he does not hold. In the following three chapters, I attempt to explain the argument that Rawls makes in each of the three parts of *A Theory of Justice*. This is followed by a chapter on some of the ways in which Rawls's theory developed after *A Theory of Justice*, and I conclude with a chapter discussing some important criticisms of justice as fairness. Although its centrality to contemporary political philosophy is generally recognized, the arguments in *A Theory of Justice* are not, in fact, widely accepted. The theory is not without weaknesses, as Rawls himself was quick to acknowledge. Still, when the most significant distortions are removed, it is far more appealing than is commonly believed. For those of us who are attracted to its principles and to its approach, the theoretical task is to rescue its core from misinterpretation and misguided criticisms. As citizens, however, our job is to help move our society in the direction of justice as we understand it.

CHAPTER I

Part 1 of A Theory of Justice – *Theory*

SOCIAL JUSTICE

The first section of *A Theory of Justice* is called "The Role of Justice," and it begins with a bold assertion of the centrality of the virtue of justice: "Justice is the first virtue of social institutions, as truth is of systems of thought." (*TJ*, 3/3) The claim is that while there may be other virtues of social institutions, they may not be achieved by sacrificing justice. If we must face a choice between justice and efficiency, for example, we are required to select justice. Justice and efficiency need not always conflict, however, and as long as we do not infringe on the requirements of justice, we may choose efficient institutional arrangements. It is important to notice that this initial announcement also indicates that the theory will primarily be a theory of the justice of social institutions. To be sure, there will be implications for individual conduct, but there are good reasons to start by considering social justice.

Having asserted the central importance of social justice, Rawls makes a further, even more dramatic claim concerning the content of social justice:

> Each person possesses an inviolability founded on justice that even the welfare of society as a whole cannot override. For this reason justice denies that the loss of freedom for some is made right by a greater good shared by others. It does not allow that the sacrifices imposed on a few are outweighed by the larger sum of advantages by many. (*TJ*, 3–4/3)

This is a criticism of utilitarianism, which holds that imposing a sacrifice on one person may be compensated for by gains to others if such a trade-off increases the overall level of happiness. In contrast, justice as fairness requires that we recognize the "inviolability" of each individual and that we not focus only on aggregate gains or losses. However, Rawls does not defend an absolutist position according to which it is never permissible to restrict individual freedoms no matter what the consequences. Such an extreme absolutism is indefensible, and as he concedes, "No doubt [these propositions] are expressed too strongly." (*TJ*, 4/4) The more moderate position that he actually defends is that it is impermissible to sacrifice an individual's basic liberties for aggregate economic gains.

By participating in social institutions in association with others we are better able to pursue our various goals. Yet our goals sometimes conflict, and we "are not indifferent as to how the greater benefits produced by [our] collaboration are distributed, for in order to pursue [our] ends [we] each prefer a larger to a lesser share." (*TJ*, 4/4) Individuals are assumed to have different and potentially conflicting conceptions of what goals are worth pursuing and which conception of a good life to affirm. Social institutions can mediate these conflicts, but it is not obvious how they should be designed in order to do this fairly. We need some principled way "for choosing among the various social arrangements which determine this division of advantages and for underwriting an agreement on the proper distributive shares." (*TJ*, 4/4) The principles of social justice are designed to do exactly this. The fundamental goal of *A Theory of Justice* is to develop an account of these principles.

Justice as fairness focuses on the justice of institutions as opposed to the many other objects that we can evaluate from the point of view of justice. We can ask, for example, whether a person is just or whether a judge's decision is just, but when we assess basic social justice, we are assessing "the basic structure of society, or more exactly, the way in which the major social institutions distribute fundamental rights and duties and determine the division of advantages from social cooperation." (*TJ*, 7/6) The basic structure of society consists in the major political, economic, and social institutions of a society "Taken together as one scheme." (*TJ*, 7/6) Although there will be implications that take us beyond the basic structure, it is this that justice as fairness aims to evaluate.

One of the reasons for starting with the justice of the basic structure is that "its effects are so profound and present from the start." (*TJ*, 7/7) This is enough to establish the importance of basic social justice. But there is another reason for the special concern with the basic structure. Whatever differences divide them, all of the members of a society must share a single basic structure. As long as individuals remain in the society – and as a simplifying assumption, we assume that they will – they have no choice but to function with the background conditions established by the basic structure. As Rawls points out in *Justice as Fairness*: "it is no defense of the principles of political justice to say to those protesting them: You can always leave the country."[1] So, while the basic structure has profound effects, it is also something that we assume individuals have no choice but to share. This distinguishes it from voluntary associations which, while they may have profound effects, are not shared by all members of a society. Furthermore, the basic structure includes a system of law which is "a coercive order of public rules" and "defines the basic structure within which the pursuit of all other activities takes place."[2] (*TJ*, 235–6/207) Backed ultimately by a threat of force, the rules of the basic structure establish the background conditions within which persons pursue their goals individually and in voluntary association with others. Because of this combination of features, there is sufficient reason to consider what justice requires of the basic structure before considering the justice of voluntary associations and individual conduct, and there is no reason to assume that the principles appropriate for the basic structure will be directly applicable to these other cases.

Most of the arguments in *A Theory of Justice* rely on the idealizing assumption that we are considering the justice of a "well-ordered society." We are interested in determining which principles of justice should govern the design of the basic structure, assuming that the members of the society will support and share those principles. Of course, we also assume that individuals will pursue different and potentially conflicting goals, and this is what gives rise to the need for justice in the first place. This is an idealization because "Existing

[1] Rawls, *Justice as Fairness*, p. 94, n. 15.

[2] As Rawls explains in *Political Liberalism*,

> political power is always coercive power backed by the government's use of sanctions, for government alone has the authority to use force in upholding its laws. In a constitutional regime the special feature of the political relation is that political power is ultimately the power of the public, that is, the power of free and equal citizens as a collective body. (p. 136)

See also Rawls, *Justice as Fairness*, p. 40.

societies are of course seldom well-ordered in this sense, for what is just and unjust is usually in dispute." (*TJ*, 5/5) In actual societies, we must also decide how to respond to the fact that not everyone complies with the requirements of ideal justice. "Obviously," Rawls comments, "the problems of partial compliance theory are the pressing and urgent matters. These are the things that we are faced with in everyday life." (*TJ*, 8–9/8) Still, it makes sense to begin with the ideal case in which we assume "full compliance" with the principles of justice. The hope is that the more complicated cases in which a society is characterized only by partial compliance will become more tractable when we understand what would be required in the ideal.

THE SOCIAL CONTRACT

While justice as fairness is part of the social contract tradition, it rejects the traditional model of a contract made from a pre-political state of nature. It relies instead on a "purely hypothetical" agreement made from an "original position of equality." (*TJ*, 12/11) The crucial feature of this initial choice situation is that

> no one knows his place in society, his class position or social status, nor does any one know his fortune in the distribution of natural assets and abilities, his intelligence, strength, and the like. I shall even assume that the parties do not know their conceptions of the good or their special psychological propensities. The principles of justice are chosen behind a veil of ignorance. (*TJ*, 12/11)

The idea is that from behind the veil of ignorance, the parties making the agreement would be unable to tailor the principles to favor themselves at the expense of others. Thus, "this initial situation is fair between individuals as moral persons, that is, as rational beings with their own ends and capable, I shall assume, of a sense of justice." (*TJ*, 12/11) The reference to "moral persons" is significant. As we have seen, in a well-ordered society, individuals have a wide variety of conceptions of the good that they will pursue rationally. But they also have a sense of justice that will put limits on permissible conceptions of the good. "Moral persons" are moved not only by their conception of the good life, but have this more complex structure of motivation. (We will consider this in more depth in chapter 3.)

We stipulate that the parties in the original position are "rational and mutually disinterested." (*TJ*, 13/12) Although the veil of ignorance prevents them from knowing their specific conceptions of the good, they are motivated to achieve the goals specified by their conception as best they can. The rationality that characterizes them "must be interpreted as far as possible in the narrow sense, standard in economic theory, of taking the most effective means to given ends." (*TJ*, 14/12) Because the parties in the original position select principles "solely on the basis of what seems best calculated to further their interests so far as they can ascertain them," (*TJ*, 584/512) they are not motivated by a sense of justice, and therefore they do not fit the description of "moral persons." The assumption of mutual disinterest is made in order to represent the diversity of conceptions of the good that the parties hold. Rawls hastens to add: "This does not mean that the parties are egoists, that is, individuals with only certain kinds of interests, say in wealth, prestige, and domination." (*TJ*, 13/12) Members of different religions, for example, may value and pursue different and conflicting spiritual aims, but these differences need not be grounded in selfishness or egoism.

Although the parties in the original position are motivated only to pursue their conception of the good, the details of this conception are unknown to them because of the veil of ignorance. The veil forces them to consider the implications of their choice of principles for everyone in the society. While they may be tempted by principles that would bestow great advantages on certain individuals, they would have no assurance that they would be the ones to benefit. While nothing in the set-up prevents the parties from choosing utilitarian principles, Rawls argues that a different conception would be a more rational choice. In their initial formulation, the two principles that Rawls favors assert the following:

> the first requires equality in the assignment of basic rights and duties, while the second holds that social and economic inequalities, for example inequalities of wealth and authority, are just only if they result in compensating benefits for everyone, and in particular for the least advantaged members of society. (*TJ*, 14–15/13)

As we will see, Rawls gives priority to the first principle over the second. In contrast to utilitarianism, these egalitarian principles do not permit the sacrifice to one person's interests to be compensated by gains to others. "The intuitive idea," Rawls says, "is that . . . the division of advantages should be such as to draw forth the willing cooperation of everyone taking part in [the scheme of cooperation], including those less well situated." (*TJ*, 15/13)

REFLECTIVE EQUILIBRIUM

The original position is only one of indefinitely many hypothetical choice situations that we might consider. However, it is privileged because it represents assumptions that we believe appropriate when attempting to identify principles of justice. The restrictions that the veil of ignorance imposes on the deliberation of the parties reflect our assumptions about what should properly count as relevant and what as irrelevant in their deliberations. "The idea here is simply to make vivid to ourselves the restrictions that it seems reasonable to impose on arguments for principles of justice, and therefore on these principles themselves." (*TJ*, 18/16) For example, "it should be impossible to tailor principles to the circumstances of one's own case." (*TJ*, 18/16) The veil of ignorance prevents exactly that. Similarly, "It seems reasonable to suppose that the parties in the original position are equal." (*TJ*, 19/17) The important point is that these conditions will themselves incorporate moral commitments. In other words, there is no assumption that we can deduce principles of justice from non-moral premises. On the contrary, Rawls declares repeatedly that he rejects such a reductionist project.[3]

Once we see that we can incorporate moral assumptions into the design of the choice situation, there is no obstacle to checking the results of the choice against the moral judgments about which we are most confident. We hope that the principles chosen in the original position match those judgments and give us principled guidance in cases where we are less confident:

> For example, we are confident that religious intolerance and racial discrimination are unjust. We think that we have examined these things with care and have reached what we believe is an impartial judgment not likely to be

[3] See, for example, *TJ*, 584–5/512, and the discussion of reflective equilibrium in chapter 5 below.

distorted by an excessive attention to our own interests. These convictions are provisional fixed points which we presume any conception of justice must fit. But we have much less assurance as to what is the correct distribution of wealth and authority. Here we may be looking for a way to remove our doubts. (*TJ*, 19–20/17–18)

If the results of the choice from the original position do not match our provisional fixed points, then we face a choice. We can either revise our considered judgments or we change the conditions of the choice situation. For Rawls, there is no way to determine ahead of time, in general, which revision would be more appropriate.

If and when we manage to attain consistency between our considered judgments and the results from the choice situation, we will have reached what Rawls calls "reflective equilibrium." This is also the name for the method of justification in which the different elements are revised to achieve consistency. If our goal were to deduce principles of justice from self-evident or non-moral premises, the method of reflective equilibrium would be blatantly circular. But that is not our goal. We come to philosophical reflection from a condition of moral uncertainty, but not complete ignorance. We should work from what we know – or what we think we know – to try to make progress in areas where we need help. The original position is "an expository device" (*TJ*, 21/19) that helps us to move toward the goal of reflective equilibrium. We will return to consider some criticisms of the idea of reflective equilibrium in chapter 5.

UTILITARIANISM

In the preface Rawls claims that "During much of modern moral philosophy the predominant systematic theory has been some form of utilitarianism." (*TJ*, vii/xvii) For Rawls, the classical utilitarianism of Henry Sidgwick represents the high point of this tradition. There is a natural way of arriving at this form of utilitarianism. If we think of an individual aiming to realize her conception of the good over a complete life, we assume that it is perfectly rational for her to impose some costs at one point in order to achieve greater gains at other points. If we then extend this model to a society as a whole, we arrive at this thought:

> Just as an individual balances present and future gains against present and future losses, so a society may balance satisfactions and dissatisfactions between different individuals . . . The principle of choice for an association of men is interpreted as an extension of the principle of choice for one man. (*TJ*, 24/21)

Thus, we generate a utilitarian conception, according to which society properly aims at maximizing the net satisfaction of the aggregated preferences of its members.

There is, however, another way to look at classical utilitarianism. We can classify ethical theories in terms of how they relate "the two main concepts of ethics," namely, the good and the right. (*TJ*, 24/21) By definition, in a teleological theory "the good is defined independently from the right, and then the right is defined as that which maximizes the good." (*TJ*, 24/21–2) A deontological theory is any theory that does not have a teleological structure. This definition is broader than is common. On this definition deontological theories are not precluded from taking into account the consequences of an action or of an institutional design. In fact, Rawls insists that "All ethical doctrines worth our attention take consequences into account in judging rightness. One which did not would simply be irrational, crazy." (*TJ*, 30/26) The relevant questions are which consequences matter and why.

Teleological theories differ from one another primarily on the basis of the good that they take to be intrinsically valuable and therefore to be maximized. While utilitarianism identifies the good with utility or the satisfaction of desire, hedonism identifies it with pleasure, and perfectionism identifies it with some pre-moral account of human excellence. But whatever the good is taken to be, teleological theories offer a powerful account of the point of morality. When we act morally, they hold, we aim to do or to produce as much good as possible. "Indeed, it is tempting to suppose that it is self-evident that things should be arranged so as to lead to the most good." (*TJ*, 25/22)

Because a teleological principle such as utilitarianism aims to maximize some aggregate good, it must be indifferent to the distribution of that good except insofar as the total is affected. "Thus there is no reason in principle why the greater gains of some should not compensate for the lesser losses of others; or more importantly, why the violation of the liberty of a few might not be made right by the greater good shared by many." (*TJ*, 26/23) The possibility of such trade-offs stands in sharp contrast to a relatively secure fixed point in our thinking about justice:

> Justice denies that the loss of freedom for some is made right by a greater good shared by others . . . Therefore in a just society the basic liberties are taken for granted and the rights secured by justice are not subject to political bargaining or to the calculus of social interests. (*TJ*, 28/25)

It is presumably true that in many circumstances utilitarianism will provide at least some support for "common sense precepts of justice and notions of natural right." (*TJ*, 28/25) Still, there may be circumstances in which it conflicts with these precepts, and even when it does not conflict, its support will be subject to many uncertainties in the calculation of aggregate utility. At root the problem is that "Utilitarianism does not take seriously the distinction between persons." (*TJ*, 27/24)

Another difficulty with utilitarianism arises from the fact that, as a teleological theory, it must define the good without reference to any moral principles. The satisfaction of any preference or desire must be given positive weight, regardless of the moral assessment we might want to make of its content. "Thus if men take a certain pleasure in discriminating against one another . . . then the satisfaction of these desires must be weighed in our deliberations according to their intensity, or whatever, along with other desires." (*TJ*, 30–1/27) This seems objectionable. We want to say that the satisfaction of those desires should not count as good at all. While the individuals who hold those desires may treat their satisfaction as good, they are objectionable and should be granted no positive weight on the scales of justice. But we can only make that assessment if we have principles available to assess the moral permissibility of conceptions of the good. Since teleological theories base the right on an independent account of the good, they cannot make such assessments.

Justice as fairness, as a deontological theory, holds that justice is not simply a matter of maximizing some independently identifiable good. The satisfaction of certain immoral or unjust preferences should not count as a good at all. If, for example, an individual "finds that he enjoys seeing others in positions of lesser liberty," the satisfaction of this preference carries no weight at all from the perspective of justice. "The principles of right, and so of justice, put limits on which satisfactions have value; they impose restrictions on what are reasonable conceptions of one's good." (*TJ*, 31/27) Rawls expresses this by saying that "the concept of the right is prior to that of the good." (*TJ*, 31/28) This phrase has the potential to mislead, and we will return to it in chapter 3, but the thought is simply that the principles of right put limits on permissible goods: "interests requiring the violation of justice have no value." (*TJ*, 31/28)

INTUITIONISM

In the absence of a systematic alternative, when we see the weaknesses of utilitarianism, we may find ourselves embracing a kind of intuitionism. Rawls's definition of intuitionism is somewhat idiosyncratic. He does not think of it as an epistemological or metaphysical theory. Rather, he defines it as any conception according to which there is "a plurality of first principles which may conflict to give contrary directives in particular types of cases" and according to which there is "no explicit method, no priority rules, for weighing these principles against one another: [in particular cases] we are simply to strike a balance by intuition, by what seems to us most nearly right." (*TJ*, 34/30) In fact, this is really a form of pluralism together with a rejection of priority rules among the first principles.

Rawls's attitude toward this form of intuitionism is very interesting:

> Now there is nothing intrinsically irrational about this intuitionist doctrine. Indeed, it may be true . . . The only way . . . to dispute intuitionism is to set forth the recognizably ethical criteria that account for the weights which, in our considered judgments, we think appropriate to give to the plurality of principles. A refutation of intuitionism consists in presenting the sort of constructive criteria that are said not to exist. (*TJ*, 39/35)

Furthermore:

> No doubt any conception of justice will have to rely on intuition to some degree. Nevertheless, we should do what we can to reduce the direct appeal to our considered judgments . . . We should do what we can to formulate explicit principles for the priority problem, even though the dependence on intuition cannot be eliminated entirely. (*TJ*, 41/36–7)

Unlike utilitarianism, intuitionism, it seems, can provide a largely correct (though perhaps incomplete) description of our considered judgments as we embark on the process of attempting to reach reflective equilibrium. As we move in the direction of reflective equilibrium, we introduce principles and priority rules that bring structure to our sense of justice, resolving conflicts and gaps. In effect, Rawls assumes that we start in a position of intuitionism, and as we move in the direction of reflective equilibrium our goal is to push back the point at which we must simply resort to intuition and undefended judgments. But exactly how far we can succeed in this endeavor is something that can only be established by actually making the effort. It is important to make this effort and reduce the direct appeal to intuitions because when we appeal to them "the means of rational discussion have come to an end," (*TJ*, 41/37) and so there is no principled way to reconcile by reason conflicting intuitions.

Justice as fairness adopts three distinct strategies for pushing back the frontier at which we appeal to intuitions. The first is that there is a limited domain of application. Our focus, as we have seen, is on the basic structure of society. We are not aiming to establish a comprehensive account of morality. Second, although it recognizes more than one fundamental principle of justice, justice as fairness establishes an ordering among them, so there is no need to balance the principles against one another according to mere intuition. Third, justice as fairness attempts to reduce the direct dependence on intuition by considering the choice of principles from the original position and therefore "substituting prudential for moral judgment." (*TJ*, 44/39) By asking what would be chosen from the original position, "we have asked a much more limited question and have substituted for an ethical judgment a judgment of rational prudence." (*TJ*, 44/39) Questions of prudential judgment will not eliminate sometimes controversial appeals to intuition altogether, but "the task is that of reducing and not of eliminating entirely the reliance on intuitive judgments." (*TJ*, 44/39)

The problem with intuitionist theories, to repeat, is that they do not give us the guidance we need when we, collectively or individually, are conflicted or uncertain about what justice requires. If we were very confident and in agreement with one another about all of our particular judgments concerning justice, there would be little need to systematize them with general principles. That is not our situation or more precisely, that is our situation only with a limited number of easy cases that form our provisional fixed points. But even these considered judgments are not assumed to be foundational or immune from critical reflection, and in the process of formulating and refining our principles we may come to revise our assessment of them as well. Justice as fairness presents "the hypothesis that the principles which would be chosen in the original position are identical with those that match our considered judgments and so these principles describe our sense of justice." (*TJ*, 48/42)

At the same time, however, Rawls recognizes that full reflective equilibrium is an ideal that is not fully reachable. He is content to establish that the two principles move us closer to this ideal than traditional rivals. In particular Rawls expresses doubt about whether the strong priority that he gives to the first principle over the second is fully adequate: "while a lexical ordering may serve fairly well for some important cases, I assume that it will not be completely satisfactory." (*TJ*, 53/46) This recognition clearly illustrates that for Rawls constructing and defending a conception of justice is a practical undertaking. It is not enough to show the theoretical possibility that some other conception may be superior. The task is to identify it as best we can.

> Objections by way of counterexamples are to be made with care, since these may tell us only what we know already, namely that our theory is wrong somewhere . . . All theories are presumably mistaken in places. The real question at any given time is which of the views already proposed is the best approximation overall. (*TJ*, 52/45)

This can only be done by spelling out the precise details of particular conceptions of justice and comparing and assessing them.

THE TWO PRINCIPLES OF JUSTICE

In chapter 2 Rawls describes the content of the two principles of justice before going on in chapter 3 to argue that they would be chosen from the original position. Yet in describing the content of the principles, he offers some remarks that are designed to "prepare the way for the favored interpretation of the two principles so that these criteria, especially the second one, will not strike the reader as extreme."[4] (*TJ*, 65) Unfortunately, some of these remarks have suggested several mistaken interpretations not only of the content of the principles themselves, but of the basic approach of justice as fairness.

As we have seen, the principles of justice are developed to evaluate the basic structure of society, which Rawls identifies with "the arrangement of major social institutions into one scheme of cooperation." (*TJ*, 54/47) The idea of treating the basic structure as a single scheme allows for the possibility that "a social system may be unjust even though none of its institutions are unjust taken separately: the injustice is a consequence of how they are combined together into a single system." (*TJ*, 57/50) Furthermore, the two principles, which are designed for the evaluation of an institutional scheme, "must not be confused with the principles which apply to individuals and their actions in particular circumstances." (*TJ*, 54/47) Yet the relationship between institutions and the actions of individuals is a subtle one. Social institutions do not have an existence independent from the actions and attitudes of the people who create, sustain, transform, or destroy them. One way in which individuals sustain institutions is simply by conforming to their rules, which set out rights, responsibilities, and procedures. Ideally, we would like to institute rules and procedures that would coordinate individuals' pursuit of their (permissible) goals in such a way that we "achieve results which although not intended or perhaps even foreseen by them are nevertheless the best ones from the standpoint of social justice." (*TJ*, 57/49) The idea would be that just as the invisible hand of an idealized market steers transactions toward efficiency, so the invisible hand of the institutions of a just basic structure would steer interactions toward justice.

The two principles of justice attempt to do exactly that. In a statement of the two principles that will be refined later,[5] Rawls presents them as follows:

> First: each person is to have an equal right to the most extensive scheme of equal basic liberties compatible with a similar scheme of liberties for others.

[4] In the original edition of *TJ*, this sentence ends not with "extreme" but with "too eccentric or bizarre." (p. 75)

[5] See the "final statement" of the two principles at *TJ*, 302–3/266–7.

Second: social and economic inequalities are to be arranged so that they are both (a) reasonably expected to be to everyone's advantage, and (b) attached to positions and offices open to all. (*TJ*, 53)[6]

Roughly, the first principle governs the design of the political structure which secures the basic liberties, while the two parts of the second principle are concerned with the institutions that regulate social and economic inequalities. An essential part of justice as fairness is the ordering among these principles. Rawls defends a strong – "lexical" – ordering of the first principle over the second, so that social and economic gains (permitted by the second principle) cannot be achieved by sacrificing the equal scheme of basic liberties (specified by the first principle). Similarly, there is a strong priority within the second principle: "One applies the second principle by holding positions open, and then, subject to this constraint, arranges social and economic inequalities so that everyone benefits." (*TJ*, 61/53)

The statement of the first principle which I quoted above is from the revised edition of *A Theory of Justice*, and it represents a subtle but significant change from the original edition, where the principle reads: "each person is to have an equal right to the most extensive basic liberty compatible with a similar liberty for others." (p. 60) Instead of referring to "liberty," the revised principle now refers to "basic liberties." Other passages throughout *A Theory of Justice* were modified in a similar way, although not all, and Rawls still sometimes refers to the first principle as a principle of "equal liberty." In *Political Liberalism*, he explains why the original formulation may be misleading:

No priority is assigned to liberty as such, as if the exercise of something called "liberty" has a preeminent value and is the main if not the sole end of political and social justice . . . Throughout the history of democratic thought the focus has been on achieving certain specific liberties and constitutional guarantees . . . The account of the basic liberties follows this tradition.[7]

6 In the original edition, the first principle reads: "each person is to have an equal right to the most extensive basic liberty compatible with a similar liberty for others." (p. 60) See the discussion below.

7 Rawls, *Political Liberalism*, pp. 291–2.

This means, of course, that the basic liberties need to be specified and defended. This was something partially addressed even in the original edition, although as we will see in chapters 4 and 5 this account changed when Rawls later revised the defense of the priority of the first principle. A preliminary list of the basic liberties includes political liberties, freedom of speech and assembly, liberty of conscience and freedom of thought, the right to hold "personal property," and rights associated with the rule of law. (*TJ*, 61/53) A full account of these basic liberties will likely depend on "the particular circumstances – social, economic, and technological – of a given society."[8] (*TJ*, 54)

The two principles impose a kind of egalitarianism – even if not strict equality – on the design of the basic structure. More specifically, they focus on the distribution of shares of "social primary goods," as opposed to levels of satisfaction, total well-being, utility, or happiness. We will examine in chapter 4 the justification for relying on primary goods and how this account changed. For now, we can simply state that they include "rights, liberties, and opportunities, and income and wealth" (*TJ*, 62/54) as well as the social basis of self-respect.[9] (*TJ*, 178/155, 440/386) The idea is that a just basic structure will aim to eliminate structural inequalities in the distribution of primary goods except when a structural inequality works to everyone's advantage relative to a baseline of equality. When we apply this requirement to different primary goods we get different results. Roughly speaking, inequalities in the scheme of basic liberties would not work to everyone's advantage. Therefore the first principle requires an equal scheme of basic liberties. Similarly, unequal opportunities would not work to the advantage of those with limited opportunities, so the second principle requires fair equality of opportunity. However, it is possible that an economic institution that allows certain structural inequalities in income and wealth among representative segments of the society might work to the advantage of everyone, including those who gain least relative to the benchmark of equality. Such an

[8] This passage was added to the revised edition and reflects Rawls's concern to specify the basic liberties rather than to assume that there is a uniform quantity of "liberty" to be maximized.

[9] In *Justice as Fairness*, Rawls considers adding medical care and "a certain amount of leisure time." (pp. 157–61; 168–76; 179) See the discussion in ch. 4.

economic institution would be just, even though it would allow some structural inequality.

Evidently Rawls believes that the first principle will be more familiar to readers, and he proceeds to attempt to clarify the content of the second principle. The two parts of the second principle function together to specify which structural inequalities are permissible and how they are to be filled by individuals. Whatever the permissible structural inequalities are, they must be filled according to procedures that are "open to all." This phrase can be given a loose or a strict interpretation. The less demanding interpretation, which Rawls calls "careers open to talents," requires merely "formal equality of opportunity in that all have at least the same legal rights of access to all advantaged social positions." (*TJ*, 72/62) This would be sufficient to rule out systems of hereditary privilege as well as discrimination based on criteria not materially relevant to positions. Historically, the achievement of this ideal was an extremely significant step, championed by many liberal reformers often under the banner of meritocracy. However, although formal equality of opportunity in this sense of non-discrimination is necessary, justice demands more. "The thought here is that positions are to be not only open in a formal sense, but that all should have a fair chance to attain them." (*TJ*, 73/63) Even under conditions of non-discrimination, fair equality of opportunity may be undermined by inequalities that can be traced to social class. The idea of fair equality of opportunity specifies that "[i]n all sectors of society there should be roughly equal prospects of culture and achievement for everyone similarly motivated and endowed. The expectations of those with the same abilities and aspirations should not be affected by their social class." (*TJ*, 73/63)

If a society were fully to satisfy the requirements of fair equality of opportunity, individuals would have a fair chance of attaining the various social positions regardless of the social class into which they were born. But this does not yet tell us which structural positions are permissible in the first place. Our preliminary statement of the second principle holds that structural inequalities are just only if they are "reasonably expected to be to everyone's advantage." But this phrase is also subject to a loose or a strict interpretation. The less demanding interpretation, which Rawls calls "the principle of efficiency," requires merely that the institutions of the basic structure satisfy the requirement of "Pareto optimality." An arrangement fails this requirement if there is some other arrangement in which there would be an improvement to at least one position without any other position becoming worse off. An arrangement satisfies this condition as long as there are no gains to be had "for free" – that is, without any loss to others. This is a weak requirement since typically there will be many different arrangements that will satisfy it – in effect, any arrangement that does not have any "waste." To take an extreme case, an arrangement in which one person is fabulously wealthy and everyone else is reduced to abject poverty may satisfy this requirement if the rich individual would not do as well under other arrangements. The principle of efficiency by itself does not provide any grounds for selecting from among these Pareto-optimal arrangements even though they may differ radically from one another. Therefore, "[t]he problem is to choose between them, to find a conception of justice that singles out one of these efficient distributions as also just." (*TJ*, 71/61)

The difference principle holds that a structural inequality is just only if the expected shares of the least advantaged position are greater than the expected shares of the least advantaged position in the absence of the inequality. If, from a position of equality, the more advantaged gain at the cost of the least advantaged, the difference principle would disallow such an inequality. Structural inequalities are permissible only when they serve to increase the total goods and when that increase works to the advantage of each position. This is possible if the "better prospects act as incentives so that the economic process is more efficient, innovation proceeds at a faster pace, and so on." (*TJ*, 78/68) Such an argument is sometimes characterized as "trickle down" economics in which gains to the wealthy "trickle down" to the poor. But it is crucial to remember that for Rawls, the baseline from which we assess prospective gains and losses is one of equality, not the inequalities that might currently exist in an actual society. If there currently are unjust inequalities, the difference principle may very well sanction losses to the wealthy in order to achieve gains for the poor. (*TJ*, 79/69) Furthermore, Rawls is careful not to claim that any particular inequality would, in fact, generate the right kinds of incentives: "The point is that something of this kind must be argued if these inequalities are to satisfy by [*sic*] the difference principle."[10] (*TJ*, 68) The burden, therefore, is on those who claim that a structural inequality is justified to show that it really would satisfy the difference principle. If they cannot do this, then the inequality is unjust.

Fair equality of opportunity and the difference principle work together to create a system of "pure procedural justice." (*TJ*, 85/74) In general, the idea of procedural justice shifts the focus from specific outcomes to the procedures that generate them. In the case of perfect procedural justice, we know what a just outcome would be, and we develop a procedure that (if followed properly) will produce that result. In the case of imperfect procedural justice, in contrast, there is no procedure that will always produce the desired result. In both of these cases we have a way of characterizing the appropriate result that is independent of the procedure itself. Rawls mentions a criminal trial as an example of imperfect procedural justice since although we may aim to convict all and only those who are in fact guilty, no procedure can rule out the possibility of so-called miscarriages of justice. In contrast, we have a case of pure procedural justice when there is no way to specify the just outcome except by constructing a procedure and actually allowing it to be carried out. It is important, of course, that the procedure be chosen correctly, and we can assess the reasons for and against different procedures. But there is no way to assess specific outcomes except by selecting the best procedure and then allowing it to generate an outcome.[11]

[10] The corresponding passage in the original edition reads: "The point is that something of this kind must be argued if these inequalities are to be just by the difference principle." (p. 78) If we assume that the society is "close-knit" and that "chain-connection" holds, we can say that the difference principle selects the most egalitarian of the efficient arrangements. A society is "close-knit" when "it is impossible to raise or lower the expectations of any representative man without raising or lowering the expectation of every other representative man." (*TJ*, 80/70) And chain-connection holds when any change that raises the prospects of the most advantaged and the least advantaged will also raise the prospects of the positions in between. (*TJ*, 80/69) Rawls assumes that these conditions hold, but the defense of the difference principle does not depend on either of these assumptions. See the discussion in Rex Martin, *Rawls and Rights* (Kansas University Press, 1985), ch. 5.

[11] Rawls also sometimes speaks of "quasi-pure" procedural justice. (*TJ*, 362/318) This is a hybrid between imperfect and pure procedural justice. It holds when we know that a just outcome must be within a certain range, but within that range we have no way of selecting the best outcome without relying on the procedure. Insofar as the procedure may generate an outcome beyond the acceptable range, we have a case that resembles imperfect procedural justice, but as long as it generates an outcome within that range, it resembles pure procedural

With these definitions, we can now make the crucial point that the actual allocation of specific goods to specific individuals is a matter of pure procedural justice. The principles of justice are not designed to determine directly which individuals are entitled to which shares of resources. Rather, they are designed to evaluate the institutional rules within which individuals come to be entitled to particular goods. When the principles refer to "inequalities," these are structural inequalities that may predictably result from the functioning of the various institutional arrangements. There is no way to answer the question of whether some allocation of goods to the particular individuals of a society is just except by instituting a fair system of rules and then allowing those individuals to interact in ways that are permissible (according to the just rules) and desirable (according to their own preferences):

> A distribution cannot be judged in isolation from the system of which it is the outcome or from what individuals have done in good faith in the light of established expectations. If it is asked in the abstract whether one distribution of a given stock of things to definite individuals with known desires and preferences is better than another, then there is simply no answer to this question. (*TJ*, 88/76)

Rawls holds that we may rely on this kind of pure procedural justice, but only if we also ensure fair equality of opportunity. It is not enough to say that the structural inequalities generated by the rules of the economic institutions work to everyone's advantage. Everyone must have a fair opportunity to fill the various positions.

We use the shares of social primary goods that individuals can expect to receive over a complete life to identify the various structural positions. Rawls clarifies and develops his defense of primary goods in subsequent work, and we will consider this in chapter 4. What is important here is that their use is not dependent on any particular conception of the good. Rather, they are designed to contribute to people's "success in carrying out their intentions and in advancing their ends, whatever these ends may be." (*TJ*, 92/79) Although some primary goods may be viewed by some people as valuable for their

justice since we have no independent grounds on which to assess it. In my opinion, most of the cases which Rawls describes as pure procedural justice are, strictly speaking, quasi-pure since some possible outcomes would be unacceptable.

own sakes, different individuals will generally use them to pursue different ends. And given the diversity of permissible ends that individuals will pursue, there is no assumption that individuals will have equal success in accomplishing their ends. Justice as fairness "does not look behind the use which persons make of the rights and opportunities available to them in order to measure, much less to maximize, the satisfactions they achieve." (*TJ*, 94/80) Once we are satisfied that the structural inequalities associated with an institutional scheme satisfy the difference principle and the positions are filled in accordance with fair equality of opportunity, then "other inequalities are allowed to arise from men's voluntary actions in accordance with the principle of free association." (*TJ*, 96/82) Against the background of just institutional arrangements the fortunes of particular individuals will wax and wane in response to their talent, effort, and luck.

DESERT

As we saw in the introduction, many critics have read Rawls as endorsing a kind of luck egalitarianism, according to which the point of just institutions is to redress any inequality for which individuals cannot be held responsible. But Rawls contrasts the difference principle with the principle of redress, which holds that "undeserved inequalities call for redress; and since inequalities of birth and natural endowment are undeserved, these inequalities are to be somehow compensated for." (*TJ*, 100/86) Like the principle of redress, the difference principle rejects utilitarianism's emphasis on "social efficiency and technocratic values." (*TJ*, 101/87) However, while the principle of redress holds that all undeserved inequalities are, as such, unjust, the difference principle rejects this view. It holds that "[t]hose who have been favored by nature, whoever they are, may gain from their good fortune only on terms that improve the situation of those who have lost out." (*TJ*, 101/87) Underlying this approach is the view that:

> The natural distribution is neither just nor unjust; nor is it unjust that persons are born into society at some particular position. These are simply natural facts. What is just and unjust is the way that institutions deal with these facts. (*TJ*, 102/87)

The way that the difference principle deals with these facts, and specifically with the sheer diversity and range of capacities and abilities, is to reward them differentially when doing so works to the advantage of the least advantaged position. Everyone in a society can benefit from the fact that their talents and abilities complement one another. This allows us to view the range and variety as a "common asset" (*TJ*, 101/87) that the society can use to work to everyone's advantage.[12]

It is sometimes objected that the difference principle interferes with the better advantaged citizens getting what they deserve. In our colloquial speech, we say that people deserve things on a variety of grounds – for example, the better team deserves to win, the criminal deserves a long prison term, workers deserve a living wage, she did not deserve the bad luck that came her way, etc. There are many different grounds for making such desert claims, and it is important to see that Rawls restricts his technical term "desert" to claims based on an assessment of moral virtue. This is most clear, perhaps, when he explains the idea of distributing goods "according to moral desert" as "[J]ustice is happiness according to virtue." (*TJ*, 310/273) Thus, Rawls takes it as a trivial and obvious fact that "We do not deserve our place in the distribution of native endowments, any more than we deserve our initial starting place in society."[13] (*TJ*, 89) That is, neither our natural capacities nor our initial social position could possibly be ours on account of our degree of moral virtue. In contrast to this restricted use, we can say that individuals have a legitimate expectation in some good when they have followed the rules of a just scheme that specifies

[12] This is related to the idea of viewing society as a social union of social unions that we will discuss in chapter 3. In the original edition, Rawls wrote: "We see then that the difference principle represents, in effect, an agreement to regard the distribution of natural talents as a common asset and to share in the benefits of this distribution whatever it turns out to be." (p. 101) Many have taken this passage to suggest that the natural assets themselves are common assets. Yet the claim concerns the distribution, not the assets themselves, and it states that the difference principle "in effect" represents it this way. In the revised edition, Rawls elaborates: "The difference principle represents, in effect, an agreement to regard the distribution of natural talents as in some respects a common asset and to share in the greater social and economic benefits made possible by the complementarities of this distribution." (*TJ*, 87) See the discussion in Rawls, *Justice as Fairness*, pp. 75–6.

[13] In the original edition, the corresponding sentence reads: "It seems to be one of the fixed points of our considered judgments that no one deserves his place in the distribution of native endowments, any more than one deserves one's initial starting place in society." (p. 104)

that entitlement. (*TJ*, 311/273) A just economic scheme, for example will specify the terms of contract that will transfer ownership of some property from one person to another. When such rules are followed, we might colloquially say that individuals deserve that property, in the sense of having a right or being entitled to it. But in Rawls's more precise language, we would say that they have a legitimate expectation in it.

So, to repeat, it is sometimes objected that the difference principle does not give people what they deserve. Now it is certainly true that the difference principle does not reward people according to an assessment of their moral virtue. But justice as fairness accepts the idea that a just scheme should respect the legitimate expectations that individuals form. The problem is that this is incomplete as a specification of distributive justice, since the idea of legitimate expectations makes reference to the idea of a just scheme of cooperation. When individuals act in ways that a just scheme specifies as entitling them to a greater share of wealth, they have a legitimate expectation in that greater share. But this leaves unspecified the properties of a just scheme. It is true that "the more advantaged are entitled to whatever they can acquire in accordance with the rules of a fair system of social cooperation. Our problem is how this scheme, the basic structure of society, is to be designed."[14] (*TJ*, 89) The difference principle provides part of Rawls's answer to this question by saying that a just scheme will allow certain social positions to have a higher expectation of goods when doing so works to the advantage of all social positions. In this way it also represents an interpretation of the ideal of fraternity: "the idea of not wanting to have greater advantages unless this is to the benefit of others who are less well off." (*TJ*, 105/90)

DUTIES AND OBLIGATIONS

The focus to this point has been resolutely on standards for the assessment of the basic structure of society. But social institutions are not independent of the actions and attitudes of individuals. On the contrary: "The social system is not an unchangeable order beyond human control but a pattern of human action." (*TJ*, 102/88) Therefore, any

[14] These sentences were added to the revised edition.

account of the justice of institutions will have implications for individual conduct. It is important to remember that this limited goal does not exhaust the moral demands of justice – to say nothing of the other virtues – that apply to individuals. Although Rawls alludes to the possibility of developing "the broader notion of rightness as fairness" (*TJ*, 111/95), that is not his project.

To clarify the principles of individual conduct, consider the analytic distinction between obligations and natural duties. Both represent moral requirements on individuals. Obligations are by definition grounded in the principle of fairness, while natural duties are not grounded in any single principle. The principle of fairness holds that:

> a person is required to do his part as defined by the rules of an institution when two conditions are met: first, the institution is just (or fair), that is, it satisfies the two principles of justice; and second, one has voluntarily accepted the benefits of the arrangement or taken advantage of the opportunities it offers to further one's interests. (*TJ*, 111–12/96)

When we voluntarily participate in a just institution, the rules and procedures of that institution will specify various benefits and burdens that accrue to us for various reasons. The benefits, we have already seen, are "legitimate expectations." The burdens are "obligations," and the principle of fairness holds that there is a moral requirement that they be fulfilled.

Two points are worth emphasizing about this narrow account of obligations. First, since the principle of fairness refers to just institutions, it does not generate obligations "to unjust institutions, or at least to institutions which exceed the limits of tolerable injustice (so far undefined)." (*TJ*, 112/96) This is not to say that in such circumstances we have no moral requirements, only that they will not be obligations in the technical sense at issue here and that an investigation of them will be part of non-ideal theory. Second, obligations "arise as a result of our voluntary acts; these acts may be the giving of express or tacit undertakings, such as promises and agreements, but they need not be, as in the case of accepting benefits." (*TJ*, 113/97) Note the implication that accepting benefits must be voluntary in the appropriate sense. This implies minimally the existence of a reasonable opportunity to turn down the benefits and thereby to escape the obligations. This is particularly significant since, as we have seen, Rawls assumes that individuals will remain members of their society over a complete life, so they cannot be said to have voluntarily accepted the benefits of participation in their society. Therefore "There is, I believe, no political obligation, strictly speaking, for citizens generally."[15] (*TJ*, 114/98) This is not to deny, however, that there is a general moral requirement on citizens to comply with the laws of a just society. The point is that this cannot be justified on the basis of the principle of fairness since there is no relevant voluntary undertaking.

This places the moral requirement of compliance under the category of natural duties, which "apply to us without regard to our voluntary acts." (*TJ*, 114/98) Some examples of these natural duties include "the duty of helping another when he is in need or jeopardy, provided that one can do so without excessive risk or loss to oneself; the duty not to harm or injure another; and the duty not to cause unnecessary suffering." (*TJ*, 114/98) But for our purposes, the most important is the duty of justice, which "requires us to support and to comply with just institutions that exist and apply to us. It also constrains us to further just arrangements not yet established, at least when this can be done without too much cost to ourselves." (*TJ*, 115/99) Although the natural duties – and the duty of justice, in particular – do not bind on account of any voluntary undertaking, we can still provide a defense of them. In particular, we can consider what support they might receive, along with the principles of social justice, from the perspective of the original position. We will consider this along with limitations on the duty of compliance in chapter 2.

THE ORIGINAL POSITION

We can now turn to the direct argument for the principles of justice. We already know that "The intuitive idea of justice as fairness is

[15] This is a change from Rawls's position in earlier work where he held that

> our moral obligation to obey the law is a special case of the duty of fair play. This means that the legal order is construed as a system of social cooperation to which we become bound because: first, the scheme is just (that is, it satisfies the two principles of justice) . . . and second, we have accepted, and intend to continue to accept, its benefits. ("Legal Obligation and the Duty of Fair Play" [1964] in Freeman, *Collected Papers*, p. 128)

to think of the first principles of justice as themselves the object of an original agreement in a suitably defined initial situation." (*TJ*, 118/102) The hypothetical choice situation must be designed in such a way that it can help us move toward reflective equilibrium. It can do this if it allows us to replace a more difficult problem with one that is more manageable but which we hypothesize has the same solution. We specify the motives and goals as well as information and options available to the parties so that when they make a rational choice, we can recognize it to be fair. Ideally, the hope is that once we have specified the information, motivation, and choices available to the parties, "[w]hat these individuals will do is then derived by strictly deductive reasoning from these assumptions about their beliefs and interests, their situation and the options open to them." (*TJ*, 119/103) The point of calling this reasoning "deductive" is not that the set-up of the choice situation is itself a matter of deduction or that empirical knowledge must somehow be excluded from all moral deliberation. Rather it is to emphasize that we assume that the parties to the hypothetical agreement are rational. This is something we stipulate along with the other features of the choice situation. Given our goal of moving toward reflective equilibrium, it is no surprise that the original position "embodies features peculiar to moral theory." (*TJ*, 120/104)

The veil of ignorance, we already know, prevents the parties from having any information that is irrelevant to the construction of principles of social justice. They do know, however, that they are selecting principles to govern the design of the basic structure of society. They also know that the society for which they are selecting the principles is in "the circumstances of justice." These are "the normal conditions under which human cooperation is both possible and necessary." (*TJ*, 126/109) Thus, the parties know that they are choosing principles for people who are "roughly similar in physical and mental powers" and who occupy "a definite geographical territory" in conditions of "moderate scarcity" in the sense that cooperative actions are neither superfluous nor will they "inevitably break down." (*TJ*, 126–7/109–10) In addition, the parties know that they will each have their own plans of life "or conceptions of the good, [which] lead them to have different ends and purposes, and to make conflicting claims on the natural and social resources available." (*TJ*, 127/110) These goals are typically embedded within "a diversity of philosophical and religious beliefs, and of political and social doctrines." (*TJ*, 127/110) Rawls would later come to call these broader frameworks "comprehensive doctrines."

We further stipulate that the parties "try to advance their conception of the good as best they can, and that in attempting to do this they are not bound by prior moral ties to each other." (*TJ*, 128/111) Although it might seem more appropriate to have the parties motivated by a sense of justice, this will not do. As we have seen, we set up the original position in an effort to help us reach reflective equilibrium, but because it is strictly hypothetical it remains up to us to determine what would be chosen from that situation. If we force ourselves to consider which principles would match the sense of justice of the parties, we simply reiterate our initial problem, and the original position would not be helpful. It is only because the parties have a different motivation than we do that the construction may advance our understanding. Of course, given the motivations that we stipulate for the parties, we must be careful to specify choice conditions so that they are led to select principles that we can recognize to be fair despite that not being their direct aim. Hence, it is crucial that the parties make their selection from behind the veil of ignorance.

To repeat a frequently overlooked point, there is no assumption that the conceptions of the good that the parties are attempting to advance are narrowly selfish:

> While these plans determine the aims and interests of a self, the aims and interests are not presumed to be egoistic or selfish. Whether this is the case depends upon the kinds of ends which a person pursues. If wealth, position, and influence, and the accolades of social prestige, are a person's final purposes, then surely his conception of the good is egoistic. His dominant interests are in himself, not merely, as they must always be, interests of a self. (*TJ*, 129/111)

The parties can no more assume that everyone will be narrowly selfish than they can assume that they all share any particular goals or single religion. The assumption of "mutual disinterest" (*TJ*, 13–14/12, 129/111–12) among the parties does not reflect an extreme individualism or selfishness, but rather the fact that they cannot assume that any particular conception of the good will be universally shared.

In the original edition of *A Theory of Justice*, Rawls introduced a complication into the motivation of parties in order to handle the problem of justice between generations. If the parties were motivated only to choose principles that advanced their conceptions of the good as well as possible given their limited information, they apparently would not be concerned to ensure the fair treatment of future generations. Thus, Rawls raises the possibility of stipulating that the parties be motivated by a "desire to further the welfare of their nearest descendants."[16] (*TJ*, original edition, p. 128) This stipulation turns out to be potentially misleading, inelegant, and unnecessary. It is potentially misleading because Rawls raises the possibility of considering the parties to be "heads of families" in order to make this intergenerational concern more vivid. This has suggested to some a latent sexism in the set-up of the original position (based on the assumption – not made by Rawls – that the representatives are male) and that the structure of the family is somehow immune from evaluation from the perspective of justice. It is inelegant because it introduces an artificial constraint into the motivation of the parties. After all, not everyone in a well-ordered society has a conception of the good which gives a prominent place to immediate descendents – not everyone will even have descendents. And finally, as we will see in chapter 2, in the years immediately after the publication of *A Theory of Justice*, Rawls came to recognize that this stipulation was unnecessary.

Given our goal of reaching reflective equilibrium, we can stipulate that the principles chosen by the parties in the original position must meet certain formal conditions that we believe "all ethical principles" must meet. (*TJ*, 130/112) The principles must be general so that they do not make reference to particular individuals. They also should be universal in that they should "hold for everyone in virtue of their being moral persons." (*TJ*, 132/114) This has the implication that it must be possible (and not self-defeating) for everyone to act on them. The principles should satisfy the publicity requirement so that the parties know they are selecting principles that will inform the public deliberations of citizens concerning the design of their

[16] The corresponding passage in the revised edition refers to a "desire to further the well-being of at least their more immediate descendants." (*TJ*, 111) But, as I argue below, this assumption should have been dropped altogether.

basic structure. In order to be able to assess institutional designs, the principles should satisfy an ordering condition. This implies that the ranks that the principles assign to arrangements should be transitive. But it also requires that the ordering be "based on certain relevant aspects of persons and their situation which are independent from their social position, or their capacity to intimidate and coerce." (*TJ* 134/116) And lastly, the principles should satisfy the finality condition. This means that when citizens deliberate about matters of basic social justice, "There are no higher standards to which arguments in support of claims can be addressed; reasoning successfully from these principles is conclusive." (*TJ*, 135/116) The principles, in other words, are to "override the demands of law and custom, and of social rules generally" as well as "considerations of prudence and self-interest." (*TJ*, 135/116–17) This is not to say that we must aim at completely expunging the influence of self-interest from our behavior. Rather, the point is that the extent and manner in which the pursuit of self-interest is permissible is to be regulated by the principles of justice, and the parties in the original position must make their selection knowing this to be the case.

The veil of ignorance prevents the parties from basing their choice of principles on considerations that we believe to be arbitrary or irrelevant to the justification of principles of justice. They do not know their social position, talents and abilities, level of intelligence and strength, conception of the good and plan of life, or particular psychological tendencies, such as "aversion to risk or liability to optimism or pessimism." (*TJ*, 137/118) In fact, because we want principles to be fair to everyone, we exclude from consideration anything that could be used to differentiate one person from another. We want to force the parties to make their choice "solely on the basis of general considerations." (*TJ*, 137/118) Further, the veil of ignorance excludes knowledge of "the particular circumstances of their own society" included "its economic or political situation," (*TJ*, 137/118) although the parties do know that their society is in the circumstances of justice. They also "know the general facts about human society . . . Indeed, the parties are presumed to know whatever general facts affect the choice of the principles of justice." (*TJ*, 137/119) Because we must determine as best we can what would be chosen in the original position, we must rely on our best understanding of the facts of political theory, sociology, social psychology, and economics. Of course, as our understanding of these fields changes, it is possible that our judgment of what would be chosen in the original position might change. This simply reflects our fallibility. The information that we provide to the parties in the original position is fallible, as is any principle based in part on such information.

Because we stipulate that the parties are equally rational, and because they are all forced to make their selection on the basis of the same general information, "each is convinced by the same arguments. Therefore, we can view the agreement in the original position from the standpoint of one person selected at random." (*TJ*, 139/120) This has led some critics to suggest that justice as fairness is not properly characterized as a "contract doctrine" at all.[17] There is something to this criticism, and Rawls acknowledges "the very important consequence that the parties have no basis for bargaining in the usual sense." (*TJ*, 139/120) Nonetheless, for reasons that we will see, the model of a contract captures important elements of justice as fairness.

So the parties in the original position aim to select principles that they expect will allow them to do as well as possible at advancing their conception of the good without knowing which specific conception of the good they hold. In order to be able to make any choice at all, "they assume that they normally prefer more primary social goods rather than less." (*TJ*, 142/123) The primary goods are not likely to be equally valuable to all life plans, and indeed in some cases certain primary goods may not contribute at all. Still, given their circumstances, this is the best that the parties can do. No matter which specific conception of the good they hold, "They know that in general they must try to protect their liberties, widen their opportunities, and enlarge their means for promoting their aims whatever these are." (*TJ*, 143/123) Given their motivation and the limitations on their information, it is rational for them to attempt "to win for themselves the highest index of primary social goods, since this enables them to promote their conception of the good most effectively whatever it turns out to be." (*TJ*, 144/125)

17 Jean Hampton, "Contracts and Choices: Does Rawls Have a Social Contract Theory?" *Journal of Philosophy*, 77 (1980).

There are three additional important stipulations in the original position. First, the parties are not moved by considerations of envy. We will return to discuss envy in chapter 3, but for now simply notice that "envy tends to make everyone worse off." (*TJ*, 144/124) There is no reason for us to have the parties be motivated by this. Second, and more importantly, the parties assume that they are capable of a sense of justice. Their choice of principles will give content to this capacity. However, the parties can take into account the psychological burden that different conceptions of justice will impose on this capacity. The importance of this point is that the parties "will not enter into agreements they know they cannot keep, or can do so only with great difficulty." (*TJ*, 145/126) That is, we stipulate that given the choice between two conceptions of justice, if the parties sincerely believe that there is only one that they will be able to comply with in all circumstances, then they must select that conception. Obviously, the prospects of being able to keep an agreement depend on a general account of human psychology. Third, the parties in the original position think of themselves as "free persons" with a "highest order interest" in developing and protecting this status:

> They do not think of themselves as inevitably bound to, or as identical with, the pursuit of any particular complex of fundamental interests that they may have at any given time, although they want to advance such interests (provided they are admissible). Rather, free persons conceive of themselves as beings who can revise and alter their final ends and who give first priority to preserving their liberty in these matters. (*TJ*, 131–2)[18]

The parties will protect this status even if it means fewer resources for the pursuit of their more particular ends. In *A Theory of Justice* this crucial stipulation may look undefended. However, as we will see in chapter 5, in subsequent work Rawls elaborates and defends this account.

THE CHOICE OF PRINCIPLES

We can now begin to consider which of the two main rivals – average utilitarianism or the two principles – it would be rational for the

[18] This passage was added to the original edition in order to clarify the grounds for the priority of the first principle.

parties in the original position to select. The two principles may seem to represent a rather extreme choice, especially when we consider that they "are those a person would choose for the design of a society in which his enemy is to assign him his place." (*TJ*, 152/132–3) Now the parties in the original position "do not, of course, assume that their initial place in society is decided by a malevolent opponent." (*TJ*, 153/133) Nonetheless, it is striking that the same principles would also be chosen if they were to make that assumption. If it is rational for the parties to choose the two principles, this must be because the set-up of the original position forces them to adopt an extremely risk-averse attitude toward their choice. We must show that the features of the original position force the parties to make a choice analogous to the "maximin rule" of choice under uncertainty.

We make a choice under uncertainty when we are selecting from available options without knowing which of a range of possible outcomes associated with each option will apply to us. The maximin rule requires us to compare the available options on the basis of the worst possible outcome for each, and to select the option whose worst outcome is least bad. That is, it "tells us to rank alternatives by their worst possible outcomes: we are to adopt the alternative the worst outcome of which is superior to the worst outcomes of the others." (*TJ*, 152–3/133) Hence, it represents an extremely risk-averse or pessimistic approach to such choices.

As we saw in the introduction, Rawls does not argue from a general commitment to the maximin principle for choice under uncertainty. "Clearly," he states, "the maximin rule is not, in general, a suitable guide for choices under uncertainty." (*TJ*, 153/133) Still, there are three conditions that contribute to the plausibility of adopting such a risk-averse principle of choice. "First, since the rule takes no account of the likelihoods of the possible circumstances, there must be some reason for sharply discounting estimates of these probabilities." (*TJ*, 154/134) Second, it is a more plausible decision rule when it is very important that some threshold level is secured while additional gains beyond that level are not as significant. The third condition is related to the second: if the consequences of falling below that minimal level are especially dire, the risk-averse attitude becomes more attractive.

When considering the choice between average utilitarianism and the two principles of justice from the original position, all three of these conditions hold. The parties have no basis for assigning probabilities to possible outcomes because of the veil of ignorance. In fact, they have very little basis for knowing in detail what the possible outcomes will be, let alone their probabilities. After all, they are only choosing the most abstract principles, not specific institutional designs. The parties do not know the particular circumstances of their society, so they cannot know which specific institutional arrangements would best satisfy the principles that they choose. "Not only are they unable to conjecture the likelihoods of the various possible circumstances, they cannot say much about what the possible circumstances are, much less enumerate them and foresee the outcome of each alternative available." (*TJ*, 155–6/134–5) The exclusion of probabilities from the deliberation of the parties is not an arbitrary stipulation but follows directly from the imposition of the veil of ignorance.[19]

If we can establish that the two principles "provide a workable theory of social justice, and that they are compatible with reasonable demands of efficiency, then this conception guarantees a satisfactory minimum." (*TJ*, 156/135) Part II of *A Theory of Justice* is largely devoted to showing precisely that the principles do provide a workable theory and that a reasonable set of institutions would be likely to satisfy them. "Moreover, this line of thought is practically decisive if we can establish the priority of liberty." (*TJ*, 156/135) As we have seen, utilitarianism would in principle allow the sacrifice of the basic liberties of some if this led to an increase in aggregate utility. If we can establish that the parties would be especially concerned to protect their basic liberties (and less concerned with additional material gains beyond the minimum threshold level), this would provide a very strong argument for the two principles of justice over a utilitarian alternative.

This point, in turn, is reinforced by the third consideration. If "other conceptions of justice may lead to institutions that the parties would find intolerable," (*TJ*, 156/135) but the two principles would prevent such possibilities, this tells strongly in favor of the conservative attitude toward the choice. If utilitarianism allows for the possibility – even if not the likelihood – of "serious infractions of liberty

[19] For a discussion of the orthodox Bayesian view that in the absence of information it is rational to assign equal probabilities to each possible outcome, see Freeman, *Rawls*, pp. 172–3.

for the sake of greater social benefits," (*TJ*, 156/135) then the parties will be reluctant to adopt such a principle. They have the option of avoiding such a possibility by guaranteeing the basic liberties directly with the two principles of justice. Again, if we can establish that the parties will be especially concerned to secure their basic liberties, we will have a "practically decisive" argument for adopting the two principles over utilitarianism. Note also that utilitarianism does not provide a direct guarantee that everyone will receive a minimally necessary share of social resources. If it were to allow some to fall below this social minimum, this too would be an intolerable outcome.[20]

Consider now what can be said, from the point of view of the original position, in favor of the principle that requires maximizing average utility. Assuming a fixed population, average utilitarianism – which requires that we maximize the average level of utility across a population – will give the same results as classical utilitarianism – which requires that we maximize aggregate utility. The two conceptions will differ, however, if we allow the size of the population to vary. Increasing the size of the population but keeping the utility profile constant will increase the total level of utility but not the average level. It seems clear that the parties in the original position would select average utilitarianism over classical utilitarianism. To see this, observe that classical utilitarianism will allow the utility level of each individual – and therefore, the average – to fall if these decreases are offset by sufficient increases in the size of the population. But the parties would have no reason to accept this. They are concerned with their own likely prospects, and their prospects are worse when average utility goes down, regardless of what happens to the aggregate. Thus, it is average, not classical, utilitarianism that serves as the main rival for the two principles of justice.

Suppose, contrary to the set-up of the original position, that the parties were to select from among a number of possible social orders in which all of the details of the various social positions, including

[20] If, however, the alternative to the two principles was a so-called "mixed conception" that secured the basic liberties and included a guaranteed social minimum, although there would be outcomes that were not preferred, none would be "intolerable." Therefore the third condition supporting the use of maximum reasoning would not hold, and the case for the two principles would be significantly weaker. We will discuss mixed conceptions in chapter 2. See also the discussion of the strains of commitment and n. 23 below.

utility levels, were known. Also suppose that a thin veil of ignorance prevented them from knowing which position they would occupy in each of these possible social orders. They know the utility levels that individuals with various combinations of talents and preferences would be likely to achieve, but they do not know which combination of talents and preferences would be their own. Given this choice, adopting average utilitarianism would maximize one's expected utility level:

> Thus if we waive the problem of interpersonal comparisons of utility, and if the parties are viewed as rational individuals who have no aversion to risk and who follow the principle of insufficient reason in computing likelihoods . . . then the idea of the initial situation leads naturally to the average principle. (*TJ*, 165–6/143)

On the other hand, to the extent that we think it rational for the parties to be risk averse – to protect themselves from the worst possible outcomes – their reasoning will resemble maximin reasoning and the two principles will become more attractive.

As we have seen, with the thicker veil of ignorance of the original position, the parties do not have a basis for identifying the various social positions associated with each conception of justice, let alone for assigning probabilities to each of them. Furthermore, the argument for average utilitarianism relies on an implicit model of the person. In order to be able to define a utility function, it assumes that all preferences are commensurable and there are "no definite highest-order interests or fundamental ends by reference to which they decide what sorts of persons they care to be . . . They are, we might say bare-persons"[21] (*TJ*, 152) since they are willing to sacrifice the satisfaction of any of their preferences if this would result in a net gain in satisfaction. This contrasts with the model of the person with highest-order interests that the parties in the original position rely on:

> They are, so to speak, determinate-persons: they have certain highest-order interests and fundamental ends by reference to which they would decide the kind of life and subordinate aims that are acceptable to them. It is these interests and ends, whatever they are, which they must try to protect. Since they know that the basic liberties covered by the first principle will

[21] This passage was added to the revised edition.

secure these interests, they must acknowledge the two principles of justice rather than the principle of utility.[22] (*TJ*, 152)

Since, as we will see more clearly in chapter 4, the basic liberties are necessary in order to protect these highest-order interests, the parties will be highly motivated to select principles that will protect their basic liberties.

Because the parties in the original position are required to protect their fundamental interests, they cannot choose principles that might result in inadequate protection. Given certain empirical assumptions, average utilitarianism very well might provide that protection. But it would not be very secure, dependent as it is on uncertain and difficult calculations. It would be far better, from the point of view of the parties in the original position, to protect these basic interests directly, and that is what the first principle of justice does. The parties are forced to make a risk-averse choice in order to ensure that their fundamental interests are protected.

It is easy to overlook the fact that we do not yet have an argument for the second principle of justice (the combination of fair equality of opportunity and the difference principle). The comparison between the two principles and average utilitarianism turns on the superiority of the first principle. The main argument for the difference principle does not come until we compare the two principles to a mixed conception, something we will consider in chapter 2. As we will see, that argument does not depend on maximin reasoning. In part, it will turn on the difficulties with relying on utility as opposed to primary goods as the object of distributive concern. So the risk aversion that Rawls attributes to the parties in the original position is much less extreme than is commonly assumed. The parties are worried about the possibility that they will be forced to sacrifice their fundamental interests, and they will select principles that will protect against that possibility. But not all violations of the difference principle would implicate their fundamental interests, and there are no good reasons to attribute an extreme risk aversion beyond their concern to protect their fundamental interests. In other words, once their basic interests are secured, the parties would not continue to select principles

[22] This passage was added to the revised edition.

based on maximin reasoning. If there are good reasons for accepting the difference principle over another conception that would also secure their basic interests, they cannot be based on an unmotivated assumption of extreme risk aversion.

ADDITIONAL CONSIDERATIONS

The choice made in the original position departs in dramatic ways from ordinary contracts. Since there are no grounds for ordinary bargaining, we can model it as the choice of one individual. Still, describing it as a contract emphasizes that it will be binding on individuals who find themselves in different circumstances with different conceptions of the good. It also suggests the conditions of finality and publicity. In addition, it implies that the choice must be made in good faith. These considerations provide additional "confirming grounds" for the two principles.

The finality condition implies that the parties view their choice as being made "once and for all." (*TJ*, 176/153) Of course, this in no way precludes us from reconsidering the choice from the original position. The point is that parties in the original position are not allowed to gamble with the possibility of an unacceptable outcome with the hope that they will be able to revisit the choice of principles in the future. We stipulate that "for an agreement to be valid, the parties must be able to honor it under all relevant and foreseeable circumstances. There must be a rational assurance that one can carry through." (*TJ*, 175/153) As we have seen, the parties assume that they will be capable of acting on the basis of a sense of justice. However, they also take into consideration the facts of moral psychology, and in particular the relative difficulty of motivating compliance with a conception. Rawls refers to this as the "strains of commitment" of a conception. It is sometimes mistakenly thought that this refers to the difficulty of effecting a transition from an existing society to one that would satisfy some conception of justice. If in an existing society some individuals profit from an unjust basic structure, it is very possible that a transition to justice will require that they give up their unjust gains. This may be psychologically (and politically) difficult, but does not tell against that conception of justice, at least as part of ideal theory.

When the parties consider the strains of commitment of various conceptions of justice, they do so from behind the veil. Because they must choose a conception that they believe in good faith they will be able to comply with, they will be especially concerned about the strains of commitment on the least advantaged. The parties would not accept principles that might result in the violation of their basic liberties if they had the option of selecting principles that would secure them. Accepting utilitarianism would require that they be willing to "acquiesce in a loss of freedom over the course of their life for the sake of a greater good enjoyed by others." (*TJ*, 176/154) Such an agreement would be extremely difficult to keep. "Indeed, we might wonder whether such an agreement can be made in good faith at all." (*TJ*, 176/154) But the parties have another option: they can secure their basic liberties directly, as the first principle of justice does. It seems that they can make no other choice in good faith. Notice that although the difference principle would minimize the strains of commitment of the least advantaged, this is not offered as an argument for it.[23] There is no requirement that the strains of commitment be minimized but only that they be limited so that there is a reasonable expectation of compliance.

A related consideration concerns the stability of a conception of justice. While the strains of commitment concern the degree of psychological difficulty needed to comply with the principles, stability concerns the tendency of a conception to generate its own support over time. That is, a conception of justice is stable when individuals raised in and living in a society satisfying that conception tend to develop and maintain a strong and effective sense of justice with that content. Stability will be a major consideration in chapter 3, but here we can observe one consideration that might weigh in favor of the greater stability of the two principles over the stability of utilitarianism. The stability of a utilitarian conception of justice depends on the willingness of individuals to make potentially unlimited sacrifices for one another. This apparently requires that the members of a society form strong bonds of identification, even with those members

[23] Presumably, although the strains of commitment of the mixed conception that we will consider in chapter 2 are greater for the least advantaged, they are still within tolerable limits since they provide a social minimum and secure everyone's basic needs. See also n. 20, above.

with whom they have no personal contact or even direct knowledge. To the extent that such strong psychological identification is difficult to achieve, utilitarianism will tend to be less stable. In contrast, the two principles appear to require only weaker identification since they define terms of mutual benefit relative to a baseline of equality. Nobody is asked to sacrifice relative to this baseline in order for others to gain. To the extent that this is correct, and to the extent that the parties in the original position would be moved by considerations of stability, this also would tell in favor of the two principles over utilitarianism.

This argument is related to a third consideration. As we have seen, utilitarianism may require significant sacrifices over the course of one's lifetime for the benefit of others. Especially in the absence of strong feelings of identification among individuals, this may tend to undermine the sense of self-respect among the least advantaged. "Self-respect is not so much a part of any rational plan of life as the sense that one's plan is worth carrying out." (*TJ*, 178/155) The two principles of justice express the idea that all individuals and plans (within the permissible range) are worthy of respect, and all individuals can properly claim a fair share of social resources with which to pursue their goals. This is likely to contribute to establishing a sense of self-respect among all. In contrast, a social structure designed along utilitarian lines may deny some individuals an opportunity to pursue their ends when resources could be more efficiently used by others. The individuals who have their ends sacrificed in this way may have more difficulty in establishing their sense of self-respect.

If different conceptions of justice tend to have different effects on the development of self-respect, this will be a matter of great significance to the parties in the original position. After all, they are to choose principles which they think will result in the greatest prospect of fulfilling their (unknown) conception of the good. But if individuals lack self-respect, it is very unlikely that their plans – whatever they are – will be achieved. If individuals think their plan is unworthy, or that they are not entitled to make claims on society in their own name, it seems quite unlikely that they will accomplish much at all. From the point of view of the parties in the original position, this would be an outcome that they would want to avoid at almost all costs. No matter what other advantages a conception of justice might have, their prospects are very poor if they lack self-respect. It is for this reason that Rawls claims that the social basis of self-respect is "perhaps the most important primary good." (*TJ*, 440/386) The two principles of justice, founded on an ideal of reciprocity and respect, would seem to provide a social basis on which self-respect can develop more fully than it would under utilitarianism.

These three related considerations – the strains of commitment, stability, and self-respect – all support the conclusion that it would be rational to choose the two principles of justice over average utilitarianism from the original position. True, this "reasoning is informal and not a proof."[24] (*TJ*, 159) Nonetheless, if enough considerations point in the same direction this may be enough to convince us of the rationality of the choice. The strains-of-commitment argument makes it especially clear that the original position forces the parties to consider the implications if the worst were to befall them. When we make agreement, we sometimes risk bad outcomes:

> But if we make an agreement, we have to accept the result; and so to give an undertaking in good faith, we must not only intend to honor it but with reason believe that we can do so . . . One cannot agree to a principle if there is a real possibility that it has any outcome that one will not be able to accept.[25] (*TJ*, 159)

The strains-of-commitment argument applies this requirement directly. As with the stability argument and the self-respect argument, the reasoning here depends on claims about moral psychology that are available to the parties in the original position. We will consider moral psychology in greater depth in chapter 3. But what lies at the bottom of these arguments is that assumption that the parties have "certain fundamental interests that they must protect if they can; and that, as free persons, they have a highest-order interest in maintaining their liberty to revise and alter these ends."[26] (*TJ*, 160) These fundamental interests are secured by the first principle (and the guarantee of a social minimum), while utilitarianism provides at most only a risky assurance that they will be protected.

[24] This passage was added to the revised edition, but see somewhat similar thoughts on p. 183 of the original edition.

[25] This passage was added to the revised edition and reinforces the considerations discussed earlier.

[26] This passage was added to the revised edition.

Our comparison of the two principles with average utilitarianism was predicated on seeing that classical utilitarianism was inferior from the point of view of the original position. But historically, classical utilitarianism has been the more important form. This suggests that its support derives not from a contract model but from something else. Rawls suggests that it is tied to "the concept of the impartial sympathetic spectator" (*TJ*, 184/161) who serves to aggregate all preferences impartially in one individual. This reveals more clearly the sense in which utilitarianism "fails to take seriously the distinction between persons." (*TJ*, 187/163) But it also reveals a contrast between average and classical utilitarianism: "Thus we arrive at the unexpected conclusion that while the average principle of utility is the ethic of a single rational individual (with no aversion to risk) who tries to maximize his own prospects, the classical doctrine is the ethic of perfect altruists." (*TJ*, 189/164–5)

The virtue of justice aims at impartially resolving conflicting claims on social resources by individuals who hold diverse conceptions of the good. Classical utilitarianism models this impartiality by aggregation in the sympathetic observer. Justice as fairness, in contrast, "define[s] impartiality from the standpoint of the litigants themselves" placed in the original position. (*TJ*, 190/165) "The fault of the utilitarianism doctrine is that it mistakes impersonality for impartiality." (*TJ*, 190/166) The problem with utilitarianism is not that it relies on sympathy or benevolence or even love. Rather, the problem is that by themselves these virtues do not tell us how to resolve conflicts among the objects or persons of concern. "The difficulty is that the love of several persons is thrown into confusion once the claims of these persons conflict." (*TJ*, 190/166) What this reveals is that the principles of justice do not replace but rather complement the sentiments of love and benevolence. "Therefore a love of mankind that wishes to preserve the distinction of persons, to recognize the separateness of life and experience, will use the two principles of justice to determine its aims when the many goods it cherishes are in opposition." (*TJ*, 191/167)

CHAPTER 2

Part II *of* A Theory of Justice – *Institutions*

Having completed the main defense of the two principles of justice, part II of *A Theory of Justice* aims to "illustrate the content of the principles of justice." (*TJ*, 195/171) The principles do not require a single institutional scheme for all circumstances, so any application needs to be sensitive to the conditions in which the principles are to be applied. This often requires that we rely on the specialized empirical knowledge that can be provided by economists, sociologists, and political scientists, among others. Philosophers have no particular expertise in these areas and so the design of institutions and policies is a quintessentially interdisciplinary task. Although the principles identify the standards and the ideals on the basis of which institutions and policies should be assessed, there is often a great deal of controversy about which designs and policies will, in fact, best live up to and satisfy these standards.

Rawls, therefore, is hesitant to consider in much detail the application of the principles to concrete circumstances, and he stresses that arrangements other than the ones he describes may also be just. Nonetheless, it is important to illustrate an institutional scheme that may plausibly be thought to realize the two principles. This is for three main reasons. First, the task of justification is not complete until we reach reflective equilibrium. Until we consider at least some main applications of the principles, we are not yet in a position to test them against many of our considered judgments and provisional fixed points. Second, the choice of principles from the original position was predicated on there being a workable institutional scheme that could meet their demands. We must show that there is, in fact, such a scheme. Finally, we will need at least a rough account of the institutions that may plausibly satisfy the two principles in order to consider their stability in part III. In addition to its intrinsic interest, then, an account of the institutions that could satisfy the principles of justice turns out to be important for the justification of the principles.

THE FOUR-STAGE SEQUENCE

Once principles of justice are available, citizens must evaluate "the justice of legislation and social policies." (*TJ*, 195/171) Even in the most favorable circumstances of a well-ordered society, we must still expect judgments often to differ when applying the principles of justice to concrete cases. Therefore, some political mechanism is necessary for "reconciling conflicting opinions of justice." (*TJ*, 196/171) Rawls assumes that this political mechanism will be specified in a constitution, so we must also judge which constitutional arrangements are just. However, no political procedure can be guaranteed to generate only just legislation. Even the most just political procedure is a matter of "imperfect procedural justice," and being imperfect, it is possible that it will issue in substantively unjust legislation. We must also ask, therefore, when the results of this imperfect procedure are "to be complied with and when they can be rejected as no longer binding. In short, [citizens] must be able to determine the grounds and limits of political duty and obligation." (*TJ*, 196/172)

It might be tempting to assume that the original position would provide a general method for resolving moral dilemmas. A moment's reflection, however, makes it clear that it is not well suited for most ordinary moral problems, including questions concerning the application of the principles of justice. After all, a proper resolution of particular moral dilemmas often requires specific knowledge of the situation – knowledge that is screened off by the veil of ignorance. Therefore Rawls presents a sequence of modifications to the original position that provides the parties with information relevant to the application of the principles. The first stage of this "four-stage sequence" is the original position itself. At the second stage, the "constitutional stage," the parties "are to decide upon the justice of political forms and choose a constitution . . . Subject to the constraints of the principles of justice already chosen, they are to design a system for the constitutional powers of government and the basic rights of citizens." (*TJ*, 196–7/172) Here, the parties have two goals:

they are to select a constitution that not only "is best calculated to lead to just and effective legislation" (*TJ*, 198/173) but is also one that implements and realizes the basic liberties specified by the first principle of justice. The veil of ignorance is relaxed so that they have access to the general facts about their particular society that may be relevant to this decision.

Once a just constitution that protects the basic liberties and defines a reasonable procedure for making laws is selected, we imagine the parties moving on to the "legislative stage" where they assess "the justice of laws and policies." (*TJ*, 198/174) At this stage the veil of ignorance is further relaxed, so that "the full range of general economic and social facts is brought to bear." (*TJ*, 199/175) In order to be acceptable, "[s]tatutes must satisfy not only the principles of justice but whatever limits are laid down in the constitution." (*TJ*, 198/174) While the constitutional stage is the appropriate perspective for implementing the first principle of justice, this legislative stage is the appropriate perspective for considering the implementation of the second principle of justice. Judgments concerning social and economic policies governed by the second principle of justice are "commonly subject to reasonable differences of opinion." (*TJ*, 199/174) This is why, as we will see, the constitutional procedure for making laws will inevitably depend on some kind of (constrained) majoritarianism.

At the final stage, the parties are concerned with "the application of rules to particular cases by judges and administrators, and the following of rules by citizens generally." (*TJ*, 199/175) The veil of ignorance is lifted completely so that "everyone has complete access to all the facts." (*TJ*, 199/175) The veil of ignorance can be fully lifted because we now have in place not only the principles of justice, a just constitutional scheme, and particular laws and policies, but we are also assuming that individuals in question are moved by the desire to act justly.

The gradual lifting of the veil is not the only change that occurs between the original position and the subsequent stages. Although Rawls does not emphasize the importance of this point, the motivation of the parties in the original position is dramatically different from that of the parties in the subsequent stages. In the original position, as we have seen, the parties are motivated solely by the goals of securing their fundamental interests and satisfying their particular, but unknown, conception of the good. The veil of ignorance forces them to make an impartial choice, and that is why the choice is of interest to us. In the subsequent stages, however, the parties are motivated by the goal of implementing and realizing the principles of justice that are already available. They have a moral motivation not present in the original position. In fact, they are trying to answer the very same questions that we are trying to answer: which constitution, laws and policies, or applications to particular cases are most just? The veil of ignorance has no essential role to play at these later stages, and it is doubtful whether the subsequent stages of the four-stage sequence can play the same useful heuristic role that the original position does. On the other hand, perhaps invoking the four-stage sequence may serve as a useful reminder that the original position is suitable only for identifying the fundamental principles of justice, not for considering their application.[1]

AN EQUAL SCHEME OF BASIC LIBERTIES

Justice as fairness looks to the constitution of a society to ensure that basic liberties are protected. It may appear that it is vulnerable to the objection that it is concerned merely with the formal protection of the liberties, especially when Rawls denies that "poverty and ignorance, and a lack of means generally" diminishes the guarantee of an equal scheme of liberties. (*TJ*, 204/179) However, Rawls intends this as an analytical point only. When adequate resources are not available, Rawls would say that this does not deprive citizens of their basic liberties. Rather, he would say that the worth of their liberties is compromised. While the first principle secures basic liberties, the second principle controls their worth. The two principles are designed to work together to achieve "a reconciliation of the liberty and equality." (*TJ*, 204/179):

> Taking the two principles together, the basic structure is to be arranged to maximize the worth to the least advantaged of the complete scheme of equal liberty shared by all. This defines the end of social justice. (*TJ*, 205/179)

[1] For further discussion of this point, see my "Having It Both Ways: Justification and Application in Justice as Fairness," *Pacific Philosophical Quarterly*, 75 (1994).

Far from being concerned only with the formal guarantee of the basic liberties, Rawls's focus is squarely on their worth, which is controlled jointly by the two principles.

To illustrate the application of the first principle, Rawls considers liberty of conscience. Since the first principle of justice requires protection of this basic liberty, we can assume that it is directly specified in a constitution. So rather than focus on the constitutional stage, Rawls has us return to the original position to consider the grounds for selecting this as a basic liberty in the first place and giving it the priority that it and the other basic liberties have over the second principle. In fact, it had better turn out that the original position can give support for equal liberty of conscience, since this is "one of the fixed points of our considered judgments of justice." (*TJ*, 206/181) Although the parties in the original position do not know whether they will hold any particular religious faith, they do know the role that such faiths play in the lives of many people. Given the possibility that they will turn out to hold religious beliefs, the parties,

> cannot take chances with their liberty by permitting the dominant religious or moral doctrine to persecute or to suppress others if it wishes. Even granting (what may be questioned) that it is more probable than not that one will turn out to belong to the majority (if a majority exists), to gamble in this way would show that one did not take one's religious or moral convictions seriously, or highly value the liberty to examine one's beliefs. (*TJ*, 207/181)

We saw that in the original position the parties "cannot enter into agreements that may have consequences they cannot accept." (*TJ*, 176/153) They would not agree to a principle that might turn out to prohibit them from practicing their religious faith, when some other principle would have permitted it. The strains of commitment would be much too high.

There are, however, limits to liberty of conscience. These limits are determined not by an assessment of the intrinsic merit or value of the different doctrines and associations. "The government has no authority to render associations either legitimate or illegitimate any more than it has this authority in regard to art and science." (*TJ*, 212/186) Rather, the limitations are determined by the requirements of an equal scheme of basic liberties for all. We should think of the government's ability to limit individual liberties as "an enabling right, a right which the government must have if it is to carry out its duty of impartially supporting the conditions necessary for everyone's pursuit of his interests and living up to his obligations as he understands them." (*TJ*, 213/187)

The language that Rawls uses in this discussion strongly anticipates the development in his later work of the ideas of a "political conception of justice" and "public reason" (see chapter 4). When the government must impose restrictions on individuals in order to maintain an equal scheme of basic liberties for all, its justification "must be based on evidence and ways of reasoning acceptable to all." This is because "a departure from generally recognized ways of reasoning would involve a privileged place for the views of some over others, and a principle which permitted this could not be agreed to in the original position." (*TJ*, 213/187) So, for example, no limitation on individual liberty of conscience can be justified simply by a reference to the doctrines of a particular religion. This reflects the grounds for toleration in the first place, which is not based on assumptions about the truth or falsity of any particular religion. It is based simply on the requirements of an equal scheme of basic liberties, and "the argument does not rely on any special metaphysical or philosophical doctrine." (*TJ*, 214/187) As Rawls explains later, "liberty of conscience and freedom of thought should not be founded on philosophical or ethical skepticism, nor on indifference to religious and moral interests." (*TJ*, 243/214) It is crucial that the argument for liberty of conscience does not deny that there may be religious truths that go beyond what can be established to everyone's satisfaction. The point is simply that no appeal is made to these contested claims when determining the limits of toleration or matters of social justice generally.

However, despite the appeal to reasoning "acceptable to all," we must consider the possibility that some individuals, perhaps based on their own religious faith, will be intolerant and will not support religious liberty. They will insist that the truth of their faith justifies the coercive use of state power to suppress dissenters. One might worry that the parties in the original position would reject the first principle on the grounds that when the veil of ignorance was lifted they might turn out to hold such an intolerant doctrine and prefer that there not be religious liberty. On the other hand, the parties certainly cannot assume that they will hold this doctrine. Rawls seems correct when he points out, "if any principle can be agreed to, it must be that of equal liberty." (*TJ*, 208/182) There appears to be an impasse precisely because this doctrine rejects the legitimate diversity built into the structure of the original position. We must either go along with the intolerant doctrine and reject the set-up of the original position, or embrace the original position and the principle of toleration embedded in the first principle of justice. But assuming that we accept the construction of the original position, what attitude should a just society have toward those who hold an intolerant doctrine?

The first thing to note is that the existence of such intolerant individuals and groups should not by itself shake our confidence that the two principles of justice are correct. Although they may reject the two principles of justice and the justification offered from the original position, the acceptability of this argument does not depend on its actually convincing everyone. If we are committed to the choice from the original position, we can simply say that those who reject a principle of toleration are mistaken or unreasonable. But second, we should restrict those who are themselves intolerant "only when the tolerant sincerely and with reason believe that their own security and that of the institutions of liberty are in danger." (*TJ*, 220/193) It is, of course, much easier to state this as a theoretical principle than to determine in practice when this line has been crossed. But the point is that some doctrines that are intolerant and reject the scheme of equal basic liberties should themselves be tolerated because they do not constitute a threat to the liberties of others.

Liberty of conscience is required because we assume that our "differences are profound and no one knows how to reconcile them by reason." (*TJ*, 220/193) However, despite holding different religious doctrines, we can each recognize this fact and therefore regulate our conduct according to shared principles. For this to work, these principles – and not any particular doctrine – must be regulative with regard to the design of the basic structure. These shared principles can form "the kernel of political morality" that can serve as "a pact of reconciliation between diverse religions and moral beliefs, and the forms of culture to which they belong." (*TJ*, 221/194) Representing the choice of principles from the original position, it seems clear that this principle of toleration would be chosen. Anything less would not be taking seriously the diversity of reasonable religions and the strains of commitment that intolerance would impose; any greater toleration of the intolerant would put in jeopardy the equal scheme of basic liberties for all.

POLITICAL LIBERTIES

The political liberties, as opposed to the civil liberties such as liberty of conscience, introduce a new complication. When we consider the application of the first principle to the political structure of society, we get the "principle of (equal) participation" which says that "all citizens are to have an equal right to take part in, and to determine the outcome of, the constitutional process that establishes the laws with which they are to comply." (*TJ*, 221/194) More concretely, this requires familiar features of a constitutional democracy, including a representative legislature; regular elections according to the precept "one person one vote"; and "firm constitutional protections for certain liberties, particularly freedom of speech and assembly, and liberty to form political associations." (*TJ*, 222–3/195)

We have already seen the distinction between the basic liberties and their worth. While the first principle guarantees an equal scheme of basic liberties for all, the worth of those liberties is controlled by the resources that individuals can devote to exercising them. Therefore, in general, the difference principle allows inequalities in the worth of a basic liberty when it works to increase the value of the liberty to the least advantaged. However, there is an additional constraint in the case of the political liberties, which are to be guaranteed their "fair value." (*TJ*, 225/197) Political liberties are competitive since when one person gains greater influence in the political process, this comes at the expense of someone else's influence. Rawls is especially concerned about the ability of those with greater wealth to exert greater influence on the political process:

> Historically, one of the main defects of constitutional government has been the failure to insure the fair value of political liberty. The necessary corrective steps have not been taken, indeed, they never seem to have been seriously entertained. Disparities in the distribution of property and wealth that far exceed what is compatible with political equality have generally been

tolerated by the legal system . . . Universal suffrage is an insufficient counterpoise; for when parties and elections are financed not by public funds but by private contributions, the political forum is so constrained by the wishes of the dominant interests that the basic measures needed to establish just constitutional rule are seldom properly presented. (*TJ*, 226/198–9)

The call for public financing of political campaigns is repeated in Rawls's later works.[2] But note also the suggestion that ensuring the fair value of political liberty might put limits on permissible disparities in the distribution of property and wealth, even beyond those imposed by the difference principle.

Other things being equal, the best constitution will be the one that is most likely to generate just legislation. But we are tightly constrained in permissible constitutional procedures by the principle of participation and the first principle's guarantee of fair value for the political liberties. Schemes such as Mill's proposal to give people with greater intelligence and education extra votes are ruled out even if such an arrangement would be more likely to produce just legislation than a scheme involving equal representation.[3] Constitutional restrictions on majority rule, on the other hand, need not produce any such inequality. Such restrictions can be justified, therefore, if a political structure including them is likely to do a better job at protecting the total scheme of basic liberties than would a structure of unconstrained majority rule. Determining which restrictions, if any, and which institutional mechanisms of enforcement would be justified depends in part on historical and empirical information about the particular society in question. There is no reason to assume that one scheme will do this best in all circumstances.

Although the basic structure of society encompasses more than just the legal and political order, these institutions occupy a special role since they are controlling with respect to the other elements. While it is not true that a society is collectively responsible only for its laws, it is through its laws that a society makes explicit, collective, and binding decisions for itself. A legal system is "a coercive order of public rules addressed to rational persons for the purpose of regulating

[2] See, for example, Rawls, *Political Liberalism*, pp. 356–63; Rawls, *The Law of Peoples*, pp. 24, n. 19, 50.

[3] See J. S. Mill, *Considerations on Representative Government* in *On Liberty and Other Essays*, John Gray, ed. (Oxford University Press, 1991), p. 338; ch. 8, paragraph 12.

their conduct and providing the framework for social cooperation." (*TJ*, 235/207) Other associations may have rules for internal governance as well, of course. "What distinguishes a legal system is its comprehensive scope and its regulative powers with respect to other associations . . . [T]he law defines the basic structure within which the pursuit of all other activities takes place." (*TJ*, 236/207)

Although the principles of justice are developed for a well-ordered society, they can offer some guidance in our non-ideal circumstances: "Existing institutions are to be judged in the light of this conception and held to be unjust to the extent that they depart from it without sufficient reason." (*TJ*, 246/216) In some circumstances, there may be sufficient reason for certain forms of paternalism. The parties,

> will want to insure themselves against the possibility that their powers are undeveloped and they cannot rationally advance their interests, as in the case of children; or that through some misfortune or accident they are unable to make decisions for their good, as in the case of those seriously injured or mentally disturbed. It is also rational for them to protect themselves against their own irrational inclinations by consenting to a scheme of penalties that may give them a sufficient motive to avoid foolish actions . . . For these cases the parties adopt principles stipulating when others are authorized to act in their behalf and to override their present wishes if necessary. (*TJ*, 248–9/218–19)

Rawls does not pursue the content of any of these principles, and it is clear that he intends such principles to be invoked only in a limited range of cases. Such "paternalistic intervention must be justified by the evident failure or absence of reason and will; and it must be guided by the principles of justice and what is known about the subject's more permanent aims and preferences, or by the account of primary goods." (*TJ*, 250/219–20) Rather than specify which specific paternalistic interventions would be justified, Rawls only aims to show that his approach does not necessarily rule out all forms of paternalism and to indicate the broad considerations that would have to be invoked in order to justify it.

Rawls concludes chapter 4 on "Equal liberty" by reflecting on the fact that "there is a Kantian interpretation of the conception of justice from which this [first] principle derives." (*TJ*, 251/221) This might suggest that this interpretation would only be of significance to those who are already interested in the work of Immanuel Kant and that it does not play an important role in Rawls's account. However, it turns out that the Kantian interpretation will be important later when we turn to considerations of stability. I will not attempt to provide even a sketch of Kant's ethical theory or to identify Rawls's criticisms of how it has traditionally been interpreted. Rather, I simply highlight the main point where Rawls thinks that his own work relates to "the high point of the contractarian tradition in Kant and Rousseau." (*TJ*, 252/222) The key element in the Kantian interpretation of justice as fairness is the following:

> By acting from these principles [of justice] persons express their nature as free and equal rational beings subject to the general conditions of human life. For to express one's nature as a being of a particular kind is to act on the principles that would be chosen if this nature were the decisive determining element. (*TJ*, 252–3/222)

The thought is that while people differ in their particular social circumstances, talents and abilities, psychological properties, and conceptions of the good, they share a common nature as free and equal beings. The original position represents this status, so we can think of the original position as "a procedural interpretation of Kant's conception of autonomy and the categorical imperative."[4] (*TJ*, 256/226) One of the more attractive features of this interpretation, Rawls believes, is that it allows us to capture elements of Kant's account without interpreting them as "purely transcendent and lacking explicable connections with human conduct." (*TJ*, 256/226)

ECONOMIC INSTITUTIONS

Rawls is almost always assumed to be a defender of "welfare-state capitalism." However, he does not use the phrase in *A Theory of Justice*. Instead, he describes what he calls a "property-owning democracy," and he came to regret not differentiating the two models more clearly. We will consider the difference between these two ideas in chapter 4, but the point I want to emphasize now is that Rawls is interested only in developing an account of one economic order that would be likely to satisfy the principles of justice. He insists that this is

[4] In the revised edition, this sentence concludes: "within the framework of an empirical theory."

not the only possibility: "Throughout [this discussion] the choice between a private-property economy and socialism is left open; from the standpoint of the theory of justice alone, various basic structures would appear to satisfy its principles." (*TJ*, 258/228)

It is much more common now than it was when Rawls was writing *A Theory of Justice* for philosophers to be well versed in – or at least to have some familiarity with – the fields of social-choice theory and welfare economics. Although clearly influenced by these fields, Rawls saw them as limited. Their greatest weakness is that they typically take preferences as given and then ask about various institutional arrangements to satisfy them. The problem is that:

> The social system shapes the wants and aspirations that its citizens come to have. It determines in part the sort of persons they want to be as well as the sort of persons they are. Thus an economic system is not only an institutional device for satisfying existing wants and needs but a way of creating and fashioning wants in the future. (*TJ*, 259/229)

The implication is that "[c]onsiderations of efficiency are but one basis of decision [concerning the design of economic systems] and often relatively minor at that." (*TJ*, 260/229)

It might be thought that any contract view would be dependent on existing desires and therefore be vulnerable to this criticism. To avoid it, we need a perspective from which to assess the justice of the basic structure that is not dependent on existing desires. It is in this context that Rawls introduces a somewhat notorious phrase, the idea of an "Archimedean point." (*TJ*, 260/230) The allusion is to Archimedes, the ancient Greek mathematician and philosopher from the third century BC, who developed the principle of the lever, and is reported to have said, "Give me the place to stand, and I shall move the earth." The "place to stand," on Rawls's analogy, is a perspective outside of existing desires. But this is not supposed to be a perspective beyond all contingencies, as some critics have assumed. On the contrary, it is dependent on many contingent features of human life including, as we will see, a thin theory of the good. The point is to generate principles of justice that do not depend on existing desires but also are not based exclusively on "a priori or perfectionist principles." (*TJ*, 263/232)

Whether or not a society allows private ownership of the means of production, and regardless of the extent of provision of public goods, "[a]ll regimes will normally use the market to ration out the consumption goods actually produced." (*TJ*, 270/239) There is little doubt that decentralized market economies have an advantage over centrally controlled command economies in terms of efficiency. Rawls notes this, but points to a "more significant advantage of a market system": "given the requisite background institutions, it is consistent with equal liberties and fair equality of opportunity. Citizens have a free choice of careers and occupations." (*TJ*, 272/240–1) Rawls is no defender of a *laissez-faire* regime, and it is crucial that market mechanisms be embedded within appropriate background political institutions; but when properly embedded in a just basic structure, markets are necessary for reasons both of individual liberty and efficiency. This is consistent with the point discussed in chapter 1 (and to be discussed again in chapter 5): a just society will rely on pure procedural justice to allocate particular goods to specific individuals. The question is how to characterize these broader economic institutions.

A theory of justice does not by itself require a particular economic scheme since the choice "depends in large part upon the traditions, institutions, and social forces of each country." (*TJ*, 274/242) However, what it can do is to "set out in a schematic way the outlines of a just economic system that admits of several variations." (*TJ*, 274/242) The detailed choice of specifics will depend on the political judgment of the society in question. Furthermore, because the "principles of justice apply to the basic structure and regulate how its major institutions are combined into one scheme," (*TJ*, 274/242) there is flexibility in the design of many individual institutions as long as the other elements are adjusted to ensure that the overall scheme is just. The example of a "property-owning democracy" is supposed to provide the outlines of one possible economic regime consistent with the principles of justice.

Given that background institutions securing the basic liberties and ensuring fair equality of opportunity are in place, Rawls suggests that economic institutions be divided into "four branches," which, he cautions, "do not overlap with the usual organization of government but are to be understood as different functions." (*TJ*, 275–6/243–4)

In other words, each of these functional roles need not correspond to a single institutional agency, but rather they can be satisfied by the joint operation of different organizational entities. The allocation branch, perhaps misleadingly named, ensures that "the price system [remains] workably competitive and . . . prevent[s] the formation of unreasonable market power" (*TJ*, 276/244) such as monopolies. It may also adjust the structure of property rights in the case of "more obvious departures from efficiency caused by the failure of prices to measure accurately social benefits and costs." (*TJ*, 276/244) Rawls does not give examples of such departures, but perhaps he has in mind the provision of goods subject to natural monopolies such as various utilities. A complementary role is played by the "stabilization branch . . . [which] strives to bring about reasonably full employment in the sense that those who want work can find it." (*TJ*, 276/244) Together, these branches "maintain the efficiency of the market economy generally." (*TJ*, 276/244) This reinforces the point that while markets will play an essential role in a just economic order, this does not imply a *laissez-faire* attitude toward them.

Markets respond to willingness and ability to play, not to need. Therefore, they "cannot be the sole device of distribution. There must be a division of labor between the parts of the social system in answering to the common sense precepts of justice." (*TJ*, 276/244) We will see how to handle these different "precepts" below. At this point, what is important is that the transfer branch aims to ensure that everyone is assured of the appropriate "social minimum." The thought is that "once a suitable minimum is provided by transfers, it may be perfectly fair that the rest of total income be settled by the price system, assuming that it is moderately efficient and free from monopolistic restrictions, and unreasonable externalities have been eliminated." (*TJ*, 277/245) Again, Rawls is cautious with this proposal, but he seems to believe that when other institutions have secured the first principle and fair equality of opportunity, such a scheme will do better at satisfying the difference principle than other institutional arrangements.

Finally, the distribution branch – again, perhaps misleadingly named – is concerned with taxation schemes and the structure of property rights. It has two goals. One goal is simply "to raise the revenues that justice requires." (*TJ*, 278/246) For this purpose, Rawls suggests that a "proportional expenditure tax may be part of the best tax scheme." (*TJ*, 278/246) In part, this is because, unlike an income tax, such an expenditure tax matches the common sense precept that one should be taxed "according to how much a person takes out of the common store of goods and not according to how much he contributes." (*TJ*, 278/246) Rawls stresses that the degree of progressivity, if any, for such a tax will depend heavily on specific circumstances, and he speculates that in a well-ordered society, a flat (i.e. proportional) tax may be more efficient than a progressive schedule. This proposal, however, is only aimed at the goal of raising revenue for the functioning of the institutions of justice, and not for the other goal of the distribution branch. Furthermore, "[i]t does not follow that, given the injustice of existing institutions, even steeply progressive income taxes are not justified when all things are considered." (*TJ*, 279/246–7)

The other goal of the distribution branch is particularly significant. It is "to preserve an approximate justice in distributive shares by means of taxation and the necessary adjustments in the rights of property." (*TJ*, 277/245) The goal, however, is not directly to satisfy the difference principle, which Rawls believes is primarily the responsibility of the transfer branch, but rather "to prevent concentrations of power detrimental to the fair value of political liberty and fair equality of opportunity." (*TJ*, 277/245) This requires, for example, imposing some form of inheritance tax to prevent the advantages gained by one generation from compounding and generating unequal opportunities in the next generation. The aim is not to eliminate all inheritances or inequalities, but only to ensure that the fair value of the political liberties and equal opportunity are not undermined.

It is here, I believe, that Rawls's account of a property-owning democracy departs sharply from the traditional model of welfare-state capitalism. Rawls does not claim that welfare-state capitalism could never satisfy the difference principle. However, when we also consider the fair value of the political liberties and fair equality of opportunity, the superiority of a property-owning democracy becomes clearer. We will examine this issue in more detail in chapter 4, but I note here that there has been a persistent and highly misleading tendency in the secondary literature to detach the difference principle from the other principles of justice and to consider it as a free-standing and independent principle of distributive justice. This is a mistake. The joint operation of all of these branches, against a background of a just constitution, is likely to satisfy all components of the two principles of justice.

Finally, Rawls mentions an "exchange branch" which is devoted to the provision of certain public goods that would not be efficiently provided through normal market mechanisms. However, in this discussion he exhibits an unusually conservative attitude which he appears to relax in subsequent work. His thought is that while a society should be free to pursue public goods that are not required by justice, it should do so only when

> the means of covering their costs are agreed upon, if not unanimously, then approximately so . . . There is no more justification for using the state apparatus to compel some citizens to pay for unwanted benefits that others desire than there is to force them to reimburse others for their private expenses. (*TJ*, 282–3/249–50)

To be sure, this is part of ideal theory and assumes that the principles are satisfied, but it is still striking that Rawls would write that mandatory taxation to support "universities and institutes, or opera and the theater . . . can be justified only as promoting directly or indirectly the social conditions that secure the equal liberties and as advancing in an appropriate way the long-term interests of the least advantaged."[5] (*TJ*, 332/291–2)

There is one further dimension of economic justice to discuss, and this concerns the problem of justice between generations. A theory

[5] Oddly, this passage comes immediately after Rawls claims that

> public funds for the arts and sciences may be provided through the exchange branch. In this instance there are no restrictions on the reasons citizens may have for imposing upon themselves the requisite taxes. They may assess the merits of these public goods on perfectionist principles, since the coercive machinery of government is used in this case only to overcome the problems of isolation and assurance, and no one is taxed without his consent. (*TJ*, 331/291)

But a political decision to impose a tax is unlikely to be a unanimous decision. Freeman reports:

> Rawls in conversation in the 1990s was surprised that others thought that *Theory* committed him to denying a democratic society the authority to publicly support perfectionist cultural institutions. His position in *Theory* is not I believe inconsistent with public opera, museums, symphonies, etc. that are supported by "user fees". But given their great costs cultural institutions are rarely supportable by user fees alone. (Freeman, *Rawls*, p. 511, n. 15)

of justice must at least give some guidance to this question since we have a provisional fixed point that it would be unjust for an existing generation to squander its resources (including material, environmental, and human) to the point where future generations would be unable to maintain a just and stable society. On the other hand excessive sacrifice for future gains (such as utilitarianism might require) seems beyond the demands of justice. The difference principle itself seems ill suited to set the appropriate rate over time since there is no reciprocity between previous and future generations. Instead, what is required is simply that societies make a contribution to developing and maintaining the conditions necessary for a stable and just basic structure. "Eventually, once just institutions are firmly established and all the basic liberties effectively realized, the net accumulation asked for falls to zero. At this point a society meets its duty of justice by maintaining just institutions and preserving their material base."[6] (*TJ*, 255) Additional savings beyond that, while permissible, are not required by justice.

This is rather imprecise, but Rawls had a difficult time reaching even this conclusion, and he made significant changes to this section in the revised edition of *A Theory of Justice*. The problem is to find a way to represent our provisional fixed point as the outcome of a choice from the original position. In the first edition, Rawls worried that the parties in the original position would have no grounds for saving at all. Therefore, as we saw in chapter 1, he stipulates that "The parties are regarded as representing family lines, say, with ties of sentiment between successive generations."[7] This assumption inserts a particular moral concern into the motivation of the parties and this threatens to undermine the heuristic value of the original position. Furthermore, it opened Rawls to the charge of sexism, as some critics argued that his approach was blind to injustice within the family.[8]

In the revised edition Rawls recognizes that a different account would suffice, although he does not revise all of the relevant passages to reflect this new approach. All that is required is that we make the parties choose a principle of savings that will apply to themselves and

[6] This passage does not appear in the original edition. [7] *TJ*, original edition, p. 292.

[8] See, for example, Deborah Kearns, "A Theory of Justice and Love – Rawls on the Family," *Politics*, 16 (1987); Susan Okin, *Justice, Gender and the Family* (Basic Books, 1989).

also that they wish earlier generations would have followed. It is true that they cannot control what earlier generations have actually done, but this is irrelevant to an assessment of what principle they would choose. "In arriving at a just savings principle (or better, limits on such principles), the parties are to ask themselves how much they would be willing to save at each stage of advance on the assumption that all other generations have saved, or will save, in accordance with the same criterion."[9] (*TJ*, 255)

THE PRECEPTS OF JUSTICE

Part of the task of reaching reflective equilibrium is to consider how well the principles of justice and the institutional scheme described above comport with the intuitive "precepts of justice." There are many such precepts, and while they conflict with one another, each has some intuitive appeal, at least within a restricted range of application. For example, the two precepts "to each according to his effort" and "to each according to his contribution" both may be appealing bases for determining wages, even though they conflict with one another. (*TJ*, 304–5/268) Worse still, there is no obvious way to combine these by, for example, assigning weights to one's effort and to one's contribution. Rawls's thought is that each of these precepts – and many others – captures a particular aspect of justice and is appropriate within a specific context or from a particular perspective. For example, from the perspective of a firm employing workers, the value of the workers' contribution is determined by their marginal productivity. From this perspective, the precept to each according to his contribution seems appropriate. On the other hand, from the point of view of the worker, effort and risk, for example, seem appropriate factors on which to base compensation.

Although different conceptions of justice may recognize a subordinate role for each of these precepts of justice and assign different weights to each of them, "[n]one of these precepts can be plausibly raised to a first principle." (*TJ*, 307/270) To attempt to do so would

[9] This passage does not appear in the original edition; however, see p. 288. See also Rawls, *Political Liberalism*, pp. 20–1, n. 22, 274; and Jane English, "Justice between Generations," *Philosophical Studies*, 31 (1977).

simply neglect other considerations that are relevant to justice. Again, consider the precept "to each according to his contribution." This precept "covers many cases of distribution in a perfectly competitive economy." (*TJ*, 308/271) But it cannot provide a complete account since:

> The marginal product of labor depends upon supply and demand . . . There is no presumption, then, that following the precept of contribution leads to a just outcome unless the underlying market forces, and the availability of opportunities which they reflect, are appropriately regulated. And this implies, as we have seen, that the basic structure as a whole is just. (*TJ*, 308/271)

Thus, while this precept fits our intuitive sense of what justice requires in many instances, its applicability presupposes that just background conditions are in place, and it therefore requires an independent account of those conditions.

Rawls gives one precept special attention, and this discussion has generated widespread misunderstanding. He concedes that this precept has great appeal: "There is a tendency for common sense to suppose that income and wealth, and the good things in life generally, should be distributed according to moral desert. Justice is happiness according to virtue." Yet, "justice as fairness rejects this conception." (*TJ*, 310/273) We discussed this issue in the introduction and chapter 1, but to repeat: the precept under consideration holds that, to the extent possible, goods ought to be distributed to particular individuals in accordance with their degree of moral virtue. Although attractive in some ways, and perhaps appropriate in some limited contexts, the idea of designing an institutional system to reward people according to their degree of moral virtue conflicts very strongly with the other precepts of justice that we have considered. It is, for example, incompatible with an economy that relies on market mechanisms that respond to supply and demand to any significant degree. "Surely a person's moral worth does not vary according to how many offer similar skills, or happen to want what he can produce." (*TJ*, 311/274)

Furthermore, recall that we are interested in identifying principles of justice for a well-ordered society as part of ideal theory. We are assuming that members of this society "have a strong sense of justice, an effective desire to comply with the existing rules and to give one another that to which they are entitled." (*TJ*, 312/274–5) Therefore Rawls continues, "we may assume that everyone is of equal moral worth." (*TJ*, 312/275) This does not strictly follow since moral worth depends on more than the degree to which one acts to promote the virtue of social justice. Still, a commitment to social justice is part of moral virtue, and this means that we cannot identify a person's overall moral worth until we have a basis for assessing what social justice requires:

> The essential point is that the concept of moral worth does not provide a first principle of distributive justice. This is because it cannot be introduced until after the principles of justice and of natural duty and obligation have been acknowledged . . . Thus the concept of moral worth is secondary to those of right and justice, and it plays no role in the substantive definition of distributive shares. (*TJ*, 312–13/275)

We must first identify a criterion for social justice (and the other virtues) before we can determine the degree to which individuals are morally virtuous.

We can clarify one reason why this precept may seem attractive by recalling from chapter 1 the idea of "legitimate expectations" in contrast to moral desert. Recall that the principle of fairness holds that when an individual voluntarily participates in an institution that is just, she acquires an obligation to act in accordance with the rules of that institution. Similarly, when an individual voluntarily participates in an institution that is just, she has a legitimate expectation that she will receive benefits in accordance with the rules of that institution. In other words, the rules of a just institution identify the mechanisms by which burdens and benefits are to be accorded to participants. The just institution of concern here is the economy of a well-ordered society, which specifies the procedures through which individuals come to acquire particular goods. We can say, if we like, that in a just economy each person gets what he or she is entitled to – or, in a loose and imprecise way, what he or she "deserves." However, the crucial point is that there is no way to identify what an individual is entitled to without first knowing what a just institutional scheme would look like. So, although justice as fairness does not aim to distribute goods according to moral virtue, "in the traditional phrase, a just scheme gives each person his due: that is, it allots to each what he is entitled to as defined by the [just] scheme itself." (*TJ*, 313/275–6)

There is, however, one area of justice in which a precept very much like the idea of rewarding people according to their moral desert seems to play a more direct role. Rawls holds that one main purpose of the criminal law "is to uphold basic natural duties," and therefore criminals usually exhibit a significant moral deficiency. (*TJ*, 314/276) Sometimes institutional rules can be viewed as presenting us with an option: we may choose whether to comply or to pay a penalty for a violation. But criminal laws are not like that. "They are not simply a scheme of taxes and burdens designed to put a price on certain forms of conduct and in this way to guide men's conduct for mutual advantage. It would be far better if the acts proscribed by penal statutes were never done." (*TJ*, 314–15/276–7) Retributive justice is appropriately sensitive to moral desert. However, it would be a serious mistake to view retributive and distributive justice as grounded on a single principle, "so that just as the one punishes certain offenses, the other rewards moral worth." (*TJ*, 315/277) Principles of retributive (and criminal) justice are necessary primarily because every society must find ways to cope with the tendency of some people to engage in immoral behavior.[10] This is an unfortunate necessity and must be addressed in partial compliance theory. Principles of distributive justice, on the other hand, are required even in a well-ordered society with full compliance as long as the circumstances of justice obtain and individuals hold different and conflicting conceptions of the good. "How justice requires us to meet injustice is a very different problem from how best to cope with the inevitable limitations and contingencies of human life." (*TJ*, 245/215) Although they respond to different problems, distributive justice has a kind of conceptual priority over retributive justice. We cannot identify injustice, let alone devise appropriate reponses to it, until we know what justice requires in the ideal, and for this we need principles of distributive justice.

[10] It may also satisfy a coordinating function, stabilizing a tendency to defect from mutually beneficial forms of social cooperation. See *TJ*, 240–1/211–13.

MIXED CONCEPTIONS AND THE PRINCIPLE OF PERFECTION

We can now return to consider two rivals to the two principles of justice. A "mixed conception" of justice is one that accepts the first principle of justice and its priority, but substitutes a different standard for the second principle. Because mixed conceptions are committed to an equal scheme of basic liberties, none is utilitarian, even if utilitarian considerations play a subordinate role as part of the second principle. For example, consider the mixed conception which retains the first principle of justice as well as fair equality of opportunity, but substitutes for the difference principle "the principle of average utility constrained by a certain social minimum." (*TJ*, 316/278) Given that the institutional arrangement sketched above to satisfy the two principles includes a guaranteed social minimum, it is somewhat unclear exactly whether or how the institutional implications of this mixed conception would differ. One advantage of the difference principle is that it gives guidance as to the level at which the social minimum should be set – namely, the level that maximizes the expected shares of primary goods for the least advantaged. This mixed conception, in contrast, apparently relies only on intuition to set this level. To be sure, this may not be a decisive objection, and relying on intuitions is not itself disqualifying: "it is evident that at some point we cannot avoid relying upon our intuitions. The difficulty with the mixed conceptions is that they may resort to these judgments too soon and fail to define a clear alternative to the difference principle." (*TJ*, 320/281)

Still, the mixed conceptions that rely in part on utilitarian considerations must face significant difficulties. The problems associated with implementing utilitarian principles are significantly greater than those associated with the difference principle. "It is necessary to arrive at some estimate of utility functions for different representative persons and to set up an interpersonal correspondence between them, and so on." (*TJ*, 320/282) The difficulties of specifying utility functions are well known and there are rival and incompatible theoretical ways of doing so. "Yet these methods involve strikingly different assumptions and presumably have very different consequences. It is a moral question which of these definitions and correspondence rules [for interpersonal comparisons], if any, are appropriate for a conception of justice." (*TJ*, 324/285) In addition to these theoretical issues, there are also practical problems associated with implementing any such proposal. First, it is clearly far more difficult to make assessments of utility levels across an entire population than it is to estimate shares of primary goods to be received by the least advantaged. In addition, the very process of estimating expected utility sets up an incentive to misrepresent one's own preferences in order to claim a larger share of resources. Shares of primary goods are public in a way that one's utility function is not. Even if people do not misrepresent their utility functions, the uncertainties and inevitable controversies in any such process are bound to generate suspicion and distrust. So even if in the ideal a mixed conception would support institutions similar to those that the two principles would support, when we recognize the practical and public role that a conception of justice is to serve, the two principles may still have a significant advantage.[11] As noted in chapter 1, the choice here – and therefore the defense of the difference principle – does not depend on the kind of maximin reasoning that leads to the rejection of utilitarianism and the selection of the first principle of justice. These considerations are less decisive than those relevant to the more fundamental choice between utilitarianism and the two principles, but that is to be expected since the two principles and this mixed conception are very similar to each other.

The final alternative conception of justice to consider is the "principle of perfection" which, in its extreme form, is a teleological theory that holds that institutions and individual duties and obligations ought to aim to "maximize the achievement of human excellence in art, science, and culture." (*TJ*, 325/285–6) A more moderate version

[11] In *Justice as Fairness*, Rawls provides a more extensive discussion of the comparison with this same mixed conception. He emphasizes that the difference principle represents an ideal of reciprocity that is lacking in other standards of distributive justice such as restricted utilitarianism, and that this, in turn, contributes to the greater stability of the two principles. (pp. 119–30) See also Joshua Cohen, "Democratic Equality," *Ethics*, 99 (1989); and Jon Mandle, *What's Left of Liberalism: An Interpretation and Defense of Justice as Fairness* (Lexington Books, 2000), pp. 134–51. In "Fairness to Goodness" [1975], Rawls adds an additional criticism: relying on a metric of utility (as opposed to primary goods) "may encourage people to develop, or claim to have developed, costly conceptions of the good in order to shift the distribution of the means of satisfaction in their direction, if only to protect themselves against the exorbitant claims of others." (Freeman, *Collected Papers*, pp. 282–3; see also "Social Unity and Primary Goods" [1982] in Freeman, *Collected Papers*, pp. 369–70)

holds that such excellence is only one of many goals to be balanced in an intuitionist theory. The problems with the more extreme form of perfectionism are clear enough. To be applicable, the principle of perfection must "provide some way of ranking different kinds of achievements and summing their values." (*TJ*, 327/287) But a specification that allows a ranking of the value of such achievements will not be able to command agreement from the parties in the original position. "They do not have an agreed criterion of perfection that can be used as a principle for choosing between institutions." (*TJ*, 327/288) The parties cannot rely on a specific standard of excellence or perfection to organize the basic structure of society any more than they can rely on a particular religion or conception of the good.

However, although no such standard of perfection can be used to underwrite the organization of the basic structure, this does not imply that such standards cannot be used for other purposes. On the contrary:

> Comparisons of intrinsic value can obviously be made; and although the standard of perfection is not a principle of justice, judgments of value have an important place in human affairs . . . While justice as fairness allows that in a well-ordered society the values of excellence are recognized, the human perfections are to be pursued within the limits of the principle of free association. Persons join together to further their cultural and artistic interests in the same way that they form religious communities. They do not use the coercive apparatus of the state to win for themselves a greater liberty or larger distributive shares on the grounds that their activities are of more intrinsic value. (*TJ*, 328–9/288–9)

This passage is of great importance given the common conservative charge that liberal principles of justice can only be based on skepticism regarding excellence. Individuals and groups are free to pursue excellence according to their own understanding, but the design of the basic structure is not dependent on any particular interpretation of excellence or a (complete) conception of human value.

One might infer that from the point of view of the basic structure that all conceptions of the good have the same intrinsic worth. Yet Rawls resists this interpretation as well:

> On the contract doctrine, then, the equal liberty of citizens does not presuppose that the ends of different persons have the same intrinsic value, nor that their freedom and well-being is of the same worth . . . We can say if we

> wish that men have equal dignity, meaning by this simply that they all satisfy the conditions of moral personality expressed by the interpretation of the initial contractual situation. And being alike in this respect, they are to be treated as the principles of justice require . . . But none of this implies that their activities and accomplishments are of equal excellence. (*TJ*, 329/289)

So, justice as fairness does not rely on any particular conception of the good or account of human excellence. But the basic liberties ensure that individuals and groups can pursue their own goals and make evaluations on the basis of their own systems of values. Furthermore, justice as fairness does not assume that these different systems of value all are of equal worth. Rather, it simply remains silent or agnostic concerning their relative merits. Such comparisons and judgments may be appropriate for individuals and groups in voluntary associations to make within a just society, but they are not appropriate bases for determining the design of the basic structure.

It is possible that a more moderate, intuitionist version of perfectionism may accord with justice as fairness on many applications to particular cases. However, with no clear method to assign weights to the different principles, this account shares the weakness of all forms of intuitionism. Furthermore, the individual principles of perfection are themselves likely to be subject to intense public controversy in their application to particular cases. Mentioning the case of "certain kinds of sexual relationships" that are said to be "degrading and shameful," Rawls notes that such judgments

> are likely to be influenced by subtle aesthetic preferences and personal feelings of propriety; and individual, class, and group differences are often sharp and irreconcilable. Since these uncertainties plague perfectionist criteria and jeopardize individual liberty, it seems best to rely entirely on the principles of justice which have a more definite structure. (*TJ*, 331/291)

POLITICAL DUTIES, CIVIL DISOBEDIENCE, AND CONSCIENTIOUS REFUSAL

With the exception of a brief interlude in chapter 1 to define and distinguish obligations and natural duties, our concern has been with institutional design. However, as we saw, social institutions are not independent of the actions and attitudes of individuals and groups. Therefore, an account of the implications of social justice for individual behavior is "an essential part of a conception of right: [these principles] define our institutional ties and how we become bound to one another." (*TJ*, 333/293) Even here it is important to recognize that the goal is not to provide a complete account of the justice of individual conduct, much less a complete account of right or morality. Again, the focus is on the requirements on individual behavior that stem from the demands of social justice.

From this perspective, it is clear that "the most important natural duty is that to support and to further just institutions." (*TJ*, 334/293) This natural duty of justice has two parts: "first, we are to comply with and to do our share in just institutions when they exist and apply to us; and second, we are to assist in the establishment of just arrangements when they do not exist, at least when this can be done with little cost to ourselves." (*TJ*, 334/293–4) There is some vagueness in this account – for example, how much cost must be borne by individuals in the name of establishing just institutions, and when exactly do institutions "apply to us"? However these questions are eventually answered, it seems clear that the parties in the original position would endorse a duty of justice knowing that this was necessary in order to support and sustain a just basic structure. A failure to place individuals under any duty of justice would leave the justice of the basic structure vulnerable to the vicissitudes of chance. The stability of a just society depends on the commitment of individuals to achieving and maintaining such an order. It is a theoretical possibility that the parties would choose to give different content to the duty of justice than what they have already chosen for the design of the basic structure, but given the publicity requirement, it is clear that they would require that individuals support institutions that satisfy the two principles. It makes sense, therefore, "to use the two principles of justice as a part of the conception of right for individuals." (*TJ*, 335/295) This does not mean that individuals must guide their ordinary conduct by a direct application of the two principles to all of the choices they make. Rather, it means that when the design of the basic structure is at stake, for example, in "the case of a citizen deciding how to vote between political parties, or the case of a legislator wondering whether to favor a certain statute," (*TJ*, 334/294) they must strive to make the institutional structure of their society conform as closely to the two principles as possible.

In addition to the duty of justice, there are other natural duties, including a duty of mutual aid. (*TJ*, 338–9/297–8) Rawls thinks that it is fairly obvious that this and others would be acknowledged from the original position. "The real difficulty lies in their more detailed specification and with questions of priority: how are these duties to be balanced when they come into conflict?" (*TJ*, 339/298) Here, Rawls glimpses the broader issues associated with the idea of "rightness as fairness," but he retreats from further investigation: "I do not know how this problem is to be settled, or even whether a systematic solution formulating useful and practicable rules is possible. It would seem that the theory of the basic structure is actually simpler." (*TJ*, 339–40/299) Although we will examine a few special cases of civil disobedience and conscientious refusal where individual duties associated with social justice conflict either internally or with broader moral considerations, no attempt is made to articulate a complete account of individual morality or even of individual justice.

When we focus on the natural duty of justice, the contrast with obligations may become elusive. The natural duty of justice entails complying with institutions that apply to us, while the principle of fairness requires accepting the burdens imposed by just institutions when we accept their benefits. The contrast concerns whether the institutions in question "must inevitably apply to us since we are born into them and they regulate the full scope of our activity" or whether the institutions apply to us only because "we have freely done certain things as a rational way of advancing our ends." (*TJ*, 344/302) Since the basic structure inevitably applies to members of a society, compliance with its demands is grounded in the natural duty of justice, not the principle of fairness. Compliance is not conditional on any voluntary undertaking, but only on the justice of the structure itself. Unlike our participation in the basic structure, we have the option of making or not making promises. Therefore, assuming that the "institution of promising" (that is, the rules which specify when and how one puts oneself under an obligation through promising and what such an obligation requires) is just, we only put ourselves under an obligation when we voluntarily make certain actions – such as saying the words, "I promise." Rawls's extended discussion of this institution is interesting and useful in its own right, but it functions as an important contrast with the unconditional nature of natural duties, including the requirement that we comply with the basic rules of a just social order. (*TJ*, 344–50/303–8)

When a just law is created by the procedures specified by a just constitution, it is clear that the natural duty of justice requires that citizens comply. The more difficult case concerns the extent of the duty to obey unjust – or not fully just – laws that have been created through a reasonably just constitutional procedure. It is sometimes denied that there is any such duty, but Rawls insists that there is, although it is not absolute: "When the basic structure of society is reasonably just, as estimated by what the current state of things allows, we are to recognize unjust laws as binding provided that they do not exceed certain limits of injustice." (*TJ*, 351/308) It is crucial that we be able to differentiate the degree to which a law or institution departs from the ideal of what justice requires. And while Rawls argues that his two principles of justice "define the most reasonable view among those on the list, other principles are not unreasonable. Indeed, some mixed conceptions are certainly adequate enough for many purposes." (*TJ*, 352/310) But if the requirement of compliance is grounded in either the duty of justice or the principle of fairness, both of which refer to the justice of the institution in question, why should not any departure at all from the most demanding standards of justice nullify the requirement to comply?

The answer becomes more clear when we recall that no political procedure can be guaranteed to produce all and only just laws. "In political affairs, perfect procedural justice cannot be achieved." (*TJ*, 353/311) We must expect that even the most just political structure will, from time to time, generate substantively unjust laws. If the duty of justice requires us to support just institutions even if they are imperfect, this means that sometimes at least we must comply with those imperfect outcomes in order to support the just institutions that generated them. In order to support the institutions of law, we must comply with the legitimate outcomes of those institutions, sometimes even when they are substantively unjust: "our natural duty to uphold just institutions binds us to comply with unjust laws and policies, or at least not to oppose them by illegal means as long as they do not exceed certain limits of injustice." (*TJ*, 354/311) To insist that we are never bound by a legitimate but unjust law is to hold that we need not support political institutions unless they instantiate perfect procedural justice. But since no political procedure can realize the ideal of perfect procedural justice, this amounts to saying we have no duty to support political institutions at all, but only their substantive outcomes when we judge them to be just. Such a doctrine is exactly what the parties in the original position reject when they embrace the duty of justice.

Even in a well-ordered society where everyone shares the same abstract conception of justice, we must expect that there will be reasonable disagreement over which specific laws or policies would be just. Economic forecasting, to take but one example, is simply not precise enough to be able to predict with great confidence the implications of various policies on the least advantaged. Individuals will often be bound by the duty of justice to comply with a legitimate law passed by the just political structure, despite the fact that they sincerely believe it to be (to some degree) unjust. As we have seen, the extent of this duty has limits. Although he does not provide a precise specification of these limits, Rawls does discuss some relevant considerations. For example, the substantive injustices must be "more or less evenly distributed over different groups in society," and the injustices must not violate the basic liberties. (*TJ*, 355/312)

Since reasonable disagreement is the norm, we must consider the status of majority rule and its limitations in justice as fairness. The only limitations on majority rule to be considered here are those that are consistent with an equal scheme of basic liberties. Various mechanisms of judicial review could be examples of this since they apply equally to all. The important point is that, consistent with the requirements of the first principle, the justification for the design of such a political procedure "rests squarely on the political ends that the constitution is designed to achieve, and therefore on the principles of justice." (*TJ*, 356/313) In other words, majority rule should be relied on only to the extent that it is "the best available way of insuring just and effective legislation . . . There is nothing to the view, then, that what the majority wills is right." (*TJ*, 356/313; cf. 296/261) The justification of a procedure of majority rule (perhaps limited by judicial review to protect the basic liberties) rests on the claim that it is more likely than other procedures to generate laws that best achieve the goals of justice. This is true – or more likely to be true – when citizens and legislators consciously aim at and vote for laws that they sincerely believe will satisfy the principles of justice. The political process is not simply a mechanism for aggregating preferences or a bargaining mechanism among private interests:

> In the ideal procedure, the decision reached is not a compromise, a bargain struck between opposing parties trying to advance their ends. The legislative discussion must be conceived not as a contest between interests, but as an attempt to find the best policy as defined by the principles of justice. (*TJ*, 357/314)

Such an account is often referred to as a form of "deliberative democracy," and it depends on the assumption that "an ideally conducted discussion among many persons is more likely to arrive at the correct conclusion (by a vote if necessary) than the deliberations of any one of them by himself." (*TJ*, 358/315) In the political process, "the exchange of opinion with others checks our partiality and widens our perspective; we are made to see things from their standpoint and the limits of our vision are brought home to us." (*TJ*, 358/315)

This model of deliberative democracy contrasts with an "ideal market process" in which individuals are assumed to act on their narrow self-interest and individuals need not have any opinion at all about the proper overall outcome. When functioning properly, an ideal market generates outcomes that are efficient with respect to those interests – with respect to the end of efficiency, it is analogous to perfect procedural justice. In contrast, as we have seen, "There seems to be no way to characterize a feasible procedure guaranteed to lead to just legislation." (*TJ*, 360/316) We know that there are some limits placed on the permissible forms of legislation – there can be no violation of the basic liberties, for example – and to this extent any legislative process is a form of imperfect procedural justice. Yet, within those limits, there seems to be no alternative, even in the ideal, to relying on the judgment of "rational legislators conscientiously trying to follow the principles of justice." (*TJ*, 362/318) Therefore, within the range of permissible legislation, we have a case of pure procedural justice. We can call such a hybrid "quasi-pure procedural justice." (*TJ*, 362/318)

Part II of *A Theory of Justice* ends by considering some cases in which the duty to comply with the law may be overridden by justifiable acts of civil disobedience or conscientious refusal. Rawls restricts his attention to cases in which a society is "nearly just, one that is well-ordered for the most part but in which some serious violations of justice nevertheless do occur." (*TJ*, 363/319) In such cases, we have a potential conflict within the demands of justice, and we must ask: "At what point does the duty to comply with laws enacted by a legislative majority . . . cease to be binding in view of the right to defend one's liberties and the duty to oppose injustice?" (*TJ*, 363/319) This discussion is not intended to be comprehensive, but only illustrative. It is also important to remember that *A Theory of Justice* was published in 1971, during the height of the Vietnam War, and some of the material incorporated into Rawls's discussion of civil disobedience dates back to a presentation at the American Political Science Association in September 1966. There can be no doubt that Rawls had the civil rights movement firmly in mind, and he notes the similarity of his understanding of civil disobedience to that in Martin Luther King's 1963 "Letter from Birmingham City Jail." (*TJ*, 364, n. 19/320, n. 19)

Rawls defines an act of civil disobedience as: "a public, nonviolent, conscientious yet political act contrary to law usually done with the aim of bringing about a change in the law or policies of the government." (*TJ*, 364/320) What is distinctive of a civilly disobedient act is that it "addresses the sense of justice of the majority of the community and declares that in one's considered opinion the principles of social cooperation among free and equal men are not being respected." (*TJ*, 364/320) As a public form of address, it is not covert or violent, and participants accept the legal consequences of their conduct. All of these components help "to establish to the majority that the act is indeed politically conscientious and sincere, and that it is intended to address the public's sense of justice." (*TJ*, 366–7/322) There is no requirement that the very law believed to be unjust be the one that is violated, nor need the violation be solely a mechanism to generate a legal challenge to the law.

Before examining the extent to which civil disobedience can be justified, there is one further element that is worth emphasizing, especially in light of the subsequent developments in Rawls's theory. Because an act of civil disobedience is addressed to the sense of justice of the citizens of a diverse society, its justification cannot be dependent on any particular religion or comprehensive moral doctrine. Rather, it must be based on what Rawls calls "political principles, that is, by the principles of justice which regulate the constitution and social institutions generally." (*TJ*, 365/321) This is the sense of "political" that Rawls later develops in *Political Liberalism* and that we will discuss in chapter 4. He elaborates: "In justifying civil disobedience one does not appeal to principles of personal morality or to religious doctrines, though these may coincide with and support one's claims; and it goes without saying that civil disobedience cannot be grounded solely on group or self-interest." (*TJ*, 365/321; cf. 384–5/337–8)

A well-ordered society should encourage citizens to make strong public appeals to the shared sense of justice when they sincerely believe that it is perpetrating a significant injustice. Citizens may express this sense through civilly disobedient acts. However, this must be balanced against the duty to support just institutions and to comply with legitimate laws. Because civil disobedience is "a political act addressed to the sense of justice of the community" it makes sense to "limit it to instances of substantial and clear injustice, and preferably to those which obstruct the path to removing other injustices." (*TJ*, 372/326) For example, when "certain minorities are denied the right to vote or to hold office, or to own property and to move from place to place, or when certain religious groups are repressed and others denied various opportunities, these injustices may be obvious to all." (*TJ*, 372/327) Of course, it would always be better to address an injustice through the established political process when that process is responsive, but sometimes the existing political structure proves itself to be indifferent. When this happens, the step to civil disobedience is not to be taken lightly, but nonetheless is sometimes justified.

Rawls's definition of civil disobedience is rather restricted, but this does not imply that other forms of non-compliance are ruled out. Conscientious refusal does not aim to appeal to the public sense of justice. Rather, it is "noncompliance with a more or less direct legal injunction or administrative order." (*TJ*, 368/323) While acts of conscientious refusal may be "grounded on political principles" and the demands of justice, they need not be, and "may be founded on religious or other principles at variance with the constitutional order." (*TJ*, 369/324) Some of Rawls's examples of conscientious refusal include the refusal of members of the Jehovah's Witnesses to salute the flag, pacifists refusing to serve in the armed forces, and covert infractions of the fugitive slave law. (*TJ*, 368–9/324) In such cases, we have the possibility of conflicts not only within justice, but more generally between the demands of compliance (itself part of the duty of justice) and other virtues and moral requirements. The example that Rawls considers, however, concerns a conflict within the ideal of justice.

Not all conscientious acts are to be tolerated. It is appropriate and necessary for a just society to put restrictions on certain actions, for example those that limit the basic liberties of others, even if those actions are grounded in deeply held religious convictions. "There is a temptation to say that the law must always respect the dictates of conscience, but this cannot be right." (*TJ*, 370/325) On the other hand, it is possible to find cases in which such refusal appears to be justified. To illustrate this possibility, Rawls writes that in some cases, pacifism as a form of conscientious refusal may be justified even though strictly speaking pacifism is incorrect – "in some situations wars of self-defense are justified." (*TJ*, 370/325) This is because:

> given the tendency of nations, particularly great powers, to engage in war unjustifiably and to set in motion the apparatus of the state to suppress dissent, the respect accorded to pacifism serves the purpose of alerting citizens to the wrongs that governments are prone to commit in their name. Even though his views are not altogether sound, the warnings and protests that a pacifist is disposed to express may have the result that on balance the principles of justice are more rather than less secure. Pacifism as a natural departure from the correct doctrine conceivably compensates for the weakness of men in living up to their professions. (*TJ*, 370–1/325)

In radically different circumstances – if governments were not prone to justify infringements on dissent in the name of security, or if the majority in a society were pacifists and the society was in danger from foreign attack – such conscientious refusal would more strongly conflict with the demands of justice. However, given actual circumstances, tolerating such acts may actually serve to increase the justice of a society, all things considered.

Although it is in principle possible to have a case of conscientious refusal that is grounded in a non-political principle (i.e. in a virtue other than justice), Rawls does not give such an example. His examples of conscientious refusal and (of course) of civil disobedience involve political justifications: they depend on "common sense principles of justice that men can require one another to follow and not upon the affirmations of religious faith and love which they cannot demand that everyone accept." (*TJ*, 385/337) A non-political defense of conscientious refusal would be far more difficult to make. It would depend on a comparison of the strength of the demands of justice to rival values, and this raises a series of issues that we will discuss in chapters 3 and 4.

Finally, it is clear that there is no mechanical decision procedure that can determine whether particular cases of civil disobedience or conscientious refusal are justified. Nor can any individual or institution be charged with making a final and authoritative determination of the permissibility of any such action. Some might object that this position "invites anarchy by encouraging everyone to decide for himself, and to abandon the public rendering of political principles." (*TJ*, 389/341) Rawls's reply is particularly revealing. He concedes that "each person must indeed make his own decision" although we will typically "seek advice and counsel" from others: (*TJ*, 389/341)

> But while each person must decide for himself whether the circumstances justify civil disobedience, it does not follow that one is to decide as one pleases . . . If [a citizen] comes to the conclusion after due consideration that civil disobedience is justified and conducts himself accordingly, he acts conscientiously. And although he may be mistaken, he has not done as he pleased . . . To the question, who is to decide? the answer is: all are to decide, everyone taking counsel with himself, and with reasonableness, comity, and good fortune, it often works out well enough. (*TJ*, 389–90/341–2)

We cannot escape responsibility for our own judgment and actions, and there can be no guarantee that our judgment will be correct or that it will always work out well enough. This is simply a result of the fact that the justice of a society depends crucially on the sense of justice of its citizens. There is little hope for the stability and the justice of a society in which most citizens are driven by narrow self-interest or hold seriously flawed conceptions of justice. But we knew that already, and such a society will likely face far more serious problems than excessive incidents of civil disobedience.

CHAPTER 3

Part III *of* A Theory of Justice – *Ends*

TWO THEORIES OF THE GOOD

One of the main goals of part III of *A Theory of Justice* is to develop an account of the stability of a well-ordered society. We have already seen that the stability of a society depends on the sense of justice of its citizens. We must now consider how people in a well-ordered society would come to acquire a sense of justice and the attitude that they would have toward that sense of justice once it is acquired. Their reflective attitude will largely be a matter of how well their sense of justice fits with their other values and goals. When they fit together well and support one another, they are said to be "congruent." To see whether and the extent to which a sense of justice fits with other elements of a person's values, we must clarify the idea of the good. Justice as fairness, in fact, relies on two theories of the good:

> The reason for doing this is that in justice as fairness the concept of right is prior to that of the good. In contrast with teleological theories, something is good only if it fits into ways of life consistent with the principles of right already on hand. But to establish these principles it is necessary to rely on some notion of goodness, for we need assumptions about the parties' motives in the original position. Since these assumptions must not jeopardize the prior place of the concept of right, the theory of the good used in arguing for the principles of justice is restricted to the bare essentials. (*TJ*, 396/347–8)

We need to develop a "thin" theory of the good for use in the original position. We need a "full" theory of the good in order to assess congruence, that is, "whether being a good person is a good thing for that person, if not in general, then under what conditions." (*TJ*, 397/349)

There is an important contrast between what we need from each of these two accounts of the good. In order to identify which principles would be chosen from the original position, we need to generate a fairly specific list of primary goods. In contrast, there is no need to develop in detail anyone's full conception of the good. We need simply to understand in general terms how a person develops and holds such a conception so that we can assess whether congruence is likely to hold. As theorists of justice, our main goal is to develop and defend a conception of justice, and this depends on a thin theory of the good. But while it may be important for each of us in our own lives to develop a (more-or-less) full conception of the good, this is not necessary in order to develop and to defend a conception of justice.

Rawls calls his broad approach to the good "goodness as rationality." The basic idea is that we say an object is "good" when it has the properties that it is rational to want in an object of its kind. This definition puts a great burden on the account of rationality, but it avoids many controversies in the philosophy of language. We often use the term "good" to express a recommendation, and this is explained by the reference to rationality in the definition. We do not need to rely on some special emotive meaning, although that is not ruled out. To see how this account applies to a person's conception of the good, first consider a simple case in which we can take for granted that an object has a certain purpose or function. An object is a good one of its kind if it has the properties that contribute to achieving its purpose. Schematically: "A is a good X if and only if A has the properties . . . which it is rational to want in an X, given what X's are used for, or expected to do, and the like." (*TJ*, 399/350–1) Given the typical uses of a knife, for example, a good knife is one that cuts well, retains its sharpness, and is easy to handle because those are the properties it is rational to want in a knife. This analysis applies not only to physical artifacts, but to people filling social roles. We can speak of a good teacher, doctor, spouse, or soldier in a similar way.

Sometimes, however, an object can serve several different, possibly incompatible functions, or it may be needed for a specialized task, in which cases an assessment of its value depends on specifying which end is the relevant one. A good knife for me will be very different from a good knife for you if I need one to hack through the jungle while you need one to filet a fish. A more complete definition explicitly specifies whose ends are served and relativizes the assessment to those ends: "A is a good X for K (where K is some person) if and only if A has the properties which it is rational for K to want in an X, given K's circumstances, abilities, and plan of life (his system of aims), and therefore in view of what he intends to do with an X." (*TJ*, 399/351) Note that this definition does not require an evaluation, either in terms of the rationality or the morality of the ends that the object will serve. A gun may be a good gun in this sense if it allows an assassin to kill efficiently. This is appropriate since we often want to assess the value of some object without assessing the end it serves. Other times, however, when we assess some object, we not only want to make such an instrumental evaluation, but we also want to make a more complete assessment, including the value of the end served. How do we assess the value of an end or system of ends?

Rawls's idea is to "adapt Royce's thought that a person may be regarded as a human life lived according to a plan" (*TJ*, 408/358) and then determine whether such a plan is rational. This is a metaphor and should not be taken to suggest that one's life must somehow fully be planned out ahead of time. Rather, the idea is simply that a person's various commitments, interests, goals, aspirations, projects, and ideals must somehow be integrated with one another to fit together into a single life. There is no suggestion that a carefully controlled life is superior to one full of spontaneity or that planning is somehow an intrinsically worthy activity. "We must not imagine that a rational plan is a detailed blueprint for action stretching over the whole course of a life. It consists of a hierarchy of plans, the more specific subplans being filled in at the appropriate time." (*TJ*, 410/360) We can think of a person's life plan as setting a kind of standard for her happiness – a person is happy to the extent that she knows herself to be successfully carrying out her life plan. And, of course, there is no assumption that everyone finds happiness in the same activities: "Since plans which it is rational to adopt vary from person to person depending on their endowments and circumstances, and the like, different individuals find happiness in doing different things." (*TJ*, 409/359)

A rational life plan satisfies two broad conditions. First, "it is one of the plans that is consistent with the principles of rational choice," and second, "it is that plan among those meeting this condition which would be chosen by him with full deliberative rationality, that is, with full awareness of the relevant facts and after a careful consideration of the consequences." (*TJ*, 408/358–9) The principles of rational choice put some constraints on life plans, but they are far from determining a unique one for a given individual. We can think of the principles of rational choice as formal requirements. They include the principle of effective means that holds that "given the objective, one is to achieve it with the least expenditure of means (whatever they are); or given the means, one is to fulfill the objective to the fullest possible extent." (*TJ*, 412/361) The principle of inclusiveness requires that a plan "is to be preferred to another if its execution would achieve all of the desired aims of the other plan and one or more further aims in addition." (*TJ*, 412/362) Finally, the principle of greater likelihood holds that among two plans with roughly the same aims, we should choose the one with the greater likelihood of success. (*TJ*, 412–13/362) In effect, these principles suffice to rule out only the most blatantly irrational, self-defeating, or inconsistent plans. They are plainly insufficient to determine a single plan.

From among the plans consistent with these formal principles, we need a way to determine which forms the basis of a person's good. In the end, Rawls holds, "we must finally choose for ourselves in the sense that the choice often rests on our direct self-knowledge not only of what things we want but also of how much we want them." (*TJ*, 416/365) More specifically, following Sidgwick,

> The rational plan for a person is the one . . . which he would choose with deliberative rationality. It is the plan that would be decided upon as the outcome of careful reflection in which the agent reviewed, in the light of all the relevant facts, what it would be like to carry out these plans and thereby ascertained the course of action that would best realize his more fundamental desires. (*TJ*, 417/366)

The basic idea is simple enough. The rational plan for a person is the plan that he would select from the permissible plans if he made the selection carefully from a position in which "he possessed full information." (*TJ*, 417/366) Rawls's rhetoric may make it sound as though he is advocating actually collecting all relevant information and then making a single, existential choice to determine one's good. He attempts to dispel this impression by noting that "a rational person will not usually continue to deliberate until he has found the best plan open to him. Often he will be content if he forms a satisfactory plan (or subplan), that is, one that meets various minimum conditions." (*TJ*, 418/367)

This account of a rational plan of life grounds the account of a person's conception of the good. But it is important to keep track of why we want such an account in the first place. We are not interested in providing guidance to individuals engaged in ordinary practical deliberation. We need the account in order to ground the use of the primary goods and to assess the stability of the principles of justice. Rawls notes this when he observes that the account of deliberative rationality is hypothetical "in a way similar to the criterion of justice." (*TJ*, 421/370) Yet there remains a crucial difference. We aim actually to identify as best we can which principles would be chosen from the original position. We are not interested in constructing anyone's actual conception of the good or plan of life. Given these limited aims, it would suffice to observe that once the formal principles rule out inconsistent plans, and we eliminate those that would only be based on false information, there still remains a broad class of permissible plans. There is no need to insist on any particular method or hypothetical choice situation (such as full information or full deliberative rationality) from which to select *the* rational plan for an individual. We can therefore avoid controversies associated with full information accounts of the good. It is obvious that false or incomplete information can result in a chosen plan being less than ideal or even downright bad for a person. However, it is not at all clear that the idea of making a choice with full information is attractive, determinate, or even coherent.[1] Fortunately, for the limited purposes of justice as fairness, we can avoid these controversies.

THE ARISTOTELIAN PRINCIPLE

In order to give some substance to this "purely formal" characterization of the good, we must rely on "certain general facts" including "the

[1] For a discussion of some of the difficulties with full information accounts, see David Sobel, "Full Information Accounts of Well-Being," *Ethics*, 104 (1994).

broad features of human desires and needs" as well as "the requirements of human capacities and abilities, their trends of maturation and growth, and how they are best trained and educated for this or that purpose." (*TJ*, 424/372–3) As part of the effort to characterize the human good in slightly less formal terms, Rawls introduces an empirical psychological principle that he calls "the Aristotelian Principle." In its initial formulation it holds that,

> other things equal, human beings enjoy the exercise of their realized capacities (their innate or trained abilities), and this enjoyment increases the more the capacity is realized, or the greater its complexity. The intuitive idea here is that human beings take more pleasure in doing something as they become more proficient at it, and of two activities they do equally well, they prefer the one calling on a larger repertoire of more intricate and subtle discriminations. (*TJ*, 426/374)

Two points call for comment. First, in this case, the "other things equal" clause is very significant. The thought is not to explain the structure of any specific individual's preferences, but rather to make a broad psychological generalization. It "formulates a tendency and not an invariable pattern of choice, and like all tendencies it may be overridden." (*TJ*, 429/376) The claim is that generally speaking, as people develop and exercise their capacities and skills, the enjoyment they take in utilizing them increases. Second, despite Rawls's examples, the point is not primarily that we like more complicated activities rather than simpler ones. Simple activities have their pleasures too, and as we develop our capacities with respect to them, in general we should expect our enjoyment in them to increase as well. Complexity is not really the point except to the extent that it is a reflection of increased skill and capacity.

The Aristotelian Principle introduces a dynamic picture of the good. If we were only concerned with satisfying our current preferences and desires, it might be unclear why we should seek to develop new ones at all. The Aristotelian Principle suggests that it will often be rational – that is, it will often serve our good – to invest in educating and developing our innate capacities. Doing so will be likely to result in higher levels of satisfaction as our capacities increase. Of course, there are limits because the costs associated with training and development may increase as skills and specialization increase. Still, "it will generally be rational . . . to realize and train mature capacities." (*TJ*, 428/376) We may or may not follow Mill and call the exercise of these "higher pleasures." The point is that the Aristotelian Principle asserts that people are generally "importantly moved not only by the pressure of bodily needs, but also by the desire to do things enjoyed simply for their own sakes, at least when the urgent and pressing wants are satisfied." (*TJ*, 431/379)

The Aristotelian Principle has been subject to many misunderstandings and mistaken criticisms. In part this is because of an example that Rawls introduces to illustrate both the content of the principle and the possibility of exceptions to it. The Aristotelian Principle is an empirical generalization that aims to explain the type of plans that individuals typically endorse. But the account of a rational plan is not dependent on this generalization. To illustrate this independence, Rawls imagines a person for whom this deep psychological fact does not hold – "someone whose only pleasure is to count blades of grass in various geometrically shaped areas." (*TJ*, 432/379) The point is not that such an activity is common. On the contrary, "we would be surprised that such a person should exist" and perhaps this activity would be evidence that he is "peculiarly neurotic." (*TJ*, 432/380) But if we assume that "his nature is to enjoy this activity and not to enjoy any other, and that there is no feasible way to alter his condition, then surely a rational plan for him will center around this activity." (*TJ*, 432–3/380) To repeat: the point is to show that the definition of a rational plan and an individual's good does not depend on the truth of the Aristotelian Principle. Still, Rawls believes that the Aristotelian Principle does characterize a deep psychological fact about most people, and therefore constitutes an empirically acceptable generalization about human goods.

One use of this empirical generalization is in developing an account of the primary goods, which are "necessary for the framing and the execution of a rational plan of life." (*TJ*, 433/380) Since the parties in the original position are to rely on primary goods, our account must not depend on the principles of justice. But in developing our thin theory of the good, we can and must draw on "the general facts about human wants and abilities, their characteristic phases and requirements of nurture, the Aristotelian Principle, and the necessities of social interdependence." (*TJ*, 434/381) We can also draw on the model of the person and the account of our highest-order interests. We will consider changes to Rawls's account of primary goods in chapter 4.

Once we have developed our thin theory of the good and, relying on the account of primary goods, constructed our principles of justice, we can insist that all further accounts of the good be compatible with those principles. For example, we can consider when a person should properly be described as good. Consistent with our earlier definition, we can say that a person is good at filling a certain role – a mother, friend, stockbroker, chef – when they have the properties that it is rational to want in a person occupying that role. If there are "broadly based" properties that "it is rational to want in persons when they are viewed with respect to almost any of their social roles," (*TJ*, 435/382) then we can say that those properties characterize a good person. At least in a well-ordered society, Rawls asserts, "the fundamental moral virtues, that is, the strong and normally effective desires to act on the basic principles of right, are undoubtedly among the broadly based properties." (*TJ*, 436/382) In a well-ordered society each member will have a normally effective sense of justice, and it is obvious that it would be rational for each to want others to have a similar sense of justice.

SELF-RESPECT

As we saw in chapter 1, Rawls claims that self-respect is "perhaps the most important primary good." (*TJ*, 440/386) This consists in "a person's sense of his own value, his secure conviction that his conception of the good, his plan of life, is worth carrying out" together with "a confidence in one's ability, so far as it is within one's power, to fulfill one's intentions." (*TJ*, 440/386) This is consistent with a thin theory of the good, and it is something that it is rational to want regardless of the particular content of one's life plan. Apathy and indifference can prevent one from achieving one's goals just as surely as a lack of basic liberties or essential resources can. "Therefore, the parties in the original position would wish to avoid at almost any cost the social conditions that undermine self-respect." (*TJ*, 440/386)

Two conditions tend to support the essential good of self-respect: "(1) having a rational plan of life, and in particular one that satisfies the Aristotelian Principle; and (2) finding our person and deeds appreciated and confirmed by others who are likewise esteemed and their association enjoyed."[2] (*TJ*, 440/386) With regard to the first point, activities and projects that can be too easily mastered and that do not present sufficient challenges are "likely to seem dull and flat, and to give us no feeling of competence or a sense that they are worth doing." (*TJ*, 440/387) With regard to the second, Rawls is here assuming that a well-ordered society will be characterized by a wide array of associations through which shared goods are jointly pursued. By participating in groups where one's conception of the good is affirmed, one comes to develop a sense of self-respect:

> Thus what is necessary is that there should be for each person at least one community of shared interests to which he belongs and where he finds his endeavors confirmed by his associates. And for the most part this assurance is sufficient whenever in public life citizens respect one another's ends and adjudicate their political claims in ways that also support their self-esteem. It is precisely this background condition that is maintained by the principles of justice. (*TJ*, 442/388)

It is unrealistic to demand that everyone affirm the same conception of the good, but it is not too much to hope that individuals might find like-minded associates and friends to affirm their sincerely embraced, permissible conceptions of the good. The principles of justice provide strong support for the development of self-respect by creating the opportunities for such associations, while at the same time fairly adjudicating the conflicts that will inevitably emerge among them.

A loss of self-respect is felt as shame. This involves a particular kind of loss that is distinct from regret, which is "the general feeling aroused by the loss or absence of what we think good for us, whereas shame is the emotion evoked by shocks to our self-respect, a special kind of good." (*TJ*, 442–3/388) Moral shame, in particular, occurs when someone recognizes that he or she lacks the virtues "that his plan of life requires and is framed to encourage." (*TJ*, 444/390) We can see how individuals are potentially vulnerable to moral shame

[2] Rawls apparently uses the terms "self-respect" and "self-esteem" interchangeably (e.g. *TJ*, 440/386). But as David Sachs argues, they are not the same. They are, however, related, and in this context Rawls probably means that the appreciation from others that we esteem can provide support to our self-respect. See David Sachs, "How to Distinguish Self-Respect from Self-Esteem," *Philosophy and Public Affairs*, 10 (1981).

if we combine the Kantian interpretation of the principles of justice with the Aristotelian Principle:

> First of all, the Kantian interpretation of the original position means that the desire to do what is right and just is the main way for persons to express their nature as free and equal rational beings. And from the Aristotelian Principle it follows that this expression of their nature is a fundamental element of their good. Combined with the account of moral worth, we have, then, that the virtues are excellences. They are good from the standpoint of ourselves as well as from that of others. (*TJ*, 445/390)

This is a particularly important passage since it reveals a core element of Rawls's argument for congruence, which is itself part of his argument for stability. It also starkly reveals how the congruence argument depends on two controversial assumptions concerning our "nature as free and equal" and that "a fundamental element" of our good consists in expressing this nature. As we will see in chapter 4, Rawls came to believe that an argument for the stability of a well-ordered society ought not to depend on these types of assumptions.

Having provided this analysis of the good, we are in a position to draw some important contrasts between the right and the good. This reveals the deep structure of justice as fairness. While a well-ordered society is characterized by a shared sense of justice, "it is, in general a good thing that individuals' conceptions of their good should differ in significant ways." (*TJ*, 447/393) Not only does society not need to reach a consensus concerning the good, there is no urgency in reaching a public understanding of what any particular individual's good consists in. We can, of course, make judgments about the good of others. But these should typically be understood as advisory, not as demands. People can agree to disagree and therefore coexist when they disagree not only about the good life for everyone, but also when they disagree about the good for some particular individual. In contrast, judgments about the principles of justice must be understood as demands, not merely as advisory. This is because, as we have seen, there can only be one basic structure, and its design will be imposed on everyone in the society.

The principles of justice are independent of the conceptions of the good that happen to prevail in a society. This is in dramatic contrast to utilitarianism, according to which the demands of justice depend on an accurate assessment of the good of each individual. One result of the utilitarian approach is that "abhorrence for certain religious or sexual practices," if held by enough people intensely enough, would be sufficient to curtail individual liberty. (*TJ*, 450/395) Perhaps a utilitarian case can be made that preserving individual liberty will, in fact, maximize overall utility in the long run. From the point of view of justice as fairness, such delicate and speculative judgments are irrelevant. "The satisfaction of these feelings has no value that can be put in the scales against the claims of equal liberty." (*TJ*, 450/395)

THE SENSE OF JUSTICE

With this account of the good in place, we can now consider the problem of stability. This is done in two stages. First, we consider the process of psychological development through which individuals acquire a sense of justice. Then we consider the issue of congruence between the right and the good and ask whether those who have developed a sense of justice will reflectively endorse it. Two points must be kept in mind throughout these discussions. First, we are only considering the acquisition and reflective endorsement of a sense of justice in a well-ordered society. A well-ordered society, recall, is one in which "everyone accepts and knows that the others accept the same principles of justice, and the basic social institutions satisfy and are known to satisfy these principles." (*TJ*, 454/397)

Second, we are interested in making a comparative judgment of relative stability between justice as fairness and its rivals, especially utilitarianism. Every society will contain, and every individual will face, some pressures and temptations away from justice. Our question concerns the relative strength of these forces and of the countervailing pressures that would tend to be generated in different well-ordered societies. "One conception of justice is more stable than another if the sense of justice that it tends to generate is stronger and more likely to override disruptive inclinations and if the institutions it allows foster weaker impulses and temptations to act unjustly." (*TJ*, 454/398) It is clear that stability, in this sense, is a virtue of just societies. If it turned out that the two principles were significantly less stable than their rivals, we would have reason to reconsider their selection and ask why they would be unable to generate their own support. On the other hand, if they are at least as stable as their rivals, this strengthens their justification.

There may be a lingering suspicion that there is something vaguely conservative about stability. This is a misconception for two reasons. First, we are not interested in the stability of whatever institutions happen to exist. We are interested in the stability of a well-ordered society. It is no virtue when an unjust basic structure or regime is entrenched and difficult to correct. Second, stability does not imply that the institutions of the basic structure are unchanging. On the contrary, as circumstances change the basic structure of society must change and adapt so that it continues to satisfy the principles of justice. The basic structure of a well-ordered society must track the demands of justice over time. The ability of a society to do this depends on the commitment of individuals to the principles of justice. Thus, the acquisition and maintenance of a sense of justice among citizens is a crucial factor in determining the stability of a just basic structure.

Traditional accounts of developmental moral psychology have been dominated by two approaches that Rawls identifies as "empiricism" (a view that he associates with Hume, Sidgwick, and to some extent Freud) and "rationalism" (associated with Rousseau, Kant, Piaget, and Kohlberg). According to empiricism – also called "social learning theory" – society must supply the moral motivation that children initially lack. In contrast, the rationalist approach holds that moral learning occurs as individuals develop their "innate intellectual and emotional capacities according to their natural bent." (*TJ*, 459/402) Instead of choosing between these models, Rawls tries to "combine them in a natural way." (*TJ*, 461/404) The idea is to "sketch the course of moral development as it might occur in a well-ordered society realizing the principles of justice as fairness." (*TJ*, 461/404) There is no claim that this process is inevitable or that there will be no deviations from this path. Rather, the idea is to present a plausible account of how a sense of justice could be acquired when things go well. We will then examine a corresponding account of the acquisition of a sense of justice in a utilitarian society. This will allow us to "contrast the psychological roots of the various conceptions of justice" (*TJ*, 462/405) and to form a tentative conclusion concerning their relative stability.

Rawls presents a sequence of three stages of psychological development. Each stage is characterized by "changes in the affective ties which belong to our final ends." (*TJ*, 493/432) The first stage, "the morality of authority," occurs in a young child's life as he or she forms bonds to particular care-givers. At this stage, the child's level of maturity is such that he or she is "not in a position to assess the validity of the precepts and injunctions addressed to him by those in authority." (*TJ*, 463/405) What is essential is that some particular individuals – Rawls assumes that they are typically the child's parents – love and express their love to the child. The child, in turn, comes to love the parents. "Although the child has the potentiality for love, his love of the parents is a new desire brought about by his recognizing their evident love for him and his benefiting from the actions in which their love is expressed." (*TJ*, 463/406) Summarizing this stage, Rawls's first psychological law holds that such bonding only occurs when the parents "manifestly first love him." (*TJ*, 463/406) As the child comes to love the parents, and to "affirm his sense of the worth of his own person," (*TJ*, 464/406) the structure of the child's desires changes. The parents come to be valued not only because of the contribution they make to the child's pre-existing desires. Because of the love and trust between them, the child comes to accept the parents' precepts and instructions, even though he or she is unable to accept or reject them on rational grounds. This generates conflicts between certain natural desires and the precepts taught and imposed by the parent which are experienced as guilt.

We can view the family as the first of many associations that the child eventually becomes part of, such as a school, clubs, a neighborhood, and eventually an entire nation. Through participation in these associations, "one learns the virtues of a good student and classmate, and the ideals of a good sport and companion." (*TJ*, 468/409) The associations to which the individual belongs will typically have various roles and norms that depend on the purposes and goals of the association. In coming to occupy roles in these associations, the individual learns that "others have different things to do depending upon their place in the cooperative scheme. Thus he eventually learns to take up their point of view and to see things from their perspective." (*TJ*, 468/410) If we assume that the rules of the association are fair and are known to be fair, and that participants generally follow them, then individuals will generally develop "friendly feelings toward them, together with feelings of trust and confidence." (*TJ*, 470/411) This is Rawls's second psychological law. As with the first, it characterizes a development of the desires and inclinations of individuals as they tend to reciprocate the treatment they have received. When other individuals act in ways that affirm our good, we come to value their well-being in return. Again, the new desires to respond by acting in accordance with the rules of the association can sometimes be overwhelmed by conflicting desires. When this happens a person will tend to "experience feelings of (association) guilt." (*TJ*, 470/412) The plausibility of this second law gains considerable support when we observe that individuals are more likely to break the rules when they observe others breaking them as well.

As a final stage, consider the limit case of the morality of associations – the role of citizen in a well-ordered society. When the basic structure of society is just and is known to be just and one's fellow citizens treat one fairly by acting in accordance with the demands of justice, one tends to acquire a desire to reciprocate and to treat others fairly too, by acting in accordance with these principles. There is, however, a difference between this case and our other associations. At least in many of our associations, and certainly the ones that we initially belong to, we know the particular individuals who occupy the various roles and positions and we come to form bonds of trust with them. However, in large associations, and certainly in a large society, our trust must be generalized to whoever is occupying a particular role – such as "citizen" – and not to specific individuals. One might worry that this generalized commitment to principles of justice involved a kind of irrational rule worship, and we will consider this below.

This generalized disposition to treat others in accordance with the principles of justice can come about in accordance with a third psychological law: "We develop a desire to apply and to act upon the principles of justice once we realize how social arrangements answering to them have promoted our good and that of those with whom we are affiliated." (*TJ*, 474/415) In this case the acquired desire is not only "to accept the just institutions that apply to us and from which we and our associates have benefited" but also "a willingness to work for (or at least not to oppose) the setting up of just institutions, and for the reform of existing ones when justice requires it." (*TJ*, 474/415) As before, these desires may not always be decisive. However, when they are sacrificed there is a tendency to feel guilt. The commitment is a generalized one aiming at fair treatment even if we do not know the specific individuals who would be harmed if we were to act unjustly. This is compatible with there being additional commitments, developed in accordance with the previous two principles, to particular individuals based on love and friendship.

At this final stage, individuals form an attachment "to these highest-order principles themselves, so that just as during the earlier phase of the morality of association he may want to be a good sport, say, he now wishes to be a just person." (*TJ*, 473/414) It is important to distinguish this account from one that emphasizes rule following for its own sake. The point is not that individuals simply come to desire to follow rules. Rather, in accordance with the Kantian interpretation, they come to desire to "express their nature as free and equal rational beings." (*TJ*, 476/417) They understand that the principles of justice ensure fair treatment of all, and they embrace this ideal whether they have direct, personal connections to those affected by their behavior or not. Rawls rejects what he calls "the doctrine of the purely conscientious act" which holds that "the highest moral motive is the desire to do what is right and just simply because it is right and just, no other description being appropriate" and that although other moral motives may be valuable, they are "less morally worthy than that to do what is right solely in virtue of its being right." (*TJ*, 477/418) This doctrine really does seem to make a fetish out of acting rightly or rule following, since it precludes any reason for acting in the prescribed way. In effect, this is an extreme form of intuitionism. In contrast, justice as fairness allows us to say and to explain what is attractive about acting on the principles of justice: for example, they involve "living with others on terms that everyone would recognize as fair from a perspective that all would accept as reasonable." (*TJ*, 478/418–19)

Although Rawls does not intend his account of psychological development to be especially controversial, it is significant that he presents it at all. It decisively refutes the common assumption that he thinks moral philosophy must be conducted in purely *a priori* terms or entirely from the perspective of the original position. It is also sometimes assumed that moral theory should be addressed to strict egoists who must be convinced that the principles of morality serve their narrow interests. This is not Rawls's project, and he assumes that such a psychological attitude would be abnormal. It would hardly tell against a conception of justice that such a psychologically stunted individual would not find it attractive. We are interested in developing principles of justice that are appropriate for individuals under favorable circumstances with relatively normal psychologies.

Rawls's core claim of moral development is that the tendency toward reciprocity "is a deep psychological fact. Without it our nature would be very different and fruitful social cooperation fragile if not impossible." (*TJ*, 494–5/433) The implications for the stability of different conceptions of justice are clear: "The most stable conceptions of justice are presumably those for which the corresponding sense of justice is most firmly based on these tendencies." (*TJ*, 495/433) The most obvious threat to the stability of a well-ordered society comes from the temptation for individuals to "free ride" on the cooperative actions of others. In the absence of strong external sanctions, the temptation to free ride can be overcome only through the internalization of either "a sense of justice or a concern for those who would be disadvantaged by their defection, [or] preferably both." (*TJ*, 497/435) The three psychological laws that we have been discussing show how an individual in a well-ordered society of justice as fairness may internalize these tendencies over time.

We are interested in the relative stability of different conceptions of justice. No doubt there will be a tendency in a well-ordered utilitarian society for children to develop and internalize a utilitarian sense of justice. But how strong will this be? What is the process by which a utilitarian conception of justice might be transferred from one generation to the next? Whatever the content, this process depends on the child's recognition that she is being treated in accordance with some principles (suitably adjusted for her level of development). But here a principle based on reciprocity has an enormous advantage over a utilitarian principle. We have assumed that a child can recognize when she is loved and that there is a tendency to respond in kind. It seems far more difficult to recognize or assess when those with whom she interacts (parents and friends) are acting in accordance with a utilitarian principle. In fact, this seems essentially impossible for infants and exceedingly unlikely for small children. Justice as fairness seems to have a dramatic advantage over utilitarianism at this first stage of moral development.

At the stage of association, utilitarianism would have to assume that "persons tend to develop friendly feelings toward those who with evident intention do their part in cooperative schemes publicly known to maximize the sum of advantages, or the average well-being." (*TJ*, 499/437) But once again, this can be difficult to recognize or assess and is therefore going to be weaker than the corresponding principle of reciprocity at the association stage. After all, "Why should the acceptance of the principle of utility . . . by the more fortunate inspire the less advantaged to have friendly feelings toward them? . . . No reciprocity principle is at work in this case and the appeal to utility may simply arouse suspicion." (*TJ*, 500/437) Again, justice as fairness seems to have a significant advantage over utilitarianism.

At the final stage utilitarian individuals would have to be willing to sacrifice their share of goods whenever doing so would lead to a greater gain to others, even when they had no personal relationship with those who gained. We would have to assume that individuals would come to acquire a utilitarian sense of justice when their interests were sacrificed for greater gains elsewhere. Again, the point is not that this is impossible, but only that the psychological mechanism that would lead to this set of desires is far weaker than the corresponding mechanism under a conception such as justice as fairness that is based on reciprocity. Overall, then, justice as fairness appears to be at least as stable as utilitarianism in terms of the strength of the psychological process leading to the acquisition of a sense of justice.

Before taking up the issue of congruence and the nature of the self, Rawls considers one loose end – what he calls "the basis of equality." It is clear that equality plays a very significant role in justice as fairness since the principles of justice obviously contain strongly egalitarian elements. More abstractly, equal justice is owed to all. We can ask: to whom is equal justice owed? This is an important question because anti-egalitarians often point out that individuals are not, in fact, equal on almost any metric. For Rawls, the short answer is that individuals are entitled to equal justice in virtue of their sharing of "moral personality."

We discussed this idea in chapter 1, where it was important to the parties in the original position, but Rawls discusses it in greater depth at this point:

> Moral persons are distinguished by two features: first they are capable of having (and are assumed to have) a conception of their good (as expressed by a rational plan of life); and second they are capable of having (and are assumed to acquire) a sense of justice, a normally effective desire to apply and to act upon the principles of justice, at least to a certain minimum degree. (*TJ*, 505/442)

When an individual has these capacities at or above the level necessary to be a fully participating member of society, she is owed equal consideration of justice. This is consistent with observing that the sense of justice may be stronger in some than in others, but as long as it reaches a certain minimal threshold, differences above that level do not affect a person's entitlement to fair treatment. Similarly, as long as a person's conception of the good is permissible (consistent with the principles of justice) she is entitled to pursue it. From the point of view of basic social justice, no further defense or justification of her goals is required. It may initially seem peculiar to base equality on a threshold conception, but on reflection, this would be so only if we implicitly assumed that moral theory had a teleological structure so that some good was to be maximized. On that assumption, we would be tempted by the view that the treatment of individuals should vary with the presence of that good. But justice as fairness rejects that teleological structure. Moral persons are themselves entitled to equal justice regardless of their contribution to any particular conception of the good. And, crucially, the parties in the original position know that they are choosing principles for a well-ordered society composed of moral persons.

CONGRUENCE

We now consider the question of congruence between a person's conception of the good and a person's sense of justice. We want to know whether in a well-ordered society "a person's rational plan of life supports and affirms his sense of justice." (*TJ*, 513/450) We have already seen an account of the development of the sense of justice, but here we are interested in the attitude that citizens will have toward their sense of justice, once acquired, from the point of view of their other values. For example, will they view it as a misfortune that they would be better off attempting to eliminate or override in order better to pursue their other goals? Congruence implies that when members of a well-ordered society reflect on their plan of life, they "will decide to maintain their sense of justice as regulative of their conduct toward one another." (*TJ*, 514/451)

Congruence is not at all a forgone conclusion even in a well-ordered society. Sometimes when we reflect on our desires, ends, and psychological attitudes, and especially when we attend to their origin, we may come to doubt their appropriateness. This is perhaps most clear in the case of attitudes that have been acquired through some kind of indoctrination. We can ask whether the promptings of a person's sense of justice are like that and worry whether they should be viewed as "simply neurotic compulsions." (*TJ*, 514/451) Of course, as we have seen, there is much that can be said in defense of the principles of justice. They are not simply undefended and arbitrary preferences. Nor are they the products of "coercive indoctrination" designed to take "unfair advantage of human weakness." (*TJ*, 515/452)

In fact, following the Kantian interpretation, we can point out that acting on the principles of justice expresses autonomy – "they are acting from principles that they would acknowledge under conditions that best express their nature as free and equal rational beings." (*TJ*, 515/452) We can also point out that the principles of justice are not merely expressions of our subjective desires since "[t]he veil of ignorance prevents us from shaping our moral view to accord with our own particular attachments and interests." (*TJ*, 516/453) The principles can be understood as objective because they are generated from "a shared point of view." (*TJ*, 517/453) The interpretations of autonomy and objectivity that Rawls here presents are controversial. They contrast with more common accounts according to which "autonomy is the complete freedom to form our moral opinions and . . . the conscientious judgment of every moral agent ought absolutely to be respected" and objectivity is a matter of satisfying whatever standards the agent, using this liberty, has decided are appropriate. (*TJ*, 518/454) The doctrine that allows absolute freedom to act according to conscience is mistaken, but we can understand its temptation:

> in times of social doubt and loss of faith in long established values, there is a tendency to fall back on the virtues of integrity: truthfulness and sincerity, lucidity and commitment, or, as some say, authenticity. If no one knows what is true, at least we can make our beliefs our own in our own way and not adopt them as handed to us by others . . . Now of course the virtues of integrity are virtues, and among the excellences of free persons. Yet while necessary, they are not sufficient; for their definition allows for most any content . . . It is impossible to construct a moral view from these virtues alone . . . But joined to the appropriate conception of justice, one that allows for autonomy and objectivity correctly understood, they come into their own. (*TJ*, 519–20/455–6)

Justice as fairness rejects the absolute authority of conscience. Instead, it presents an objective set of principles to be used in assessing the permissibility of conscientiously held values. Nonetheless, within these broad principles, there is considerable scope for diverse conceptions of the good.

Given this diversity of conceptions of the good in a well-ordered society, are the shared principles of justice sufficient to establish the good of community? As we will see in chapter 5, some critics have doubted this. But in a well-ordered society the principles can underwrite the value of community, at least when understood in a certain way, and therefore can provide further support for the congruence of the right and the good. To understand this special sense of community, consider first a contrasting model. The idea of a "private society" is one in which, first,

> the persons comprising it . . . have their own private ends which are either competing or independent, but not in any case complementary. And second, institutions are not thought to have any value in themselves, the activity of engaging in them not being counted as a good but if anything as a burden. (*TJ*, 521/457)

In such a society, individuals value (and are motivated to comply with the requirements of) social institutions only to the extent that they contribute to their private ends. It is possible, even if not likely, that in such a society individual interests would align in such a way that outcomes were fair. Yet such a society "is not held together by a public conviction that its basic arrangements are just and good in themselves, but by the calculations of everyone" concerning their personal ends. (*TJ*, 522/458)

A well-ordered society of justice as fairness is not a private society in this sense. Individuals are assumed to have acquired a sense of justice and to be motivated by an intrinsic desire to treat others fairly. This assumption captures a deeper understanding of "the social nature of mankind" (*TJ*, 522/458) than a private society represents. Even the model of a private society can recognize that "society is necessary for human life" and that our interests and abilities are shaped by society. (*TJ*, 522/458) However, it fails to recognize that we can realize our goods in ways that complement those of others. A basic fact about human existence is that "[t]he potentialities of each individual are greater than those he can hope to realize." (*TJ*, 523/458) When different individuals aim to realize different potentials, they can appreciate and value the complementary goods that they collectively achieve. "When men are secure in the enjoyment of the exercise of their powers, they are disposed to appreciate the perfections of others, especially when their several excellences have an agreed place in a form of life the aims of which all accept." (*TJ*, 523/459) An example of such a "social union" is an orchestra, in which each of the musicians, with their complementary skills, makes a distinctive contribution to the overall goals which are valued for their own sake. Other examples of social unions include the broad collective projects of science and art, families and friendships, religion and culture.

While most societies contain countless social unions, a well-ordered society of justice as fairness can itself be understood as a social union of social unions. "Both characteristic features are present: the successful carrying out of just institutions is the shared final end of all the members of society, and these institutional forms are prized as good in themselves." (*TJ*, 527/462) The claim is not that everyone holds a shared conception of the good. What is shared is a sense of justice and the recognition that the shared goal of a just society can only be realized as a collective achievement. While this goal is regulative in the sense that it determines the permissibility of other values and ends, it does not establish a dominant end to which all other values are related instrumentally. Individuals are assumed to have diverse plans that are all compatible with this regulative sense of justice. A well-ordered society reflects this deep sense of sociability, and citizens will value their sense of justice that makes this possible.

If we combine the Kantian interpretation (according to which we are free and equal moral beings) and the Aristotelian Principle (according to which our good is found in ways that express our nature and capabilities) we reach the following conclusion:

> the collective activity of justice is the preeminent form of human flourishing. For given favorable conditions, it is by maintaining these public arrangements that persons best express their nature and achieve the widest regulative excellences of which each is capable. At the same time just institutions allow for and encourage the diverse internal life of associations in which individuals realize their more particular aims. (*TJ*, 529/463)

At least in a well-ordered society, to the extent that the Kantian interpretation and the Aristotelian Principle hold, the right and the good are congruent. Individuals who have acquired a sense of justice will recognize it to be valuable. Rawls makes several other complicated arguments for congruence that will take us into the next section. It is important to emphasize at this point that the initial argument for the two principles of justice does not depend on either the Kantian interpretation or the Aristotelian Principle. However, when we ask about the stability of a conception, we need to consider assumptions about the values that individuals will affirm. And this requires that we draw on empirical claims about moral psychology and provide an account of values beyond basic social justice.

This dependence on empirical psychology is even clearer in the discussion of envy. We initially discussed envy when considering the psychology of the parties in the original position. In that context, it was up to us to specify the psychological properties in any way that was appropriate to our purposes. The motive of pure envy is often irrational in the sense that it involves hostility to the good of others even though their good does not detract from one's own. Therefore, it made sense to exclude it from the psychological make-up of the parties in the original position. Regardless of whether it is irrational, however, we must now ask whether it would likely be prevalent in a well-ordered society "to such an extent that the society system becomes unworkable and incompatible with human good." (*TJ*, 531/465) If so, it might tend to undermine the stability of such a society. Presumably, in any society some individuals will feel envious of the specific condition of others. "Particular envy" is the result of competition over some specific good or position. General envy, in contrast, is that which is "experienced by the least advantaged towards those better situated . . . [with respect to] the kinds of goods and not for the particular objects they possess." (*TJ*, 531/466) Our question concerns the extent of general envy in a well-ordered society.

Rawls speculates that three conditions contribute to "hostile outbreaks of envy." He follows Nietzsche in holding that individuals are vulnerable to envy when they "lack a sure confidence in their own value and in their ability to do anything worthwhile." (*TJ*, 535/469) This tendency is exacerbated when the contrast between one's own condition and the success of others is publicly visible and emphasized. And finally, these conditions are more likely to generate envy when individuals "see their social position as allowing no constructive alternative to opposing the favored circumstances of the more advantaged." (*TJ*, 535/469) Although no society can completely eliminate the possibility of general envy, it seems that a well-ordered society of justice as fairness will mitigate this tendency by addressing each of these three conditions. While some other conceptions of justice may be even more egalitarian than justice as fairness, it is fair to say that under the two principles "the spread of income and wealth should not be excessive in practice, given the requisite background institutions." (*TJ*, 536/470) Furthermore, it is assumed that individuals will pursue whatever permissible conception of the good they affirm and will have the opportunity to do so in association with others with whom they share their values. This will tend to support their self-respect and confidence in the worth of their goals. And finally, the public affirmation of fair equality of opportunity will reduce the feeling that individuals are trapped with no alternative but to oppose the good fortune of the more advantaged.

Contrary to the claims of some conservative writers who hold that "the tendency to equality in modern social movements is the expression of envy," (*TJ*, 538/471) justice as fairness makes no such appeal. The parties in the original position are not motivated by envy, nor does envy inform the set-up of the original position itself. Indeed, Rawls is hostile to most expressions of envy. Unlike envy, however, resentment is a moral feeling because its explanation makes essential reference to moral principles. This means that feelings of resentment, unlike feelings of pure envy, can be assessed in terms of the defensibility of the principles on which they are based. If, in fact, an individual is being treated unfairly, resentment toward this situation may be an appropriate response. Such a judgment depends, of course, on a proper assessment of what fairness requires in that context. A sense of justice, therefore, may generate proper feelings of resentment. Such feelings are not blind hostility toward those who are more advantaged but are grounded in an appropriate opposition to injustice.

The limits on the inequality of income and wealth help to prevent generalized envy, but the equality of the basic liberties is also significant. As we have seen, "if the persons in the original position know that their basic liberties can be effectively exercised, they will not exchange a lesser liberty for greater economic advantages."[3] (*TJ*, 474–5) Notice the implication that there may be circumstances in which the basic liberties cannot be effectively exercised. In such cases it may be an urgent matter to secure the economic conditions that provide for the effective exercise of the basic liberties. A trade-off would have to be made, however, only if the guarantee of the basic liberties were actually an impediment to the necessary economic development. Rawls does not speculate about when, if ever, this might be the case. Instead, he simply notes that "[t]he equal liberties can be denied only when it is necessary to change the quality of civilization so that in due course everyone can enjoy these freedoms."[4] (*TJ*, 475) Under reasonably favorable conditions in which the basic liberties can be exercised effectively, the parties in the original position would reject possible economic gains that could be achieved only by infringing the guarantee of equal basic liberties.

Between the original edition and the revised edition of *A Theory of Justice*, the grounds for the priority of the first principle shift. In the original edition, Rawls argued that as the wealth of society increases further marginal increases become less and less important compared with securing the basic liberties. In effect he assumed that

[3] The corresponding passage in the original edition of *TJ* reads: "The supposition is that if the persons in the original position assume that their basic liberties can be effectively exercised, they will not exchange a lesser liberty for an improvement in their economic well-being, at least not once a certain level of wealth has been attained." (p. 542)

[4] The corresponding passage in the original edition reads: "The denial of equal liberty can be accepted only if it is necessary to enhance the quality of civilization so that in due course the equal freedoms can be enjoyed by all." (p. 542)

all rational conceptions of the good share a certain broad structure. But even if this assumption of diminishing marginal gains to wealth is correct, it is not at all clear that it can secure Rawls's conclusion. At most, such an argument can establish that as the wealth of a society increases, the trade-off between the basic liberties and economic gains should favor the basic liberties more and more. But this falls far short of establishing the lexical priority of the first principle over the second. More importantly, this argument makes the principles of justice dependent on the conceptions of the good that individuals happen to hold.

Largely in response to the criticisms of H. L. A. Hart, in the revised edition Rawls changed the argument for the priority of the basic liberties.[5] The new argument depends not on the actual structure of preferences that individuals happen to have, but on the account of the two moral powers that characterize the moral person. As we saw above, we assume that moral persons have a capacity for a sense of justice and a capacity for a conception of the good. This in turn generates "highest-order interests" in maintaining these capacities at the level necessary to be fully participating members of a cooperative scheme. We will discuss Rawls's elaboration of this argument in chapter 4, but in the revised edition of *A Theory of Justice*, his discussion is brief but suggestive:

> The parties conceive of themselves as free persons who can revise and alter their final ends and who give priority to preserving their liberty in this respect . . . They must first secure their highest-order interest and fundamental aims (only the general form of which is known to them), and this fact is reflected in the precedence they give to liberty; the acquisition of means that enable them to advance their other desires and ends has a subordinate place. (*TJ*, 475–6)[6]

This argument does not depend on an empirical survey of the actual structure of individual preferences. Rather, it is tied to the requirements for developing and maintaining the two moral powers. In order to develop and to maintain the capacity to reflect on and revise

[5] H. L. A. Hart, "Rawls on Liberty and Its Priority" [1973] in *Reading Rawls: Critical Studies on Rawls' "A Theory of Justice,"* Norman Daniels, ed. (Stanford University Press, 1989). Responding to Hart's critique also resulted in the change in the first principle from "liberty" to "the basic liberties" that we discussed in chapter 1.

[6] This passage does not appear in the original edition.

a person's conception of the good, she must be assured of liberty of conscience and the other basic liberties. The same holds with respect to our capacity for a sense of justice. While each individual will have specific ends that he or she takes to be worth pursuing, these are subordinate to the development and maintenance of the two moral powers.

DOMINANT ENDS AND THE SELF

We can now consider the issue of congruence from a slightly different perspective. Let us continue to think of happiness as the condition of a person who knows that his or her rational plan is going well and is confident that this good fortune will continue. On this understanding, "happiness is not one aim among others that we aspire to, but the fulfillment of the whole design itself." (*TJ*, 550/482) As we have seen, Rawls holds that the content of this inclusive aim is determined by one's rational plan of life, which itself can be identified through deliberative rationality. One element of deliberative rationality that we have not yet mentioned is the idea of analysis. Given an abstract and general characterization of some goal, we may seek to determine what would count as achieving it in some specific circumstances. For example, if I aim to become a successful artist, I have to determine whether to measure success in terms of sales, displays in prestigious galleries, published reviews, my own assessment, or some other standard or combination of standards. Each of these interpretations can be further specified, given particular circumstances – how much money, how many displays or reviews, in which locations, etc. Sometimes such an analysis will show that potential conflicts among general goals can be eliminated or finessed given the actual conditions in which we find ourselves. However, we must expect that in any circumstances some goods will conflict and we will simply have to make a choice: "we may narrow the scope of purely preferential choice, but we cannot eliminate it altogether." (*TJ*, 552/483)

The necessity for a "purely preferential choice" arises when "there is no ready standard of comparison to decide between [aims] when they conflict." (*TJ*, 552/484) If there is no standard for comparison of different values or ends, we can say that they are incommensurable. Some theorists insist, however, that all goods are commensurable.

One tempting way to make sense of the idea of commensurability is through the idea of a dominant end. If there were a dominant end, then "the procedure for making a rational choice . . . would then be perfectly clear: deliberation would always concern means to ends, all lesser ends in turn being ordered as means to one single dominant end." (*TJ*, 552/484) In fact, it may appear unclear how a rational choice could ever be made in the absence of a dominant end. This model of deliberation is attractive and influential. However, it is only plausible to the extent that we can identify a determinate content for the dominant end. It cannot be happiness as we have defined it, since this is an inclusive end that incorporates diverse goals without imposing or assuming any ordering among them. "The extreme nature of dominant-end views is often concealed by the vagueness and ambiguity of the end proposed." (*TJ*, 554/485) When pressed to identify the content of the dominant end, Rawls believes it becomes clear that there is no such end. "Human good is heterogeneous because the aims of the self are heterogeneous." (*TJ*, 554/485)

Arguably the most influential attempt to carry though dominant-end reasoning identifies the dominant end with the feeling of pleasure. Because we find pleasure in diverse activities, it may appear that this type of hedonism avoids the narrowness of other dominant ends. Nonetheless, it is as unreasonable as any other dominant end:

> We need only note that once pleasure is conceived, as it must be, in a sufficiently definite way so that its intensity and duration can enter into the agent's calculations, then it is no longer plausible that it should be taken as the sole rational aim. Surely the preference for a certain attribute of feeling or sensation above all else is as unbalanced and inhuman as an overriding desire to maximize one's power over others or one's material wealth. (*TJ*, 556–7/488)

If this is correct – if there is no dominant end that defines our good – then this raises a difficulty for teleological theories. "In a teleological theory any vagueness or ambiguity in the conception of the good is transferred to that of the right." (*TJ*, 559/490) If our good is to some degree simply a matter of the preferences that we happen to have, a teleological theory carries this indeterminacy over into the principles of right and justice. It seems, however, that principles of justice are not matters of mere preference in the way that our conception of the good is, at least in part. A teleological theory has great difficulty resolving this dilemma, "[a]nd this suggests that the structure of teleological doctrines is radically misconceived: from the start they related the right and the good in the wrong way." (*TJ*, 560/490–1)

A dominant end, if there were one, would not only provide a procedure for rational resolution of practical choices. It would also provide an understanding of the unity of the self. Rejecting the existence of a dominant end forces us to look elsewhere for an understanding of our unity:

> It is not our aims that primarily reveal our nature but rather the principles that we would acknowledge to govern the background conditions under which these aims are to be formed and the manner in which they are to be pursued. For the self is prior to the ends which are affirmed by it; even a dominant end must be chosen from among numerous possibilities. There is no way to get beyond deliberative rationality. (*TJ*, 560/491)

Some critics, to be discussed in chapter 5, point to this passage as evidence that Rawls holds that we are "unencumbered" selves. We have already seen that Rawls holds that we are characterized by a complex motivation structure: a sense of justice, a conception of the good, and highest-order interests in maintaining these capacities. The point of this passage is that we should understand our unity not in terms of the pursuit of a single dominant end but rather in terms of our commitments to principles of justice and to one of many permissible conceptions of the good. "Now the unity of the person is manifest in the coherence of his plan, this unity being founded on the higher-order desire to follow, in ways consistent with his sense of right and justice, the principles of rational choice." (*TJ*, 561/491–2)

The parties in the original position do not assume that they will aim to maximize pleasure or any other particular goal. They want to establish conditions under which each can "fashion his own unity" by developing a coherent and rational life plan compatible with the principles of right. (*TJ*, 563/493) We do this "only gradually," (*TJ*, 561/492) against a background of

> many associations . . . [that represent] countless ideals and forms of life that have been developed and tested by innumerable individuals, sometimes for generations. Thus in drawing up our plan of life we do not start de novo;

we are not required to choose from countless possibilities without given structure or fixed contours. (*TJ*, 563–4/493–4)

In addition to forming our plan of life against a background of already existing associations and traditions, the priority of right means that the principles of justice constrain the permissible plans of life. Even with these constraints, however, there remains an ineliminable element of purely personal choice in the determination of one's plan of life and therefore in one's good.

Although the priority of right implies that the principles of justice constrain permissible plans, the principles of justice do not establish a dominant end because they are not "all controlling." (*TJ*, 565/495) While they rule out some conceptions of the good, they leave room for a wide variety of permissible ways of life. These permissible conceptions of the good are equally permissible, and the selection among them does not have to be justified in terms of the contribution that they make to the goal of social justice or any other end. Indeed, no public justification is required at all. Rather than starting with a dominant end which subordinates all rational actions from the beginning, justice as fairness specifies a sequence of constraints within which diverse goods can be embraced and pursued. We begin with the broadest constraints established by the principles of justice themselves. As individuals commit themselves to specific goals and participate in specific associations they put themselves under further constraints and obligations.

We are finally in a position to pull together the main arguments for the congruence of the right and the good. Recall that "what is to be established is that it is rational (as defined by the thin theory of the good) for those in a well-ordered society to affirm their sense of justice as regulative of their plan of life." (*TJ*, 567/497) Presumably, congruence would not hold in at least some non-well-ordered societies. In a well-ordered society of justice as fairness, however, we assume that individuals have already acquired a sense of justice in accordance with the moral psychology outlined above. This greatly simplifies our task, since we are not attempting to justify justice to an egoist. "Rather, we are concerned with the goodness of the settled desire to take up the standpoint of justice." (*TJ*, 568/498) Our question is whether an individual with a sense of justice in a well-ordered society would want to eliminate or subordinate his sense of justice to his more particular aims.

First, consider that even individuals who might be tempted to view their sense of justice as burdensome, we can assume, would view some relationships of affection and fellow feeling as part of their good. Therefore, they would have to differentiate between those relationships where they aim to treat others fairly and those where they do not. In a well-ordered society it may become difficult to identify and select who will be harmed by one's defection from justice. By eliminating or suppressing our sense of justice, we very well might end up doing harm to the particular individuals toward whom we have sentimental attachments. Maintaining our sense of justice "protects in a natural and simple way the institutions and persons we care for and leads us to welcome new and broader social ties." (*TJ*, 571/500)

A second argument for congruence is based on the Aristotelian Principle. When we view a well-ordered society as a social union of social unions, we can see that participating in it realizes to a unique degree our human sociability. By fully participating in such a society we "bring to fruition our latent powers" and collectively accomplish goals that we simply could not achieve individually. "Yet to share fully in this life we must acknowledge the principles of its regulative conception, and this means that we must affirm our sentiment of justice. To appreciate something as ours, we must have a certain allegiance to it." (*TJ*, 571/500)

Finally, a third argument for congruence is based on the Kantian interpretation. Once the argument from the original position is complete, we can see that "[t]he desire to act justly and the desire to express our nature as free moral persons turn out to specify what is practically speaking the same desire." (*TJ*, 572/501) This desire has a feature that distinguishes it from others. Typically, desires can vary in strength and be balanced against potentially competing desires without altering their content:

> But the desire to express our nature as a free and equal rational being can be fulfilled only by acting on the principles of right and justice as having first priority. This is a consequence of the condition of finality: since these principles are regulative, the desire to act upon them is satisfied only to the extent that it is likewise regulative with respect to other desires . . . Therefore

in order to realize our nature we have no alternative but to plan to preserve our sense of justice as governing our other aims. (*TJ*, 574/503)

The ideal of expressing this nature is a desire unlike others that can be part of a plan. Rather, it concerns the structure of the plan as a whole and how the specific desires are ordered and combined within the plan. It is a matter of the plan's being consistent with the principles of justice and right:

> Of course, this does not mean that the realization of our nature as a free and rational being is itself an all or nothing affair. To the contrary, how far we succeed in expressing our nature depends upon how consistently we act from our sense of justice as finally regulative. What we cannot do is express our nature by following a plan that views the sense of justice as but one desire to be weighed against others. (*TJ*, 575/503)

We can judge the many gradations of justice that characterize different individuals. The point is that when we subordinate the principles of justice to other ends, we are no longer expressing our nature in our plan. And to the extent that our good consists in expressing our nature, our good is consistent with and indeed must be regulated by the principles of justice.

MORAL JUSTIFICATION

The congruence argument depends on assuming that individuals have already acquired a sense of justice and that they exercise it in a well-ordered society. It does not aim to establish that there can be no conflict between one's good and the principles of justice in other circumstances, nor does it aim to show that developing a sense of justice will serve one's other interests even in a well-ordered society. Similarly, the overall argument for the principles of justice is also limited since it does not aim to convince a moral skeptic. This reflects Rawls's understanding of the nature of moral argument. One common understanding of moral argument is Cartesian, which "presumes that first principles can be seen to be true, even necessarily so; deductive reasoning then transfers this conviction from premises to conclusion." (*TJ*, 578/506) Alternatively, one could attempt "to introduce definitions of moral concepts in terms of presumptively non-moral ones, and then to show by accepted procedures of common sense and the sciences that the statements thus paired with the asserted moral judgments are true." (*TJ*, 578/506) Rawls rejects both of these approaches: "There is no set of conditions or first principles that can be plausibly claimed to be necessary or definitive of morality and thereby especially suited to carry the burden of justification." (*TJ*, 578/506)

Instead, we should think of morality as Socratic. "There is no reason to suppose that [morality's] first principles or assumptions need to be self-evident, or that its concepts and criteria can be replaced by other notions which can be certified as non-moral." (*TJ*, 578–9/507) The original position, in particular, should not be understood as foundational, self-evident, non-moral, or morally neutral. It is, rather, a device that is designed to help us reach reflective equilibrium. But is reflective equilibrium – assuming we can reach it – justification enough? To answer this question, we need to consider the nature of justification:

> Justification is argument addressed to those who disagree with us, or to ourselves when we are of two minds. It presumes a clash of views between persons or within one person, and seeks to convince others, or ourselves, of the reasonableness of the principles upon which our claims and judgments are founded. Being designed to reconcile by reason, justification proceeds from what all parties to the discussion hold in common. (*TJ*, 580/508)

In order to resolve disagreements or uncertainties, we look for areas of agreement and confidence to serve as premises, and we construct arguments from them. Obviously, it will not always be easy to find premises that are strong enough to resolve the disagreements and uncertainties that we face. But "one of the aims of moral philosophy is to look for possible bases of agreement where none seem to exist. It must attempt to extend the range of some existing consensus and to frame more discriminating moral conceptions for our consideration." (*TJ*, 582/509)

The construction of the original position is an attempt to gain a perspective on the problem of social justice from which we can extend the range of agreement. The idea is that while each of the features of the original position is individually reasonable and justifiable, they are jointly sufficient to establish that the two principles of justice are superior to their main rivals. "We should like it to happen that the superiority of a particular view (among the currently known) is the result, perhaps the unexpected result, of this newly observed consensus." (*TJ*, 582/510) Even if we succeed in this, it is still possible that some other as-yet-unknown or unconsidered conception of justice might be superior. Rawls is surprisingly sanguine about this possibility: "I doubt, however, that the principles of justice (as I have defined them) will be the preferred conception on anything resembling a complete list." (*TJ*, 581/509) The bare possibility of a superior conception of justice is not troubling. What one must do to make good the possibility is actually to present another conception of justice and defend its superiority from the point of view of the original position. Alternatively, one could argue that some other choice of perspective is preferable to the original position. One great advantage of the original position, however, is that it allows us to consider a moral question "solely on the basis of what seems best calculated to further [the parties'] interests so far as they can ascertain them. In this way we can exploit the intuitive idea of rational prudential choice." (*TJ*, 584/512)

It is worth repeating one final time that while the choice within the original position is non-moral, the construction of the original position itself incorporates moral assumptions. The original position helps us to recognize an impartial, but not impersonal, perspective. This perspective is "not from a certain place beyond the world, nor [from] the point of view of a transcendent being; rather it is . . . [one] that rational persons can adopt within the world." It recognizes the diversity of individuals and their goods and allows them to "bring together into one scheme all individual perspectives and arrive together at regulative principles that can be affirmed by everyone as he lives by them, each from his own standpoint." (*TJ*, 587/514)

CHAPTER 4

After A Theory of Justice

A POLITICAL CONCEPTION OF JUSTICE

The publication of *A Theory of Justice* generated a huge secondary literature, a small portion of which we will examine in chapter 5. In a few cases, such as the changes to the formulation of the first principle prompted by criticisms made by H. L. A. Hart, Rawls responded directly by clarifying or revising elements of the theory. But by far the most significant developments in Rawls's work after *A Theory of Justice* were due to his own ultimate dissatisfaction with the argument for the congruence between the right and the good. This was an area that was – and continues to be – badly neglected in the secondary literature, and according to Samuel Freeman, "Rawls once said (in conversation) that he thought the congruence argument was one of the most original contributions he made in *A Theory of Justice*, and that he was puzzled why it did not attract more comment."[1] In this section, we will explore the problem he found in the congruence argument in *A Theory of Justice* and how this prompted him to develop the idea of a political conception of justice. In the next section, we will look at two areas where these developments allowed Rawls to strengthen the arguments made in *A Theory of Justice*, namely, the reliance on primary goods and the priority of the first principle over the second. In the final section, we will consider some clarifications that Rawls made concerning the ideal of a property-owning democracy and its relation to the model of welfare state capitalism.

[1] Samuel Freeman, "Congruence and the Good of Justice" in *Justice and the Social Contract*, p. 143, n. 2. In an interview conducted in 1991 Rawls commented that the third part of the book "was the part I liked best." ("John Rawls: For the Record," p. 44) See also Freeman, *Rawls*, p. 6.

In the introduction to *Political Liberalism*, first published in 1993, Rawls refers to "a serious problem internal to justice as fairness, namely . . . that the account of stability in Part III of *Theory* is not consistent with the view as a whole." He continues: "I believe all differences are consequences of removing that inconsistency. Otherwise these lectures take the structure and content of *Theory* to remain substantially the same."[2] This last point is often overlooked. The idea of a political conception of justice entails a revision concerning how the congruence argument is understood, but the structure of the main argument for the principles of justice remains largely unaffected by this change. In fact, leaving aside the issue of stability, recasting justice as fairness as a "political conception of justice" allows us to strengthen the arguments in *A Theory of Justice*.

The stability argument in *A Theory of Justice*, recall, aims to establish that a well-ordered society of justice as fairness would tend to be stable – or at least as stable as a well-ordered society based on rival conceptions of justice. The argument has two parts. First, Rawls argues that individuals raised in a well-ordered society of justice as fairness would tend to acquire a sense of justice at least as strong as the corresponding sense of justice acquired by individuals raised in different well-ordered societies. This argument depends on empirical principles of developmental moral psychology. They key elements of this argument are unaffected, although presented differently, when justice as fairness is understood as a political conception of justice.[3] Second, Rawls asks what attitude adults in a well-ordered society would tend to have toward their own sense of justice once it has been developed in the normal way. The aim is to show that once acquired in this way, a regulative sense of justice is not "irrational and injurious to our good." (*TJ*, 489/428) In other words, this second dimension of stability depends on showing that in a well-ordered society of justice as fairness, the right and the good would be congruent. And it is this complicated argument, almost completely neglected by the secondary literature, that Rawls came to believe was inconsistent with justice as fairness as a whole.

[2] Rawls, *Political Liberalism*, p. xvi, cited in this chapter parenthetically.

[3] See Rawls, *Justice as Fairness*, pp. 195–8.

It is important that the arguments for the two principles of justice do not depend on any particular conception of the good. This is crucial because the need for justice itself is due to the existence of diverse conceptions of the good and the resulting conflicts concerning how social resources should be used. If the principles of justice depended on a prior identification of the correct or best conception of the good, they could not serve the role of fairly adjudicating these conflicts. Rawls emphasizes this throughout *A Theory of Justice*. Indeed, at times, he goes even further, suggesting that the principles of justice "define a pact of reconciliation between diverse religions and moral beliefs, and the forms of culture to which they belong." (*TJ*, 221/194) The implication here is that the justification of the principles of justice should be independent not only of any particular conception of the good, but also of any particular religion, system of moral beliefs, or cultural form. As we noted in chapter 1, a conception of the good typically will fit into such a wider system of beliefs – either religious, philosophical, or moral – that Rawls would later call such a "comprehensive doctrine."

The argument for the congruence of the right and the good, however, does assume that the members of a well-ordered society will hold a certain comprehensive – or partially comprehensive – doctrine. The issue is not simply that we can give a "Kantian interpretation" to justice as fairness. Nor is it Rawls's claim that "the Kantian interpretation of the original position means that the desire to do what is right and just is the main way for persons to express their nature as free and equal rational beings." (*TJ*, 445/390) Rather, the problem is that the argument relies on this (and related) assumptions to argue that citizens would view "this expression of their nature is a fundamental element of their good." (*TJ*, 445/390) The problem is even more apparent when Rawls claims that "the collective activity of justice is the preeminent form of human flourishing." (*TJ*, 529/463) Rawls never suggests that all citizens will affirm the same conception of the good. But when making the congruence argument, he assumes that they will view their sense of justice as regulative of their other values because by doing so they express their nature. Rawls came to doubt that all reasonable people would value the expression of this nature over all else.[4] A well-ordered society would likely contain reasonable individuals who would reject the Kantian interpretation and the pre-eminent role it gives to moral autonomy. They would hold, in other words, a different comprehensive doctrine from the one expressed by the Kantian interpretation. The congruence argument cannot establish that the right and the good are congruent for those reasonable people, even in a well-ordered society.

While coming to recognize that not all reasonable people would accept the same comprehensive doctrine, Rawls himself continued to endorse the Kantian interpretation. In his Dewey Lectures, published as "Kantian Constructivism in Moral Theory" in 1980, we get a further elaboration of the Kantian doctrine.[5] However, by the time *Political Liberalism* was published in 1993, Rawls had abandoned the search for a general argument that would establish the congruence of the right and the good. Although he continued to claim that reasonable individuals would place great weight on the importance of social justice and other political virtues, he no longer aimed to establish that all reasonable people must view justice as regulative or, more generally, how they would integrate social justice with their comprehensive values.[6] Indeed, it seems clear that there is no single argument that will be able to establish congruence between the principles of justice and the other values affirmed by all of the various reasonable comprehensive doctrines since they differ from one another precisely in what they value and why. Each reasonable comprehensive doctrine provides its own account of the various non-political values and how basic social justice fits into its world view. But if this is the case, it seems to put into doubt whether a society in circumstances of reasonable pluralism could be stable.

This raises exactly the central question of *Political Liberalism*. Instead of aiming to establish that congruence would hold in a well-ordered society of justice as fairness, the goal is to consider how

[4] In addition to the Kantian interpretation, Rawls apparently came to doubt another part of the congruence argument, namely, the idea that individuals will necessarily come to value the complementarity of different conceptions of the good that allows us to view society as a social union of social unions. See *PL*, 388, n. 21. However, compare *PL*, 204, 320–3.

[5] Rawls, "Kantian Constructivism in Moral Theory," [1980] reprinted in Freeman, *Collected Papers*.

[6] See, for example, *PL*, 208–9.

stability is even possible in a society characterized by a reasonable pluralism of comprehensive doctrines. As Rawls states at the beginning of *Political Liberalism*:

> the problem of political liberalism is: How is it possible that there may exist over time a stable and just society of free and equal citizens profoundly divided by reasonable though incompatible religious, philosophical, and moral doctrines? Put another way: How is it possible that deeply opposed though reasonable comprehensive doctrines may live together and all affirm the political conception of a constitutional regime? (*PL*, xviii; cf. 4)

Stability, therefore, remains a central concern. Indeed, the relevant concept is "stability for the right reasons," (*PL*, xxxvii) since even if the stability of a political regime could be achieved through coercive threats, this would not count as the right kind. (*PL*, 143) Stability requires that "citizens have a normally effective sense of justice and so they generally comply with society's basic institutions, which they regard as just." (*PL*, 35; cf. 141) But if individuals are generally motivated to act according to the principles of justice, they must view such actions as in some sense good or valuable. All citizens must "share one very basic political end, and one that has high priority: namely, the end of supporting just institutions and of giving one another justice accordingly." (*PL*, 202) The congruence argument in *A Theory of Justice* was supposed to establish that citizens of a well-ordered society would reflectively endorse the value of that basic end. In *Political Liberalism*, we do not have an argument that all individuals will view their sense of justice in this way.[7] Rather, we ask: how is it even possible for citizens to share a normally effective sense of justice when they do not share a comprehensive doctrine?

The answer, in a phrase, is that there must be an overlapping consensus of reasonable comprehensive doctrines. While citizens differ in their deep religious, philosophical, and moral convictions, they can still share a conception of justice for the basic structure. Justice is not usually viewed as independent of these other broader concerns. Most comprehensive doctrines aim to justify a conception of justice

[7] All reasonable people will view their sense of justice in this way, but this claim depends on a specific understanding of the concept of the reasonable. See the discussion in my "The Reasonable in Justice as Fairness," *Canadian Journal of Philosophy*, 29 (1999).

by showing how it is grounded or justified in terms of a broader doctrine. Such grounding is not objectionable. But in order to serve as the focus of an overlapping consensus, we must be able to detach a conception of justice from these background doctrines where there is reasonable disagreement. We must, in other words, rely on a political conception of justice that has the following properties: (1) "it is a moral conception worked out for a specific kind of subject . . . the 'basic structure' of society" (*PL*, 11); (2) it is "presented as a freestanding view" – that is, "it is neither presented as, nor as derived from, such a [comprehensive] doctrine applied to the basic structure of society, as if this structure were simply another subject to which that doctrine applied" (*PL*, 12); and (3) it "is expressed in terms of certain fundamental ideas seen as implicit in the public political culture of a democratic society." (*PL*, 13)

Although a political conception of justice is presented as a freestanding view and not dependent on any particular comprehensive doctrine, it can also be seen as "a module, an essential constituent part, that fits into and can be supported by various reasonable comprehensive doctrines that endure in the society regulated by it." (*PL*, 12) Each reasonable comprehensive doctrine that is part of the overlapping consensus can provide its own deep foundations for the political conception of justice, relating it in systematic ways to other values and beliefs. More specifically, each can explain in its own terms why for political purposes citizens are to be viewed as free and equal and society is to be viewed as a fair system of cooperation. As we will see, political liberalism works from these models of the person and of society that are implicit in the public political culture of a democratic society.

Some critics have assumed that since a political conception is expressed in terms of ideas found in the public culture of a society, it represents a kind of relativism that abandons the idea of a proper justification. This misreading combines with a misunderstanding of the idea of an overlapping consensus to suggest that Rawls's main concern is to come up with principles that could serve as a compromise among the comprehensive doctrines that happen to hold influence and power in a society at any given time. This is clearly mistaken. Rawls takes pains to distinguish an overlapping consensus from the idea of a *modus vivendi*. One way that conflicting parties may reach an agreement is through a negotiated compromise. If no side is able to impose its preferred option on the others, each might be willing to accept a second- or third-best option on the condition that the others abandon their first choice and compromise as well. This is the model of a *modus vivendi*, and Rawls notes that "its stability is contingent on circumstances remaining such as not to upset the fortunate convergence of interests." (*PL*, 147) To be sure, such an agreement may represent progress if the alternative is no agreement at all. Europe took an immense step toward justice in the seventeenth century when it was able to establish a *modus vivendi* following the wars of religion. However, in a true overlapping consensus each reasonable comprehensive doctrine affirms the political conception as correct given the circumstances and not as a compromise at all. Each reasonable comprehensive doctrine will affirm more than the political conception – for example, in areas beyond the basic structure – but it will view the political conception as correct as far as it goes.

The requirement that a political conception be expressed in terms of ideas that are "implicit in the public political culture of a democratic society" does not replace the demand that the political conception be a correct conception of justice. In addition to being correct, a political conception must also be able to command widespread allegiance in a society. As Charles Larmore explains,

> Rawls often writes that the basis of his political liberalism is drawn from notions implicit in our political culture. That does not mean that it is important only that these notions are widely affirmed, and not that they express valid principles. The point is rather that valid principles, which are also alien to a culture, can be of no help in solving its problems of finding terms of political association amid reasonable disagreement about the good life.[8]

The terms of the public political culture can be shared by different reasonable comprehensive doctrines, and so they are not tied to any one in particular. A political conception of justice must present itself as freestanding (not tied to any particular comprehensive doctrine) but at the same time justified in terms of these shared fundamental ideas.

[8] Charles Larmore, *The Morals of Modernity* (Cambridge University Press, 1996), pp. 149–50.

PUBLIC REASON AND LEGITIMACY

Agreement over principles of justice alone would not ensure stability of the right kind. What matters for stability is not only the shared allegiance to abstract principles, but also a common deliberative perspective that allows citizens to apply the principles collectively to design their basic institutions and social policies. Rawls calls this framework "public reason."[9] Public reason is the collective reason that a democratic society employs when addressing "what the political conception of justice requires of society's basic structure of institutions, and of the purposes and ends they are to serve." (*PL*, 213) It is to be expressed in public declarations of politicians and officials – and especially the Supreme Court – when addressing, in their official capacities, matters of basic social justice. But it is also to guide the deliberation and actions of individuals in their role as citizens of a democracy when matters of basic social justice are at stake. Like a political conception of justice, which public reason includes, public reason draws on the public political culture of a liberal democracy but does not depend on any one particular comprehensive doctrine. When jointly addressing constitutional essentials and matters of basic justice,

> citizens are to conduct their fundamental discussions within the framework of what each regards as the political conception of justice based on values that the others can reasonably be expected to endorse and each is, in good faith, prepared to defend that conception so understood. This means that each of us must have, and be ready to explain, a criterion of what principles and guidelines we think other citizens (who are also free and equal) may reasonably be expected to endorse along with us. (*PL*, 226)

The requirement that others "reasonably be expected to endorse" the basic framework implicitly carries the rider "without giving up their own reasonable comprehensive doctrine." Public reason is the reason of the public when addressing matters of basic justice, and this cannot be predicated on acceptance of any single comprehensive doctrine. On the contrary, it assumes the continued existence of a diversity of reasonable comprehensive doctrines.

[9] Through the 1990s Rawls's view of public reason developed. I present here what I take to be his final account as expressed in "The Idea of Public Reason Revisited" [1997] in Freeman, *Collected Papers*.

Citizens have a moral duty – the duty of civility – to try to meet this ideal. The ideal of public reason provides a standard for evaluating whether a certain type of argument is appropriate and successful. (This is why there should not be legal sanctions against failures to meet this ideal any more than there should be legal sanctions against any other kind of bad argument. Such failures are legally protected by freedom of speech.) On a narrow reading, this ideal would imply that it is not appropriate for citizens ever to cite their own comprehensive doctrine in support of their political conclusion since others cannot reasonably be expected to share the doctrine. However, Rawls rejects this narrow reading in favor of a wide view according to which we may "introduce into political discussion at any time our comprehensive doctrine, religious or nonreligious, provided that, in due course, we give properly public reasons to support the principles and policies our comprehensive doctrine is said to support." (*PL*, 453) This last condition is called "the proviso."

Rawls's account of public reason has been widely criticized as being too restrictive and discriminatory against religious doctrines.[10] In reply, it is important to emphasize, first, that the scope of public reason is limited to collective decisions concerning constitutional essentials and matters of basic social justice. Rawls leaves it as an open question whether and to what extent public reason should apply to non-fundamental matters, such as ordinary policy decisions. (*PL*, 214–15) Furthermore, the ideal of public reason applies only when an argument is addressed to the public at large. In a context in which one is addressing only those who share a particular comprehensive doctrine it is perfectly appropriate to rely on that particular view. There is no violation for members of a particular religion, say, to work out their understanding of how some sacred text properly applies to some political issue. And finally, with the proviso, there is only a violation if an argument drawing on a comprehensive doctrine is not also presented "in due course" in terms that other reasonable people can be expected to accept.

[10] See, for example, Nicholas Wolterstorff, "The Role of Religion in Decision and Discussion of Political Issues" in *Religion in the Public Square: The Place of Religious Convictions in Political Debate*, Robert Audi and Nicholas Wolterstorff, eds. (Rowman and Littlefield, 1997); Christopher Eberle, *Religious Conviction in Liberal Politics* (Cambridge University Press, 2002).

But what if people continue to insist that this framework is unfair since it rules out an argument that they sincerely believe to be correct but which depends essentially on their particular comprehensive doctrine? At this point the charge of unfairness should be turned around. As Freeman observes: "The unfairness seems to lie on the side of those who suggest that there is no duty of civility upon people, who are religiously or otherwise motivated, to be able to justify or explain themselves to other reasonable persons who reject their comprehensive doctrines."[11] To the extent that they insist on making such arguments, they are being unreasonable. This is not to deny that they may be perfectly reasonable in other areas or that their conclusions follow from their premises which themselves might be reasonable. But it is they who are failing to recognize that others may reasonably reject their comprehensive doctrine and that justification is owed to them in terms that they could reasonably accept.

To see that this would be unreasonable, recall that the design of a society's basic institutions is regulated and enforced through the political structure. Hence, "political power is always coercive power backed by the government's use of sanctions." (*PL*, 136; cf. *TJ*, 235/207) It is one thing to hold a certain comprehensive moral, religious, or philosophical view to be correct and to believe that others who disagree are mistaken. But it is another to insist that one's comprehensive doctrine can properly be coercively imposed on others who do not share it or that one's comprehensive doctrine can provide grounds for coercion against those who reject it. In light of this contrast, the liberal principle of legitimacy can be stated as follows:

> our exercise of political power is proper and hence justifiable only when it is exercised in accordance with a constitution the essentials of which all citizens may reasonably be expected to endorse in the light of principles and ideals acceptable to them as reasonable and rational. (*PL*, 217; cf. xlvi, 137)

Although reasonable comprehensive doctrines will disagree about other matters, they can agree that coercion with regard to the basic structure of society requires a special type of justification that appeals to the reasonableness of the persons subjected to its coercive demands.

[11] Freeman, *Rawls*, p. 412.

They will, of course, ground this requirement in different ways. Just as different religions can endorse free religious faith each for their own doctrinal reasons while endorsing one particular view as correct, so too a full overlapping consensus involves a shared commitment to a political conception of justice and to public reason.

The restrictions on acceptable arguments that the requirements of public reason and the duty of civility impose are not external impositions. A reasonable comprehensive doctrine limits itself. Some defenders of public reason have drawn a parallel with the exclusion of illicitly acquired evidence in a court of law. However, there is an important difference between these two cases since sometimes evidence that would be relevant to establishing guilt is excluded in order to serve some other goal judged to be of great value. In the case of public reason, however, each reasonable comprehensive doctrine will recognize that arguments that exceed the limits of public reason are inappropriate when addressed to the general public and when matters of basic justice are at stake. That is, there are no arguments that a reasonable comprehensive doctrine will recognize as appropriate and relevant that it will be prohibited from making. Reasonable citizens will ground the duty of civility in their own comprehensive doctrine. They will hold, therefore, each for their own reasons, that an argument that depended exclusively on their comprehensive doctrine alone would provide an inadequate basis for establishing the requirements of basic social justice.

Public reason is the collective reasoning of a democratic society when it addresses matters of basic social justice. A philosophical account of public reason should do no more than specify "the public reasons in terms of which such questions are to be politically decided." (*PL*, li) The framework should not, in general, dictate the specific outcomes of public deliberations. These are matters for citizens to determine collectively, giving arguments that they sincerely believe could be shared by their fellow citizens. For most policy matters, public reason could potentially endorse a range of possible options. Any one of these decisions could be legitimate – in accordance with the liberal principle of legitimacy – even if we do not believe them to be equally just. On the other hand, we can identify broad constraints on the kinds of reasons that can properly be cited and therefore constraints on the possible range of legitimate outcomes. Specifically, in order to be compatible with the constraints of public reason and the duty of civility, the reasons must be grounded in a liberal political conception of justice. That is, it must: (1) specify certain "basic rights, liberties and opportunities"; (2) assign "special priority to those rights, liberties, and opportunities, especially with respect to claims of the general good and of perfectionist values"; and (3) ensure that all citizens have "adequate all-purpose means to make effective use of their liberties and opportunities." (*PL*, 6) If a conception of justice were to fail to give priority to a scheme of basic liberties or fail to provide everyone with adequate resources, there would be some citizens to whom such a conception could not be justified. Such a conception could not be supported within the space of public reason.

Justice as fairness is obviously one such liberal conception, and if the congruence argument is dropped, it can easily be presented as a political conception.[12] But justice as fairness is not the only liberal political conception of justice. For example, the mixed conception that we considered in chapter 2 that rejects the difference principle in favor of utilitarianism constrained by a minimum floor (and accepts fair equality of opportunity and the first principle) is also a liberal conception. The idea of public reason does not dictate any single political conception of justice:

> It is crucial that public reason is not specified by any one political conception of justice, certainly not by justice as fairness alone. Rather, its content – the principles, ideals, and standards that may be appealed to – are those of a family of reasonable political conceptions of justice and this family changes over time. (*PL*, l–li)

Although Rawls argues that justice as fairness is the most reasonable, he recognizes that other liberal political conceptions are also reasonable and potentially legitimate. (*PL*, xlvi–xlvii, 6, 442) The ideal of public reason entails a liberal political conception, but it is possible that reasonable citizens may come to different conclusions about which is the most reasonable. If the citizens of a liberal democracy collectively (even if not unanimously) favored some other liberal political conception, that decision could be legitimate, even if not, according to Rawls's own judgment, fully just.

[12] For example, Rawls offers an interpretation of the construction of the original position that is political in the appropriate sense. See *PL*, 22–8.

Neither Rawls himself nor the secondary literature has fully explored the implications of there being not only one but a family of reasonable and potentially legitimate conceptions of justice.[13] Recall that the problem with the congruence argument was that it was too utopian since we cannot expect or demand that all citizens of a well-ordered society share the same (partially) comprehensive doctrine on which the argument was based. In *Political Liberalism* Rawls asks how stability is even possible without a shared comprehensive doctrine, and he answers that it is possible when there is an overlapping consensus on a political conception of justice. This, too, is utopian since we cannot expect all reasonable people to share a single political conception of justice. We can only realistically hope that they will each endorse one in a family of reasonable, liberal conceptions. With suitable changes to the account of an overlapping consensus, this may be enough to show that stability is possible. What is required, in addition to each citizen endorsing some liberal conception of justice, is that each also recognizes the reasonableness of other liberal conceptions and the liberal principle of legitimacy. If they do this, then they can view as legitimate whatever political conception is collectively (although not universally) endorsed, even if they do not think it is the best one. They can therefore recognize political decisions based on it to be morally binding, even if they do not believe them to be fully just. In *Political Liberalism*, therefore, stability ultimately depends on the liberal principle of legitimacy, rather than a single conception of justice, being the focus of an overlapping consensus.

Given the diversity of reasonable comprehensive doctrines, it is unrealistic to suppose that we could have a general argument that would establish the congruence of the right and the good even in a well-ordered society. The question of congruence requires that we examine the relationship between justice and various non-political values. For this reason the issue of congruence cannot be addressed from within the limits of a political conception of justice and public reason:

[13] See Joshua Cohen, "For a Democratic Society" in Freeman, *The Cambridge Companion to Rawls*, pp. 129–31.

> Thus it is left to each citizen, individually or in association with others, to say how the claims of political justice are to be ordered, or weighed, against nonpolitical values. The political conception gives no guidance in such questions, since it does not say how nonpolitical values are to be counted. This guidance belongs to citizens' comprehensive doctrines. (*PL*, 386–7)

Stability requires that citizens "judge (by their comprehensive view) that political values either outweigh or are normally (though not always) ordered prior to whatever nonpolitical values may conflict with them." (*PL*, 392) Because this requires weighing political against non-political values, this exceeds the limits of a political conception of justice. The most we can do from within a political conception is to establish that political values, such as basic social justice, "are very great values and hence [are] not easily overridden." (*PL*, 139) Each reasonable comprehensive doctrine will, however, also endorse other important values that may conflict, and we cannot simply assume that from the point of view of each comprehensive doctrine the value of social justice will always be greater.

The congruence argument in *A Theory of Justice* does not successfully establish what Rawls originally intended, namely, that congruence would hold for all (or most) citizens of a well-ordered society. It can only reach this conclusion by assuming that all citizens share the same (partially) comprehensive doctrine of the Kantian interpretation. But not all would. Still, the congruence argument represents an example of how one reasonable comprehensive doctrine can establish the regulative value of justice. Other reasonable comprehensive doctrines must establish the value of justice in relation to other values in their own terms. In effect, the Kantian interpretation becomes just one member of an overlapping consensus that supports justice as fairness, and other reasonable comprehensive doctrines will have to embed a political conception of justice in their own larger framework. Rawls does not claim that such an overlapping consensus is inevitable – still less that one already exists. In *Political Liberalism*, he is interested in answering the question of how is stability even possible:

> *PL* makes no attempt to prove, or to show, that such a consensus would eventually form around a reasonable political conception of justice. The most it does is to present a freestanding liberal political conception that

does not oppose comprehensive doctrines on their own ground and does not preclude the possibility of an overlapping consensus for the right reasons. (*PL*, xlv–xlvi)

But even Rawls's account of an overlapping consensus on a single liberal political conception turns out to be unrealistic since we cannot expect all reasonable people to endorse the same conception. Stability is still possible, however, if citizens generally accept one of a family of liberal political conceptions, recognize the other members of that family to be reasonable, and accept the liberal principle of legitimacy.

THE POLITICAL CONCEPTION OF THE PERSON

The conceptual tools that were generated by the development of a political conception of justice can be used to strengthen elements of justice as fairness not directly concerned with stability. In this section I will discuss two of them, both related to the model of the person already present in *A Theory of Justice* but further developed in *Political Liberalism*. As we saw above, a political conception of justice draws on ideas found implicit in the public political culture of a democratic society. Specifically, it relies on the understanding of society as a fair system of cooperation and an understanding of citizens as free and equal moral persons. As we saw, Rawls notes in *A Theory of Justice* that equal justice is owed to all "moral persons":

> Moral persons are distinguished by two features: first they are capable of having (and are assumed to have) a conception of their good (as expressed by a rational plan of life); and second they are capable of having (and are assumed to acquire) a sense of justice, a normally effective desire to apply and to act upon the principles of justice, at least to a certain minimum degree. (*TJ*, 505/442)

As long as individuals exhibit these capacities at a level above a minimal threshold, they are entitled to equal justice.[14] These two capacities represent our "fundamental interests" and, as we saw in

[14] In *A Theory of Justice* Rawls does not assume that this sufficient condition is necessary:

> Whether moral personality is also a necessary condition I shall leave aside. I assume that the capacity for a sense of justice is possessed by the overwhelming majority of mankind, and therefore this question does not raise a serious practical problem . . . We cannot go far wrong in supposing that the sufficient condition is always satisfied. Even if the capacity were necessary, it would be unwise in practice to withhold justice on this ground. The risk to just institutions would be too great. (*TJ*, 506/442–3)

chapters 1 and 3, and as we will see again below, the parties in the original position are very highly motivated to protect them. This is a crucial step in the argument for the selection of the two principles of justice, but in *A Theory of Justice* the grounding of these "highest-order interests" seems underdeveloped and undefended.

Consider more specifically the capacity to have a conception of the good. There is more to this capacity than might at first appear. Moral persons, who have the capacity for a conception of the good, conceive of themselves as free in the following sense:

> They do not think of themselves as inevitably bound to, or as identical with, the pursuit of any particular complex of fundamental interests that they may have at any given time, although they want the right to advance such interests (provided they are admissible). Rather, free persons conceive of themselves as beings who can revise and alter their final ends and who give first priority to preserving their liberty in these matters. (*TJ*, 131–2; cf. 152)[15]

In *A Theory of Justice*, this priority is grounded in the Kantian understanding of moral autonomy, which states that "[p]roperly understood, then, the desire to act justly derives in part from the desire to express most fully what we are or can be, namely, free and equal rational beings with a liberty to choose." (*TJ*, 256/225; cf. 515/452) When we interpret justice as fairness as a political concept, however, the Kantian interpretation becomes just one of many reasonable doctrines. This seems to leave the highest-order interests unsupported and therefore to place the choice of the first principle in doubt.

In *Political Liberalism* individuals are still understood to have these same two moral powers, but they are no longer grounded in the partially comprehensive doctrine of the Kantian interpretation. Instead, they are assumed – as citizens – to have these moral powers "[i]n order to fulfill their political role." (*PL*, xliv) The political role of citizen is given, in turn, by an understanding of society as "a fair system of social cooperation between free and equal persons viewed as fully cooperating members of society over a complete life." (*PL*, 9) This conception of society is "implicit in the public culture of a

In *Political Liberalism*, however, he suggests that moral personality is "*necessary* and sufficient . . . for being counted a full and equal member of society in questions of political justice." (*PL*, 302, my emphasis)

[15] This passage was added to the revised edition.

democratic society," (*PL*, 15) and therefore does not exceed the limits of the political.

As in *A Theory of Justice*, equal justice is owed to all citizens who have the two moral capacities above a minimal level. This level is now specified by the requirements of full participation in a fair system of cooperation. A sense of justice is necessary for participation in a fair system of social cooperation in part because cooperation is not merely coordinated activity:

> Cooperation involves the idea of fair terms of cooperation: these are terms that each participant may reasonably accept, provided that everyone else likewise accepts them. Fair terms of cooperation specify an idea of reciprocity: all who are engaged in cooperation and who do their part as the rules and procedure require, are to benefit in an appropriate way as assessed by a suitable benchmark of comparison. (*PL*, 16)

If a fair system of cooperation is to be based on an ideal of reciprocity, individuals must generally have "the capacity to understand, to apply, and to act from the public conception of justice which characterizes the fair terms of social cooperation." (*PL*, 19) But this just is the capacity to have a sense of justice – the first of the two moral powers.

A fair system of cooperation also requires "an idea of each participant's rational advantage, or good." (*PL*, 16) The capacity for a conception of the good ensures that individuals hold some goals to be worth pursuing and are therefore not indifferent to how they are treated. Without such a capacity, there would be no basis or occasion for assessing whether individuals are treated fairly. On the basis of this capacity citizens are understood to be free in a particular sense since they "are seen as capable of revising and changing [their] conception [of the good] on reasonable and rational grounds, and they may do this if they so desire." (*PL*, 30) The capacity to reflect on and to revise one's conception of the good allows us to say that citizens "are viewed as capable of taking responsibility for their ends." (*PL*, 33) In particular, they view themselves as being able to revise their ends when they conflict with the demands of justice.[16] Typically, of course,

[16] I have argued elsewhere that there will inevitably be conflicts internal to a conception of the good, and that therefore the capacity to revise one's conception of the good can also be understood as part of the capacity to pursue rationally one's ends. See *What's Left of Liberalism*, pp. 62–5.

such revisions will be based on other values that they hold. There is no requirement that individuals be able to revise their doctrine of the good from some value-free perspective – whatever that would mean. Nor is there any requirement that individuals be able to revise their ends easily or in some single act of the will. (*PL*, 31; *TJ*, 568/498) Nor is there any implication that an individual's good is only valuable if it is subject to constant critical scrutiny and re-evaluation. Such an assumption could only be based on some comprehensive doctrine, and it would be inappropriate to incorporate it in our political model of the person. Rawls is explicit on this point: "Of course, many persons may not examine their acquired beliefs and ends but take them on faith, or be satisfied that they are matters of custom and tradition." (*PL*, 314) Still, for political purposes, we view persons as being responsible for their conception of the good. This allows us to set up a:

> "social division of responsibility": society, citizens as a collective body, accepts responsibility for maintaining the equal basic liberties and fair equality of opportunity, and for providing a fair share of the primary goods for all within this framework; while citizens as individuals and associations accept responsibility for revising and adjusting their ends and aspirations in view of the all-purpose means they can expect, given their present and foreseeable situation. (*PL*, 189)

We will discuss the connection to primary goods below.

This understanding of the person as free and equal, and as having the two moral powers necessary to fulfill the role of citizen, is developed as part of a political conception of justice and need not be extended to areas beyond matters of basic social justice. For example, when we say that for political purposes individuals are treated as equals, this means that they are entitled to equal justice. This does not imply that their accomplishments from a comprehensive point of view are of equal worth – a point Rawls had already made in *A Theory of Justice*. (*TJ*, 329/289; cf. 94/80–1) Similarly, we do not imply anything about the metaphysical status of free will when we say that for political purposes citizens are viewed as free in the sense that they have the capacity to revise and take responsibility for their conception of the good. Some critics charge that Rawls's account is incompatible with the way some religious believers view their own faith. They do not view their faith as a "choice" but rather as a "calling." However, holding a citizen responsible for her comprehensive doctrine and conception of the good for political purposes is perfectly compatible with her believing (on the basis of a comprehensive doctrine) that her doctrine is given to her by God and is not subject to her arbitrary choice. In fact, it seems somewhat surprising that defenders of religious doctrines would diminish the significance of the political liberty to revise one's faith. After all, in circumstances of reasonable pluralism, it would be especially important to someone of religious faith that others be viewed as being capable of revision their views. To reject this model would seem to preclude anyone who is not already there from coming to the true faith.

For our purposes the important point about this political model of the person is that citizens have a fundamental, "higher-order" interest in developing and maintaining each of the two moral powers at the level necessary to fulfill their role as citizen. (They also have a third higher-order interest in achieving their determinate conception of the good.)[17] (*PL*, 74) Again, such interests were present in *A Theory of Justice*, but they are developed more fully in the context of a political conception of justice. In particular it is with reference to these higher-order interests that Rawls now justifies the use of primary goods. In *A Theory of Justice* primary goods were identified as "things that every rational man is presumed to want." (*TJ*, 62/54) Unfortunately, this may have suggested that primary goods were to be identified as the essential means "for achieving the final ends which a comprehensive empirical or historical survey might show that people usually or normally have in common." (*PL*, 308) Instead, we can now say that "given the political conception of citizens, primary goods specify what their needs are – part of what their good is as citizens – when questions of justice arise." (*PL*, 188; cf. *TJ*, xiii) That is, the primary

[17] In "Kantian Constructivism in Moral Theory," Rawls says that the interests in realizing and exercising the two moral powers are "highest-order" interests, and he observes that they are "supremely regulative" so that "whenever circumstances are relevant to their fulfillment, these interests govern deliberation and conduct." In contrast, the interest in fulfilling the determinate conception of the good is merely a "higher-order" interest since "it is in essential respects subordinate to the highest-order interests." ("Kantian Constructivism in Moral Theory" in Freeman, *Collected Papers*, pp. 312, 313) *Political Liberalism* claims that they are "higher-order interests" perhaps because Rawls does not believe that all reasonable comprehensive doctrines will view them as supremely regulative.

goods are necessary in order to develop and maintain the two moral powers as well as effectively to pursue reasonable conceptions of the good.

This account provides strong support for the basic liberties in particular, which are, of course, primary goods, since they provide "the background institutional conditions necessary for the development and the full and informed exercise of the two moral powers." (*PL*, 308) Liberty of conscience, for example, directly protects both moral powers, for without it individuals would not be free to reflect on their sense of justice and conception of the good and to revise each if necessary. Liberties of speech and association are also necessary to protect these capacities for the same reason, since reflection typically and most effectively proceeds in dialogue with others. Similarly, "freedom of movement and free choice of occupation against a background of diverse opportunities . . . allow the pursuit of diverse final ends and give effect to a decision to revise and change them, if we so desire." (*PL*, 308) Other items can be added to the list of primary goods if they prove to be important in serving the higher-order interests. Medical care is an obvious example, since over the course of everyone's life there will be times when illness or accident interferes with their ability to participate fully in society. In such circumstances medical care becomes necessary for a return to full functioning in the cooperative system. (*PL*, 184) As with the detailed specification of the other primary goods, judgments about health care policy must be made from the legislative stage of the four-stage sequence, because it "depends in part on information about the prevalence of various illnesses and their severity, the frequency of accidents and their causes, and much else."[18] Income and wealth are primary goods because they serve the third higher-order interest, that is, they "are needed

[18] Rawls, *Justice as Fairness*, p. 173. Rawls excludes from consideration severe and chronic disabilities that prevent people from participating fully in a fair scheme of cooperation. This is not because he thinks there are no duties owed to such individuals. The point is that the natural duties "have no necessary connection with institutions or social practices" (*TJ*, 114/98) and he "take[s] it as obvious, and accepted by common sense, that we have a duty towards all human beings, however severely handicapped." (Rawls, *Justice as Fairness*, p. 176, n. 59) His strategy is to develop an understanding of what justice requires among free and equal citizens who are fully cooperating members of society. Once that has been worked out we can attempt to extend the account to address those who are unable to participate fully. See the discussion in Samuel Freeman, "Frontiers of Justice: The Capabilities Approach vs. Contractarianism," *Texas Law Review*, 85 (2006), pp. 411–18.

to achieve directly or indirectly a wide range of ends, whatever they happen to be." (*PL*, 308) Rawls's understanding of wealth is very broad. It "consists of (legal) command over exchangeable means for satisfying human needs and interests."[19] He specifically mentions that "people have control over wealth not only as individuals but also as members of associations and groups" including, in a property-owning democracy, "stockholders of a corporation," and "in a socialist economy, the workers in the firm [who] control its capital and means of production."[20]

This account of primary goods leaves us with a subtle puzzle, however. The parties in the original position are motivated strictly by their unknown yet determinate conception of the good. Why would they give priority to selecting principles that would allow them to develop and maintain the two moral powers? One possible answer is simply that when the veil of ignorance is lifted, they may find that their comprehensive doctrine places great weight on moral autonomy and reflection on one's values. Such a doctrine will value the development of the capacity to reflect on and revise one's conception of the good far beyond the minimal level necessary to fulfill the role of citizen. But the parties cannot assume that they will hold such a doctrine, so they cannot assume that the continued development of the two moral powers beyond the minimal level necessary will itself be part of their determinate conception of the good.

Again: the parties are choosing principles on the basis of their assessment of which will be likely to lead them to do as well as possible, where success is measured in terms of their (unknown) conception of the good. They are to make this assessment on the assumption that the principles chosen would generally inform the sense of justice of the citizens of a well-ordered society. If they were to choose principles that did not secure the adequate development of the two moral powers, this would affect not only themselves but others in their society as well. They would be choosing principles that would result in a society in which many citizens – perhaps even they themselves – would be unable to participate fully because they lacked

[19] John Rawls, "Fairness to Goodness" [1975] in Freeman, *Collected Papers*, p. 271.
[20] *Ibid.*, p. 272.

one or both of the moral powers. It is this outcome that the parties would want to avoid at almost any cost, since they would properly judge that their prospects of achieving their conception of the good in such a society would be quite poor. "Clearly, the public knowledge that everyone has an effective sense of justice and can be relied upon as a fully cooperating member of society is a great advantage to everyone's conception of the good." (*PL*, 316) The parties will give this high priority to securing the two moral powers only up to the point at which they are capable of full participation in the fair system of cooperation. They cannot assume anything about how they will value moral autonomy beyond that point.

Other things equal, the parties in the original position would want to secure a larger share of wealth and resources with which to pursue their conception of the good. But they would not want to secure a larger share at the cost of creating a society in which many individuals lacked the two moral powers. It would be far more costly in terms of their own conception of the good to live in a society in which many others did not have an adequate sense of justice or a capacity to take responsibility for their conception of the good. Since the basic liberties "are the background institutional conditions necessary for the development and the full and informed exercise of the two moral powers," (*PL*, 308) the parties would want to secure these prior to any additional gains in wealth. Hence, they would give priority to the first principle of justice over the second.

On the other hand, we might think that in conditions of extreme deprivation, the resources needed for basic human functioning would take priority over securing basic liberties. Rawls acknowledges the point:

> the first principle covering the equal basic rights and liberties may easily be preceded by a lexically prior principle requiring that citizens' basic needs be met, at least insofar as their being met is necessary for citizens to understand and to be able fruitfully to exercise those rights and liberties. (*PL*, 7)

Rawls does not make the details of such a principle explicit. He seems to assume that its idea is implicit in the first principle. As we saw in chapter 3, already in *A Theory of Justice* the priority of the first principle holds only in circumstances in which the basic liberties can be effectively exercised.[21]

A PROPERTY-OWNING DEMOCRACY

The most common interpretations of justice as fairness assume that it is a form of luck egalitarianism and that it supports a form of welfare-state capitalism. Neither is correct. *Political Liberalism* makes it clear that Rawls is interested in developing an account of society as a fair system of cooperation among individuals understood as free and equal citizens holding a diverse range of reasonable comprehensive doctrines. Once his account of distributive justice, and therefore his account of the justice of economic institutions, is understood in this light, it becomes clearer that these common interpretations are mistaken. We discussed luck egalitarianism in the introduction and we will return to it again in chapter 5. In this section, we will consider Rawls's support for what he calls a "property-owning democracy." The account of a property-owning democracy does not depend on the idea of a political conception of justice, and it was already implicit in *A Theory of Justice*. Still, it was only after the publication of *A Theory of Justice* that Rawls came to make explicit the contrast between a property-owning democracy and welfare-state capitalism. In the preface for the revised edition, written in 1990, he noted that if he were to have rewritten *A Theory of Justice* he would have distinguished these models more sharply. (*TJ*, xiv)

When *A Theory of Justice* was published in 1971, the dominant cleavage among theories of economic justice was between those that defended some form of capitalism and those that defended some form of socialism. There were many variations and sometimes bitter disputes within each of these ideologies, but before attending to such details, a theory had to declare which side it was on. In *A Theory of Justice*, however, Rawls rejects this assumption: "Throughout [this discussion] the choice between a private-property economy and socialism is left open; from the standpoint of the theory of justice alone, various basic structures would appear to satisfy its principles."

[21] See pp. 474–5 in the revised edition and p. 542 in the original edition for slightly different expressions of this idea.

(*TJ*, 258/228) This is not to say, of course, that all forms of private property or all socialist economies would satisfy his principles, but only that some versions of each might. Any just socialism would have to be embedded within a genuinely democratic political structure and rely heavily on market mechanisms; any just private-property regime would have to provide the resources to keep the political process independent of private wealth and to ensure that "property and wealth [were] kept widely distributed." (*TJ*, 225/198) But Rawls's refusal to be pigeonholed as either a defender of capitalism or of socialism was apparently too subtle for some critics. Since he does not come down squarely on one side or the other, they leaped to the conclusion that, as Benjamin Barber claimed, he must "have nothing to say" about the choice of economic institutions: "To assert that, so far as a theory of justice is concerned, there is nothing to choose between capitalism and socialism is so striking a claim that to cite it nearly obviates the need to comment on it."[22]

What Rawls actually says, as we saw in chapter 2, is that the principles of justice cannot by themselves determine whether a just regime would allow or prohibit private ownership of the means of production. While one of the basic liberties is "the right to hold and to have the exclusive use of personal property," the emphasis here is on "personal" property because that is required "for a sense of personal independence and self-respect, both of which are essential for the development and exercise of the moral powers." (*PL*, 298) In contrast there is no basic liberty to ownership of the means of production, nor is there one to "participate in the control of means of production and natural resources, which are to be socially owned." (*PL*, 298) Principles of justice do not directly dictate a decision for all circumstances concerning the permissibility and extent of private or collective ownership of the means of production:

Which of these systems and the many intermediate forms most fully answers to the requirements of justice cannot, I think, be determined in advance. There is presumably no general answer to this question, since it depends in

[22] Benjamin Barber, *The Conquest of Politics* (Princeton, 1988), p. 81. Cf. John Gray, "Contractarian Method, Private Property and the Market Economy" in his *Liberalisms: Essays in Political Philosophy* (Routledge, 1989), p. 161; and Barry Clark and Herbert Gintis, "Rawlsian Justice and Economic Systems," *Philosophy and Public Affairs*, 7 (1978), p. 304.

large part upon the traditions, institutions, and social forces of each country and its particular historical circumstances. (*TJ*, 274/242)

It is possible that in some circumstances, only one (broad) economic scheme would be just. But given the complexities of economic institutions and the lack of precision in economic forecasting, it is far more likely that a range of schemes would appear to be compatible with the principles of justice. What is important in such circumstances is that the decision concerning the extent of private ownership of the means of production be made through a society's legitimate political mechanisms.

Although Rawls consistently holds that a democratic socialism could be just, he concentrates on the requirements of justice for a society which allows private ownership of the means of production. It is easy to lose track of the various considerations in *A Theory of Justice* that are relevant to the assessment of economic systems. For example, I quoted above the remark about the importance of keeping property and wealth widely distributed and of keeping the political process independent of private wealth. (*TJ*, 225/198) The first principle of justice, therefore, has distributive implications. Similarly, Rawls asserts, "[f]ree market arrangements must be set within a framework of political and legal institutions which regulates the overall trends of economic events and preserves the social conditions necessary for fair equality of opportunity." (*TJ*, 73/63) Fair equality of opportunity, therefore, has distributive implications. When Rawls focuses directly on economic institutions, he assumes:

> that the basic structure is regulated by a just constitution that secures the liberties of equal citizenship . . . and the fair value of political liberty in maintained . . . I assume also that there is fair (as opposed to formal – equality of opportunity . . . [The government] also enforces and underwrites equality of opportunity in economic activities and in the free choice of occupation. This is achieved by policing the conduct of firms and private associations and by preventing the establishment of monopolistic restrictions and barriers to the more desirable positions. Finally, the government guarantees a social minimum either by family allowances and special payments for sickness and employment [*sic* – surely he means "unemployment"], or more systematically by such devices as a graded income supplement (a so-called negative income tax). (*TJ*, 275/243)

In order to be just, a society must devise institutions that can reasonably be expected to achieve all of these aims.

As we saw in chapter 2, Rawls divides the distributive responsibilities of the government into various "branches." These are to be understood as functional roles, not institutional structures. It is all too easy to focus exclusively on the "transfer branch" that established a social minimum. (*TJ*, 276/244) Such a narrow focus neglects the important distributive roles of the "allocation branch," which adjusts taxes, subsidies, and "changes in the definition of property rights" in order to keep markets competitive; the stabilization branch, which works to maintain "reasonably full employment" and "the free choice of occupation"; and the distribution branch, which "imposes a number of inheritance and gift taxes . . . [in order] gradually and continually to correct the distribution of wealth and to prevent concentrations of power detrimental to the fair value of political liberty and fair equality of opportunity." (*TJ*, 276–7/244–5) All of these have important implications for the distribution of wealth in a just society. If one ignores these, and loses track of the priority Rawls places on the distributive effects of the fair value of the political liberties and of fair equality of opportunity, one might be tempted to conclude that the main requirement of economic justice was the provision of a safety-net by the transfer branch. And, indeed, Rawls is almost always read in this way – as a defender of a form of welfare-state capitalism.

This is, however, a serious distortion of justice as fairness. The problem with the model of welfare-state capitalism is that it does not take seriously the goal of maintaining the conditions under which citizens can interact with one another as equals. Instead, it limits itself to maintaining a minimum share of resources for all, without concern for the terms of interaction among individuals.[23] On this model, distributive justice requires adjustments of the distribution of resources to ensure that nobody falls below a certain threshold of income or wealth. There is no commitment to ensuring that the political liberties have fair value or that there is fair equality of opportunity, nor is there any assessment of the operation of the markets

[23] It is worth noting that the term "welfare" in the phrase "welfare state" differs from the typical economic or philosophical understanding of welfare as a measure of well-being.

or consideration of the terms with which individuals operate within markets. There is no problem if the terms of interaction are radically unequal, as long as the outcomes can be adjusted so that nobody falls through the safety-net. As a result, such a scheme "permits very large inequalities in the ownership of real property (productive assets and natural resources) so that the control of the economy and much of political life rests in few hands."[24] Such a society is likely to "develop a discouraged and depressed underclass many of whose members are chronically dependent on welfare. This underclass feels left out and does not participate in the public political culture."[25] The possibility of an underclass withdrawing into "apathy and resentment" and becoming alienated from the main social institutions was already an explicit concern in *A Theory of Justice*. (*TJ*, 226/198)

As an alternative to welfare-state capitalism, Rawls advocates what he calls a "property-owning democracy," taking the term from the economist J. E. Meade.[26] Such an arrangement allows private ownership of the means of production, but it aims to "put in the hands of citizens generally, and not only of a few, sufficient productive means for them to be fully cooperating members of society on a footing of equality."[27] The idea is that when individuals are able to interact on a footing of real and not only formal equality, the possibility of class exploitation is undermined. Although private ownership of the means of production is often taken to be the defining characteristic of capitalism, the absence of class exploitation marks a crucial contrast between a property-owning democracy and capitalism. Hence, Rawls presents it as an alternative to capitalism. But the label is not what is important. The key point is that there must be a strong institutional effort to ensure that individuals are able to maintain the conditions that allow them to interact from a "footing of equality." If such conditions were incompatible with private ownership of the means of production, then the case would be made for some form of socialism. For Rawls, however, such a case has not been made. Although the

[24] Rawls, *Justice as Fairness*, p. 138. [25] *Ibid.*, p. 140.

[26] J. E. Meade, *Liberty, Equality and Efficiency* (New York University Press, 1993). Rawls also cites Richard Krouse and Michael McPherson, "Capitalism, 'Property-Owning Democracy,' and the Welfare State" in *Democracy and the Welfare State*, Amy Gutmann, ed. (Princeton University Press, 1988). On the history of the term, see Amit Ron, "Visions of Democracy in a 'Property-Owning Democracy': Skelton to Rawls and Beyond," *History of Political Thought*, 29 (2008).

[27] Rawls, *Justice as Fairness*, p. 140.

world has witnessed precious few experiments with property-owning democracy, the record is comparable with the lack of truly democratic socialist regimes.

What is fundamental is not the extent to which a society allows private ownership of the means of production but whether it has institutions that ensure that citizens can interact as equals. What is required is "to put all citizens in a position to manage their own affairs on a footing of a suitable degree of social and economic equality."[28] In a just society the least advantaged are not treated as "objects of our charity and compassion, much less our pity – but those to whom reciprocity is owed as a matter of political justice among those who are free and equal citizens along with everyone else."[29] A property-owning democracy aims to ensure this "not by the redistribution of income to those with less at the end of each period, so to speak, but rather by ensuring the widespread ownership of productive assets and human capital (that is, education and trained skills) at the beginning of each period, all this against a background of fair equality of opportunity."[30] Once again, this contrasts importantly with the model of welfare-state capitalism, according to which shares of resources are adjusted at the end of each period to ensure that nobody falls through the safety-net. It is true that a property-owning democracy must also provide some kind of guaranteed minimum as a social safety-net, but if the other elements of the economy are working properly, it will rarely be used.

The contrast between adjustments occurring at the beginning or end of each period is metaphor. The end of one period is always the start of the next, so there may seem to be little institutional difference between adjusting the results of one and setting the terms of the next. Still, the contrast reveals how Rawls thinks about the requirements of economic justice. The point goes beyond issues of institutional design and helps reveal why justice as fairness is not a form of luck egalitarianism. For Rawls economic justice is concerned not with achieving any particular outcome in terms of the distribution of goods. Rather, it is concerned with achieving and maintaining fair terms for citizens freely to pursue their permissible goals through interaction and cooperation as equals.

[28] *Ibid.*, p. 139. [29] *Ibid.* [30] *Ibid.*

CHAPTER 5

Criticisms of A Theory of Justice

Given the absolute centrality of Rawls's work to contemporary political philosophy, it would be impossible to attempt anything like a comprehensive survey of the secondary literature which now contains many thousands of works. Instead we will focus on a few themes that have figured prominently in the critical literature. In the first section we will consider some criticisms of the idea of reflective equilibrium and Rawls's method of justification. This will highlight an important contrast between how Rawls conceives of the project of justice as fairness and a common understanding of the tasks of moral philosophy. The second and third sections will examine the so-called "communitarian" critique of Rawls. There are several distinct views that are often given this label, and we will focus on two of the most important. This will bring out more clearly how Rawls thinks about the virtue of justice and the degree of flexibility and sensitivity to different circumstances that he allows. In the last two sections we will consider two criticisms that focus on economic justice – first the libertarianism of Robert Nozick and then the radical egalitarianism of G. A. Cohen. This will allow us to bring out more clearly how Rawls thinks about distributive justice and the contrast between justice as fairness and luck egalitarianism.

FOUNDATIONALISM AND REFLECTIVE EQUILIBRIUM

In the preface to *A Theory of Justice* Rawls comments that "I have avoided extensive methodological discussions . . . Occasionally there are methodological comments and asides, but for the most part I try to work out a substantive theory of justice." (*TJ*, ix/xix) His primary goal, as we have seen, is to defend a conception of justice that is superior to its main traditional rivals, utilitarianism and intuitionism. Although he does not claim that no improvements to his conception are possible, Rawls thinks that a society that organized its basic structure according to this conception would be a more just and stable society than one that organized itself on a utilitarian conception. But, in general, what kinds of arguments might establish the superiority of one conception of justice over another? How would we know – or even have grounds to believe – that one conception was superior to another in the first place?

As we saw in chapter 1, the answer that Rawls gives is that a conception of justice is justified when we endorse it from a state of reflective equilibrium. If we were to reach such a state, we would have "done what we can to render coherent and to justify our convictions of social justice." (*TJ*, 21/18) Ultimately, the justification of a conception of justice "is a matter of the mutual support of many considerations, of everything fitting together into one coherent view." (*TJ*, 21/19) There is no reason not to take Rawls at his word when he says that it is a matter of "everything" fitting together. Anything that is potentially relevant, that might be part of an argument for or against a conception of justice, may be included – particular moral judgments about specific cases, general moral principles, still-more abstract procedural restrictions on acceptable moral arguments, comprehensive value systems, scientific theories, metaphysical doctrines, and much else. The method of reflective equilibrium is a declaration of inclusion: all considerations are welcome to apply and none is ruled out ahead of time. In this regard neither substantive moral convictions nor abstract principles nor meta-ethical doctrines enjoy a guaranteed priority over the others. The idea of reflective equilibrium rejects both the methodological priority that David Gauthier gives to "theory rather than intuition"[1] as well as that which Thomas Nagel gives to "intuitions over arguments."[2] It rejects, as well, the view that Michael Smith endorses when he claims that "philosophers have surely been right to give meta-ethical questions a certain priority over questions in normative ethics" and that "we should do normative ethics only after we have given satisfactory answers to certain questions in meta-ethics."[3]

[1] David Gauthier, *Moral by Agreement* (Oxford University Press, 1986), p. 269.
[2] Thomas Nagel, *Mortal Questions* (Cambridge University Press, 1979), p. x.
[3] Michael Smith, *The Moral Problem* (Blackwell, 1994), p. 2.

Understood in this inclusive sense, the idea of reflective equilibrium – unlike, for example, contractarianism – is hardly a "method" at all.[4] As we will see, however, there is an important and controversial point about the role of philosophy lurking in this seemingly trivial position. This can be most clearly revealed by considering some of the criticisms that it has generated.

We begin our work toward achieving reflective equilibrium and justifying a conception of justice by noting that there are some judgments that,

> we now make intuitively and in which we have the greatest confidence... There are questions which we felt sure must be answered in a certain way. For example, we are confident that religious intolerance and racial discrimination are unjust. We think that we have examined these things with care and have reached what we believe is an impartial judgment not likely to be distorted by the excessive attention to our own interests. (*TJ*, 19–20/17–18)

These considered judgments serve as provisional fixed points. They are, however, rather unsystematic and do not yet have the support of a general conception of justice, which, after all, is what we are trying to generate. In an early criticism of the idea of reflective equilibrium, Peter Singer challenged the reliance on such provisional fixed points, asking,

> Why should we not rather make the opposite assumption, that all the particular moral judgments we intuitively make are likely to derive from discarded religious systems, from warped views of sex and bodily functions, or from customs necessary for the survival of the group in social and economic circumstances that now lie in the distant past?[5]

[4] Compare Samuel Freeman: "It is only the nihilistic idea that our moral capacities themselves are unreliable no matter what the circumstances, and that morality and justice are simply illusory, that is incompatible with reflective equilibrium." (*Rawls*, p. 35) Elijah Millgram also doubts that reflective equilibrium should properly be called a "method," arguing that "if *anything* you do counts as an instance of Method X, then Method X is not a *method*." (*Ethics Done Right: Practical Reasoning as a Foundation for Moral Theory* (Cambridge University Press, 2005), p. 9, his emphasis) But he goes on to mischaracterize the idea of reflective equilibrium when he states that it involves revising one's theory "when one does not *like* the consequence." This leads him to conclude that reflective equilibrium amounts to "intellectual dishonesty." (p. 10, his emphasis) But the idea of reflective equilibrium does not tell us to revise our theory when we do not like the consequences. It tells us to consider revising the theory when we have reason to believe that the theory or its consequences are incorrect, whether we like them or not.

[5] Peter Singer, "Sidgwick and Reflective Equilibrium," *The Monist*, 58 (1974), p. 516.

It is possible that our provisional fixed points may turn out to be incorrect, even if we do not think that this is likely. But it is important to see that reaching reflective equilibrium is not only a matter of identifying principles that fit our pre-theoretical moral judgments. Unfortunately, Rawls may encourage this picture when he compares the task of a moral theorist to that of a linguist attempting to describe the grammar of a natural language. (*TJ*, 47/41) After all, it might be said, the linguist does not presume to dictate revisions to the language but merely identifies the hidden structures that bring systematic order to complicated data.[6] This might suggest that the achieving of reflective equilibrium is essentially a "curve-fitting" problem, in which we attempt to subsume particular data points under a simple general principle. However, using terminology that he introduced in 1974, Rawls rejects this idea of "narrow" reflective equilibrium in favor of "wide" reflective equilibrium.[7] Already in *A Theory of Justice* he points out that we are not merely "smoothing out . . . certain irregularities" in our sense of justice as it already stands. (*TJ*, 49/43) Rather, we are open to all relevant considerations, moral and non-moral, abstract and particular. Although Rawls is sometimes accused of holding a "monological" view, an effort to reach reflective equilibrium requires that we engage with the views of others.[8] This is because "the exchange of opinion with others checks our partiality and widens our perspective; we are made to see things from their standpoint and the limits of our vision are brought home to us."(*TJ*, 358/315) Through such dialogue and reflection "a person's sense of justice may or may not undergo a radical shift." (*TJ*, 49/43)

Singer is right to suggest that our provisional fixed points are not beyond criticism and are therefore not suitable to play a foundational role. We must check them against more general principles and commitments. This is exactly what we do in our effort to reach reflective

[6] See also Rawls's comment that "[t]here is a definite if limited class of facts against which conjectured principles can be checked, namely, our considered judgments in reflective equilibrium." (*TJ*, 51/44) However, notice that here it is only once we have reached reflective equilibrium that we are in a position to check our principles.

[7] See "The Independence of Moral Theory" [1975] in Freeman, *Collected Papers*, p. 289.

[8] See, for example, Jürgen Habermas, *Moral Consciousness and Communicative Action*, Christian Lenhardt and Shierry Weber Nicholsen, trans. (MIT Press, 1990), p. 66. Rawls denies this in *Political Liberalism*, p. 383. The charge is surely due to an excessive emphasis on and misinterpretation of the original position. See also his discussion of "general and wide, or what we may refer to as full, reflective equilibrium" in *Political Liberalism*, p. 384, n. 16.

equilibrium. By the same token, however, it is possible that our more general principles and ideals might themselves be the product of an indefensible ideology. Once this possibility is conceded, it is clear that our abstract principles cannot play a foundational role either. We can do no better than to reflect critically on our commitments at all levels and to work from where we are most confident to where we are least confident. To repeat: our goal is to try to identify principles of justice that we think, on reflection, we should endorse. The idea of reflective equilibrium allows us to introduce any considerations we take to be relevant to that process.

The criticism that Richard Brandt levels against the idea of reflective equilibrium is in some ways an extension of Singer's. Brandt recognizes that particular intuitions do not play a foundational role in reflective equilibrium. However, he argues that our moral beliefs, even if fully coherent, stand in need of independent grounds of justification. There is "no reason to think" that a coherent system of normative beliefs "is better justified than a less coherent one . . . unless some of the beliefs are initially credible – and not merely initially believed – for some reason other than their coherence."[9] He continues: "The fact that a person has a firm normative conviction gives that belief a status no better than fiction. Is one coherent set of fictions supposed to be better than another?"[10] Brandt concludes that justification must come from outside the system of our normative beliefs – specifically, from "the ordinary methods of science and observation."[11] Otherwise what looks like justification "may be no more than a reshuffling of moral prejudices."[12]

R. M. Hare also believes that justification must come from outside of a system of moral beliefs.[13] Since the idea of reflective equilibrium "make[s] the *truth* of the theory *depend on* agreement with people's opinions," this undercuts justice as fairness's claim to objectivity.[14] Rawls allegedly fails to make the "simple distinction" between "the view that thinking something can make it so (which is in general false)

[9] Richard Brandt, *A Theory of the Good and the Right* (Oxford University Press, 1979), p. 20.
[10] *Ibid.* [11] *Ibid.*, p. 22. [12] *Ibid.*
[13] Unlike Brandt, Hare believes that moral philosophy can and should be based "entirely on the formal properties of the moral concepts as revealed by the logical study of moral language." R. M. Hare, "Ethical Theory and Utilitarianism" in *Utilitarianism and Beyond*, Amartya Sen and Bernard Williams, eds. (Cambridge University Press, 1982), p. 25.
[14] R. M. Hare, "Rawls' Theory of Justice" [1973] in Daniels, *Reading Rawls*, p. 83.

and the view that if we are to say something sincerely, we must be able to accept it (which is a tautology)."[15] Hare holds that Rawls asserts the former, and therefore is reduced to "advocating a kind of subjectivism, in the narrowest and most old-fashioned sense."[16] But Rawls never suggests that our thinking something makes it so. On the contrary, the effort to reach reflective equilibrium is the effort to figure out what we should think about justice. If our thinking something made it true, there would be no effort required in order to select principles – any principles that we happened to believe would be true simply because we believed them. Hare gives no evidence that Rawls holds such a view. It is almost as though Hare cannot believe that Rawls would be asserting what Hare considers to be a tautology. But given a common understanding of the goals and methods of philosophy – an understanding shared by Hare – asserting the importance of reflective equilibrium is not at all trivial.

Hare sees Rawls's repudiation of the project of providing secure foundations for moral beliefs as a repudiation of philosophy itself. Because Rawls bases his justifications in part on substantive moral commitments, Hare believes that he is not restricting himself to the method that is "proper and peculiar" to philosophers and therefore "run[s] the risk of doing no more for the topic of justice than journalists and politicians."[17] Jürgen Habermas agrees that most of what Rawls is doing is not philosophy properly so-called: "What moral *theory* can do and should be trusted to do is to clarify the universal core of our moral intuitions and thereby to refute value skepticism. What it cannot do is make any kind of substantive contribution."[18] When Rawls does make a substantive contribution, he is speaking not as a philosopher but "simply as a committed liberal in his society."[19] In some ways, this view harkens back to the position of T. D. Weldon that we saw in the introduction.

[15] *Ibid.* [16] *Ibid.*, p. 82. [17] *Ibid.*, p. 95.

[18] Habermas, *Moral Consciousness and Communicative Action*, p. 211.

[19] Jürgen Habermas, "Life-Forms, Morality and the Task of the Philosopher" [1984] in *Autonomy and Solidarity*, rev. edn., Peter Dews, ed. (Verso, 1992), p. 199. Habermas does not intend this as an objection. He himself writes frequently on particular moral and political issues and he argues that philosophers should "forget about their professional role and bring what they can do better than others into a common business. But the common business of political discourses among citizens nevertheless stays what it is. It is not a philosophical enterprise." (pp. 199–200)

But the proper aims and methods of philosophy are exactly what are at stake. One often-dominant tradition says that philosophy should aim to provide secure foundations for various disciplines from outside the ground-level domain of enquiry. Scientific foundations must be provided for normative investigations; epistemological foundations must be provided for scientific investigations; logical or metaphysical foundations must be provided for epistemology. Only by securing foundations from outside of the domain of investigation can the body of knowledge be secured against a skeptical challenge. Any attempt to provide "internal" justifications does no more than "reshuffle" existing beliefs.

So while from one perspective the idea of reflective equilibrium is trivial, from another it represents a powerful statement of liberation from traditional foundational views about philosophy. This became explicit in Rawls's 1974 Presidential Address to the American Philosophical Association, entitled "The Independence of Moral Theory." There, he argued against the still-common view that "Moral philosophy is . . . secondary to metaphysics and the philosophy of mind as well, which are in turn secondary to the theory of meaning and epistemology."[20] Despite the suggestion of his title, Rawls is not asserting that ethical theory is unrelated to other areas of philosophy such as meta-ethics and epistemology. Rather, he holds that the dependence goes both ways:

> I have urged, then, that moral theory is, in important respects, independent from certain philosophical subjects sometimes regarded as methodologically prior to it. But I do not care for independence too strictly understood; an idea I like better is that each part of philosophy should have its own subject matter and problems and yet, at the same time, stand directly or indirectly in relations of mutual dependence with the others.[21]

In fact, Rawls suggests that progress in meta-ethics is likely to be made only after we have a better understanding of ground-level moral theories. The nineteenth- and early twentieth-century developments in logic and set theory lay the groundwork for "the extraordinary deepening of our understanding of the meaning and justification of

[20] John Rawls, "The Independence of Moral Theory" [1975] in Freeman, *Collected Papers*, p. 287.

[21] *Ibid.*, p. 302.

statements in logic and mathematics . . . Once the substantial content of moral conceptions is better understood, a similar transformation may occur." (*TJ*, 51–2/45) Thomas Nagel summarizes the thought this way: "Rawls believes that it will be more profitable to investigate the foundations of ethics when there are more substantive ethical results to seek the foundations of."[22] So the idea of reflective equilibrium highlights Rawls's non-trivial and indeed controversial rejection of a traditional conception of philosophy as a foundational enterprise.[23]

By insisting that substantive moral reflection that is based in part on our considered judgments Rawls is tapping into another philosophical tradition. In his 1917 essay, "On the Need for a Recovery in Philosophy," John Dewey famously wrote: "Philosophy recovers itself when it ceases to be a device for dealing with the problems of philosophers and becomes a method, cultivated by philosophers, for dealing with the problems of men."[24] Specifically, he criticized "the submergence of recent philosophizing in epistemology – that is, in discussions of the nature, possibility, and limits of knowledge in general, and in the attempt to reach conclusions regarding the ultimate nature of reality from the answers given to such questions."[25] Philosophers, he thought, must overcome the tendency to engage in the "disparagement of the things of ordinary qualitative experiences, those which are esthetic, moral, practical."[26] Rawls did not stress this connection to the American pragmatists, and this lineage has been almost completely neglected in the secondary literature, but already in his 1950 doctoral dissertation he noted that "[t]he origin of rational reflection has been frequently discussed by pragmatists who have asserted the doctrine that rational thought (i.e., empirical or scientific inquiry) begins, or is stimulated by confusion, doubt, and perplexity."[27]

[22] Thomas Nagel, "Rawls on Justice" [1973] in Daniels, *Reading Rawls*, p. 2.

[23] See also Rawls, *Justice as Fairness*, p. 31.

[24] John Dewey, "The Need for a Recovery of Philosophy" [1917] in *The Essential Dewey*, vol. 1, Larry Hickman and Thomas Alexander, eds. (Indiana University Press, 1998), p. 68.

[25] *Ibid.*, p. 55.

[26] John Dewey, "Experience, Knowledge and Value: A Rejoinder" [1939] in *The Philosophy of John Dewey*, Paul Schilpp and Lewis Hahn, eds., 3rd edn. (Open Court, 1989), p. 524.

[27] John Rawls, *A Study in the Grounds of Ethical Knowledge* (PhD Dissertation, Princeton University, 1950), p. 212, n. 1. He then cites Peirce and Dewey. In *A Theory of Justice*, the connection is made only indirectly through references to Goodman and Quine. (*TJ*, 20, n. 7/18, n. 7, 579, n. 33/507, n. 34)

The effort to reach reflective equilibrium does, indeed, begin in perplexity. It is not simply a matter of summarizing what we already know, as we saw Richard Rorty suggest in the introduction.[28] There are conflicts and tensions within our thinking, and on some issues we simply do not know what to think with any confidence at all. In an effort "to provide guidance where guidance is needed," (*TJ*, 20/18) it is perfectly appropriate to appeal to our considered judgments. Rawls hypothesizes that the construction of the original position may help this effort. He submits the "hypothesis that the principles which would be chosen in the original position are identical with those that match our considered judgments." (*TJ*, 48/42) As Joshua Cohen points out, the choice from the original position "provide[s] a *unified rationale*" for the principles of justice, thus explaining both our provisional fixed points as well as providing answers to questions about which we are much less confident.[29] Rawls shows how such an effort to reach reflective equilibrium can be philosophically respectable, even if philosophers have no claim to an authoritative position in such a process.

SANDEL AND COMMUNITY

One of the most persistent criticisms of Rawls, and one that set the agenda for much work in political philosophy in the 1980s and 1990s, is that justice as fairness is objectionably individualist in one way or another. Many different criticisms advanced under this heading have been labeled forms of "communitarianism." These positions are often united by little more than their opposition to the alleged excessive individualism of justice as fairness, so it is not surprising that there are many disparate ways in which they think the value of community should properly be respected. I will consider only two of the most important of these criticisms. Both hold that community is in some important way left out or denigrated in justice as fairness, but

[28] Rorty holds that "the most philosophy can hope to do is to summarize our culturally influenced intuitions about the right thing to do in various situations" as a way of "heightening the sense of shared moral identity that brings us together in a moral community." ("Human Rights, Rationality, and Sentimentality," p. 171) Cf. "The Priority of Democracy to Philosophy" [1988] in *Objectivity, Relativism, and Truth: Philosophical Papers*, vol. I (Cambridge University Press, 1991), pp. 184–5.

[29] Cohen, "Democratic Equality," p. 729.

they disagree about how. Michael Sandel argues that the substantive value of participation in and identification with a community is neglected, while Michael Walzer claims that it should be left up to a community to determine which substantive values to embrace. There is a significant contrast between these two critiques. While Sandel argues that justice as fairness neglects a substantive good – the good of identification with one's community – Walzer denies that a theory of justice should be dictating any particular goods. Instead he holds that it should be left up to particular communities to decide which specific values to affirm. Sandel recognizes this contrast when he writes that "[t]he mere fact that certain practices are sanctioned by the traditions of a particular community is not enough to make them just."[30] On this basis, Sandel holds that he is "not, strictly speaking, communitarian."[31] But he clearly does hold that justice as fairness neglects community in an important way, so there is little harm done in applying this label as long as we keep in mind the diverse ways in which community can figure into a communitarian critique of justice as fairness.[32]

In 1982 Sandel's *Liberalism and the Limits of Justice* "first elicited the label 'communitarian' and brought about the retrospective recruitment of other writers to that flag."[33] Sandel aims to show that the vision of a just society as understood by deontological liberalism, and by justice as fairness in particular, is "flawed."[34] Indeed, he holds that "in some cases, justice is not a virtue but a vice."[35] This is a dramatic assertion, but for Sandel it follows from his claim that justice "is a remedial virtue, whose moral advantage consists in the repair it works on fallen conditions."[36] The need for justice itself reveals this morally fallen condition, and the achievement of justice, even if fully satisfied, cannot restore a superior pre-fallen state. Justice, according to Sandel, can indeed be a virtue, "but only conditionally, as physical courage is to a war zone."[37] It would be better to escape from the conditions that give rise to the need in the first place.

30 Sandel, *Liberalism and the Limits of Justice*, p. xi. 31 *Ibid.*, cf. p. 186.

32 I discuss this further in ch. 4 of *What's Left of Liberalism?*

33 Stephen Mulhall and Adam Swift, *Liberals and Communitarians*, 2nd edn. (Blackwell, 1996), p. 40.

34 Sandel, *Liberalism and the Limits of Justice*, p. 1. 35 *Ibid.*, p. 34.

36 *Ibid.*, p. 32. 37 *Ibid.*, p. 31.

The analogy to the war zone is telling, and other communitarians make use of it as well.[38] The thought is that concerns about justice emerge only when individuals think of themselves as isolated and indifferent, if not hostile, to one another. When individuals are conceived of in that way their relations can – at best – only be artificially mediated by principles of justice. Justice is only the "first virtue" in societies where "the resolution of conflicting claims among mutually disinterested parties is the most pressing social priority."[39] But this overlooks another supposedly more attractive possibility: that we abandon the valorization of choice above all else and recognize and value the unchosen, constitutive attachments that make us who we are. This approach avoids the "metaphysical embarrassment"[40] of the liberal individual, according to which our values are the products of choice and cannot implicate our identities. More importantly, as Sandel explains in later work, this flawed voluntarist model of the self leaves us unable to,

> make sense of our moral experience, because it cannot account for certain moral and political obligations that we commonly recognize, even prize. These include obligations of solidarity, religious duties, and other moral ties that may claim us for reasons unrelated to a choice. Such obligations are difficult to account for if we understand ourselves as free and independent selves, unbound by moral ties we have not chosen. Unless we think of ourselves as encumbered selves, already claimed by certain projects and commitments, we cannot make sense of these indispensable aspects of our moral and political experience.[41]

Recognizing our shared and unchosen constitutive commitments allows us to make sense of these moral virtues. It also undercuts the need for the virtue of justice.

There is a significant disagreement between Sandel and Rawls, but it may be obscured by a series of misinterpretations of Rawls's position. Sandel holds that for the argument from the original position to work, we must presuppose "the pictures of the unencumbered self, a self understood as prior to and independent of purposes and

[38] Alasdair MacIntyre, "Modern politics is civil war carried on by other means." (*After Virtue*, 2nd edn. (Notre Dame, 1984), p. 253).

[39] Sandel, *Liberalism and the Limits of Justice*, p. 30. [40] *Ibid.*, p. 14.

[41] Michael Sandel, *Democracy's Discontent* (Harvard University Press, 1996), pp. 13–14.

ends."[42] But the fact that the parties in the original position do not know their conception of the good does not imply that we do not. Nor does it imply that we cannot think of some of our ends and values as essential to our self-conceptions. Rawls himself notes this very point, referring to Royce's idea that "an individual says who he is by describing his purposes and causes, what he intends to do in his life." (*TJ*, 408/358) When Rawls comments that "the self is prior to the ends which are affirmed by it," (*TJ*, 560/491) he is not making a point about the depth of our identification with our goals. He is arguing against a teleological understanding of morality according to which there is one dominant good that ought to structure our deliberations and self-conception.

Far from holding the atomistic picture of society that Sandel and other communitarians attribute to him, Rawls takes pains to distance himself from it. As we saw in chapter 3, he distinguishes a well-ordered society of justice as fairness from the idea of a "private society." (*TJ*, 521/457) In such a society, human sociability is understood merely as the fact that we develop our abilities to speak and to think only in a social context and that coordinated activities often are mutually beneficial. Our deeper sociability is found in the idea of a social union, in which "human beings have in fact shared final ends and they value their common institutions and activities as good in themselves." (*TJ*, 522/458) Moreover, they value and appreciate the collective goods that can only be achieved because of the complementarity among the talents and abilities that individuals choose to develop and pursue. In addition to containing "countless social unions of many different kinds,"[43] (*TJ*, 527/462) a well-ordered society can itself also be understood as a special kind of social union – a social union of social unions. This implies that citizens of a well-ordered society share a common end, which it is not hard to identify: they share the goal of achieving and maintaining basic social justice.

This serves to highlight the real disagreement between Rawls and Sandel. Sandel suggests that the shared goal of just institutions simply is too thin to sustain a deep sense of identification and commitment.

[42] Michael Sandel, "The Procedural Republic and the Unencumbered Self," *Political Theory*, 12 (1984), p. 86.

[43] See also Rawls, *Political Liberalism*, p. 146, n. 13.

A superior alternative would be to overcome the disagreements that give rise to the need for justice in the first place. This is made clear at the conclusion of *Liberalism and the Limits of Justice*:

> justice finds its occasion because we cannot know each other, or our ends, well enough to govern by the common good alone. This condition is not likely to fade altogether, and so long as it does not, justice will be necessary. But neither is it guaranteed always to predominate, and in so far as it does not, community will be possible, and an unsettling presence for justice.[44]

Implicit in this view is the assumption that the need for justice is due primarily to epistemic deprivation. If we only knew "each other, or our ends, well enough" we could overcome the conflicts that necessitate appeal to the remedial virtue of justice.

However, a clearer recognition of our ends would not dissolve the need for justice unless we assume that our ends – our true ends, perhaps – would not conflict. Here we have a deep disagreement with Rawls, who holds that "it is, in general, a good thing that individuals' conceptions of their good should differ in significant ways." (*TJ*, 447/393) In *Political Liberalism* Rawls argues that the diversity of reasonable comprehensive doctrines is "the natural outcome of the activities of human reason under enduring free institutions. To see reasonable pluralism as a disaster is to see the exercise of reason under the conditions of freedom itself as a disaster."[45] The need for justice arises not because of our inability to "know each other, or our ends," or because of excessive selfishness or individualism, but because of the diversity of reasonable ends, which is itself the result of the exercise of reason in circumstances of freedom.

Principles of justice are needed to mediate fairly the conflicts among reasonable conceptions of the good. To do this, a conception of justice must not simply substitute one system of ends for all others. Certainly, it will posit certain necessary ends and rule out others as well as identify certain impermissible means. However, it must leave room for the diversity of goods that gives rise to the need for justice in the first place. Although the principles of justice must take precedence over specific conceptions of the good, this does not make them "all controlling." (*TJ*, 565/495) It is a mistake to think that

[44] Sandel, *Liberalism and the Limits of Justice*, p. 183.
[45] Rawls, *Political Liberalism*, pp. xxiv–xxv.

"once the principles of justice are given precedence, then there is a dominant end that organizes our life." (*TJ*, 465/495) In a well-ordered society unity is found in the shared conception of justice that citizens affirm. But it is not a "community" if by that we mean that there is a single comprehensive doctrine affirmed by all. Such a community "is no longer a political possibility for those who accept the constraints of liberty and toleration of democratic institutions."[46] Although a well-ordered society contains many such communities within it, it cannot be one itself without eliminating the conditions of freedom that give rise to many different and conflicting doctrines and values.

WALZER AND THE SOCIAL MEANING OF GOODS

A very different approach to community is found in the work of Michael Walzer. Unlike Sandel, Walzer does not question whether an increase in justice would be a moral improvement. However, Walzer holds that the demands of justice are relative to the values affirmed in particular communities. The problem with justice as fairness, he suggests, is that it is not sufficiently sensitive to the variations among the values affirmed by different societies. In effect, he argues, justice as fairness aims to impose its own external blueprint of a just society without sufficient sensitivity to the specific values affirmed in particular societies. In that sense, it is disconnected and undemocratic.[47]

For Walzer, "Justice is relative to social meanings."[48] In order to determine whether some good has been distributed justly, we must first identify the meaning of that particular good in the particular society in question. Only then can we judge whether the distribution of that good is consistent with its meaning. Different goods, with different meanings, must have different distributive mechanisms: "When meanings are distinct, distributions must be autonomous."[49] Thus, we get the idea of distinct "spheres of justice" corresponding to the different meanings of different goods. Injustice occurs when

[46] *Ibid.*, p. 201; cf. p. 40.

[47] See Walzer's claims that any effort to formulate principles of justice not based on local meanings is "an authoritarian business." ("Philosophy and Democracy," *Political Theory*, 9 (1981), p. 381)

[48] Michael Walzer, *Spheres of Justice* (Basic Books, 1983), p. 312.

[49] *Ibid.*, p. 10.

the distribution of a good is inconsistent with its meaning but is determined by – is "dominated by" – some other good from outside its sphere. For example, if an inequality in wealth, unobjectionable in itself, results in unequal political influence, one sphere unjustly dominates another. If political influence is determined by wealth, it is not being distributed according to its democratic meaning (that at least is its meaning in a democracy): "What democracy requires is that property should have no political currency, that it shouldn't convert into anything like sovereignty, authoritative command, sustained control over men and women."[50] An inequality in wealth is only unjust if it dominates the distribution of some other good.[51] (It is worth noting that Rawls, too, finds the influence of inequalities in wealth on political equality to be one of the most serious defects that contemporary liberal democracies face.)[52]

This account of justice, which Walzer calls "complex equality," tries to avoid imposing any distributive standard that is not based on the values endorsed by a particular society. As Richard Arneson notes, "This 'distribution according to social meanings' norm is an empty vessel, the content of which could be anything."[53] In order to fill this empty vessel and to generate a determinate standard, we need to identify the meaning of the good in question and to determine the corresponding distributive mechanism. Unfortunately, Walzer gives us very little help in understanding how to make such judgments, although his work is filled with numerous (often contentious) examples. Joshua Cohen points out that "[i]n all these cases the values of the political community *are identified through its practices*... The existing practices serve as evidence – in fact as the only evidence – for the account of the 'collective consciousness'."[54] If we base the meaning of a good on the existing distributive mechanism alone, it is hard to see how we could ever generate critical distance from the practices and conclude that some other distributive mechanism would

[50] *Ibid.*, p. 298.

[51] *Ibid.*, p. 107: "once we have blocked every wrongful exchange and controlled the sheer weight of money itself, we have no reason to worry about the answers the market provides."

[52] See *TJ*, 225–6/198–9; *Political Liberalism*, pp. lvi, 356–63.

[53] Richard Arneson, "Against 'Complex Equality'" in *Pluralism, Justice, and Equality*, David Miller and Michael Walzer, eds. (Oxford University Press, 1995), p. 240.

[54] Joshua Cohen, "Book Review of *Spheres of Justice*," *The Journal of Philosophy*, 83 (1986), p. 463.

be superior. We face what Cohen calls the "simple communitarian dilemma."[55]

Not all forms of immanent critique are conservative, and in an effort to avoid this dilemma we might appeal not only to the existing practices but also to the attitudes and understandings of the individuals in the society. After all citizens may be critical of their own institutions, and we might seek to explain such attitudes by claiming that the institutional mechanisms do not correspond to the meaning the good has for them. The problem is that virtually any good will have different meanings for different citizens. We cannot simply appeal to the shared understanding of the majority, even if there is one, for as Walzer observes, "a majority of the citizens . . . might well misunderstand the logic of their own institutions or fail to apply consistently the principles they professed to hold."[56] We will often – maybe even typically – be forced to conclude that some good does not have a single meaning in a society. In such a case, no distributive mechanism could possibly be just. If there are genuinely different interpretations of some good, Walzer argues, "then it might be (morally) necessary to work out a political accommodation. Politics must sometimes substitute for justice, providing a neutral frame within which a common life slowly develops."[57] It is unclear exactly what a "neutral frame" would be, but what is clear is that for Walzer justice is impossible to attain until "a common life" – by which he must mean a shared interpretation of the meaning of the good in question – has developed. The contrast with justice as fairness, which assumes a diversity of conceptions of the good, is once again clear.

Walzer's suggestion that justice as fairness is insensitive to differences among societies is a common one. There seems to be a widespread assumption that Rawls aims to identify a scheme of institutions that all societies must follow. This is a mistaken impression for at least three reasons. First, the parties in the original position do not directly select among various institutional schemes. The original position is designed to address "one of the most general of all choices which persons might make together, namely . . . the choice

[55] *Ibid.*, p. 464. [56] Walzer, *Spheres of Justice*, p. 99.

[57] Michael Walzer, "'Spheres of Justice': An Exchange," *New York Review of Books*, July 21, 1983, p. 44. Compare *Spheres of Justice*, p. 313.

of the first principles of a conception of justice which is to regulate all subsequent criticism and reform of institutions." (*TJ*, 13/11–12) These abstract principles, when combined with specific information regarding particular societies, specify a range of permissible institutional arrangements. The four-stage sequence allows us to incorporate information that is relevant to the application of the principles to particular societies. "In the original position the only particular facts known to the parties are those that can be inferred from the circumstances of justice." (*TJ*, 200/175) In the subsequent stages, however, "the general facts about their society are made available to them." (*TJ*, 200/175) This means that the decisions made at subsequent stages will not be universal in the way that the principles themselves are intended to be. Although a society will be just according to justice as fairness when it satisfies the two principles, different institutional mechanisms will do this most effectively (or even minimally adequately) in different circumstances.

Second, a just society will have a democratic political structure that allows it to make decisions for itself. Obviously, this provides the opportunity for different societies to make different decisions and to diverge from one another in significant ways. It also presents them with the possibility of making unjust decisions. This is because, as we have seen, "there is no scheme of procedural political rules which guarantees that unjust legislation will not be enacted." (*TJ*, 198/173) Is it acceptable for a society to make a democratic decision that departs from the requirements of the two principles? That depends on what is meant by "acceptable." On the one hand, Rawls holds that such a departure would be unjust – or at least it would not be fully just. On the other hand, as long as the injustice is not too great, a democratic decision may still be legitimate and therefore binding on citizens. While his most extensive discussion of legitimacy is found in *Political Liberalism*,[58] already in *A Theory of Justice* Rawls argued that "our natural duty to uphold just institutions binds us to comply with unjust laws and policies, or at least not to oppose them by illegal means as long as they do not exceed certain limits of injustice." (*TJ*, 354/311) Thus, the sense in which Rawls intends to "impose" limitations on a society's democratic decisions is very attenuated. A

[58] See, for example, pp. 216–17.

Rawlsian citizen will advocate decisions and policies in accordance with the two principles, but if a democratic polity makes a decision that she believes to be unjust, within certain limits she will continue to recognize the legitimacy of that decision.

Finally, turning to the issue of distributive justice more narrowly, Rawls does not believe that his principles require any specific allocation of goods to particular individuals. The specific allocation of goods is a matter of pure procedural justice. It is unpredictable, and we should not expect or demand that all societies that satisfy the principles of justice will be characterized by any single pattern of distribution. The next section will consider this issue in more depth.

NOZICK AND DISTRIBUTIVE EQUALITY

Within three years of the publication of *A Theory of Justice*, Robert Nozick, Rawls's colleague at Harvard, published *Anarchy, State, and Utopia*, a book that many people take to be the definitive libertarian reply to Rawls.[59] Nozick is critical of Rawls's egalitarianism and presents his so-called "entitlement theory of justice" as an alternative that emphasizes individual rights and liberty. This framing of the contrast led to a widespread image of a stand-off between those (like Rawls) who value equality and those (like Nozick) who value liberty. As Alasdair MacIntyre represents the dispute:

> Rawls makes primary what is in effect a principle of equality with respect to needs . . . Nozick makes primary what is a principle of equality with respect to entitlements. For Rawls how those who are now in grave need came to be in grave need is irrelevant; justice is made into a matter of present patterns of distribution to which the past is irrelevant.[60]

Furthermore, according to MacIntyre, no principled resolution of this dispute is possible, "[f]or how can a claim that gives priority to equality of needs be rationally weighed against one which gives priority to entitlements?"[61] Nozick himself encourages this interpretation, suggesting that any egalitarian conception of justice will objectionably interfere with individual liberty and rights.

[59] Nozick, *Anarchy, State, and Utopia*. [60] MacIntyre, *After Virtue*, p. 248.
[61] *Ibid.*, p. 249.

Nozick contrasts historical principles of distributive justice, of which his entitlement theory is one, with end-result principles. An end-result principle is "patterned if it specified that a distribution is to vary along with some natural dimension."[62] Nozick suggests that "[a]lmost every suggested principle of distributive justice is patterned: to each according to his moral merit, or needs, or marginal product, or how hard he tries, or the weighted sum of the foregoing, and so on."[63] And obviously equality is a pattern of distribution as well. Nozick does not find it surprising that Rawls would endorse a patterned principle of distributive justice, since "[a] procedure that founds principles of distributive justice on what rational persons who know nothing about themselves or their histories would agree to *guarantees that end-state principles of justice will be taken as fundamental.*"[64]

In contrast, Nozick's entitlement theory relies on historical principles that recognize that "past circumstances or actions of people can create differential entitlements or differential deserts to things."[65] The specification of the entitlement theory requires that we identify two principles. First, we need a principle for the just acquisition of goods that were previously not owned – a principle of "original acquisition." Second, we need a principle for the just transfer of goods that are already owned from one person to another. Then the entitlement theory simply says:

1. A person who acquires a holding in accordance with the principle of justice in acquisition is entitled to that holding.
2. A person who acquires a holding in accordance with the principle of justice in transfer, from someone else entitled to the holding, is entitled to the holding.
3. No one is entitled to a holding except by (repeated) applications of 1 and 2.[66]

Nozick acknowledges that additional principles will be necessary in order to correct violations of the principles of original acquisition and transfer. And strikingly, referring to the difference principle specifically, he suggests the possibility that "some patterned principles of distributive justice [may serve] as rough rules of thumb meant to approximate the general results of applying the principle

[62] Nozick, *Anarchy, State, and Utopia*, p. 156. [63] *Ibid.*, pp. 156–7.
[64] *Ibid.*, pp. 198–9. [65] *Ibid.*, p. 155. [66] *Ibid.*, p. 151.

of rectification of injustice."[67] Still, in the ideal, if there were no violations of the first two principles, the entitlement theory would not require that the distribution of goods conformed to any pattern.

Nozick supports the view that only an entitlement theory like his is consistent with liberty with his famous "Wilt Chamberlain" example. Under the heading "How liberty upsets patterns," he writes:

> suppose a distribution favored by one of these non-entitlement conceptions is realized. Let us suppose it is your favorite one and let us call this distribution D_1; perhaps everyone has an equal share, perhaps shares vary in accordance with some dimension you treasure. Now suppose that Wilt Chamberlain is greatly in demand by basketball teams, being a great gate attraction . . . The season starts, and people cheerfully attend his team's games; they buy their tickets, each time dropping a separate 25 cents of their admission price into a special box with Chamberlain's name on it. They are excited to see him play; it is worth the total admission price to them . . . Is he entitled to the income? Is this new distribution D_2, unjust?[68]

For Nozick, the answer is obvious, since under D_2 nobody has grounds to complain that they were treated unjustly: certainly not Chamberlain or the individuals who "were entitled to dispose of the resources to which they were entitled (under D_1)."[69] Nor are their grounds for third parties to complain: "After someone transfers something to Wilt Chamberlain, third parties *still* have their legitimate shares; *their* shares are not changed."[70] Nozick concludes that "no end-state principle or distributional patterned principle of justice can be continuously realized without continuous interference with people's lives."[71] Hence, it appears that a commitment to any egalitarian distributive principles really will conflict with a commitment to individual liberty.

Strictly speaking, however, Nozick is in no position to determine whether the distribution D_2 is just until we have specified the principles for original acquisition and just transfer. As Jonathan Wolff points out,

> The entitlement theory is not completely stated until we are told the precise content of Nozick's principles of justice in acquisition, transfer, and rectification, and so we should expect a detailed statement and justification of

[67] *Ibid.*, p. 231. [68] *Ibid.*, pp. 160–1. [69] *Ibid.*, p. 161. [70] *Ibid.* [71] *Ibid.*, p. 163.

Nozick's versions of these principles. But again at a crucial point, we are offered nothing like this.[72]

Nozick assumes that the transfers that occur in the Chamberlain example are consistent with any reasonable principle of just transfer because they are voluntary. But what exactly are the fans doing when they put 25 cents in the box? They are attempting to follow their society's rules for just transfer. Without such rules, there would be no mechanism for making this exchange. But Nozick cannot generate the rules of just transfer from some prior account of voluntary transfers, because without the rules no transfers would be possible at all – voluntary or otherwise. The mistake is clear when Nozick asks rhetorically, "[i]f the people were entitled to dispose of the resources to which they were entitled (under D_1), didn't this include their being entitled to give it to, or exchange it with, Wilt Chamberlain?"[73] This is a bluff. We don't know whether they are entitled to give it to Chamberlain until we know what the rules of just transfer are, and calling the transfer to Chamberlain "voluntary" does not answer this question. Nozick simply assumes without argument that property rights must include a right to transfer the full market value of the property. But this is not the only possible scheme of property rights and, in fact, is arguably in tension with Lockean principles that he claims as inspiration.[74]

Suppose, for example, we thought that individuals had the right to transfer not the full market value of their holdings but only 80 percent, with the remaining 20 percent transferred to the poorest

[72] Jonathan Wolff, *Robert Nozick: Property, Justice and the Minimal State* (Stanford University Press, 1991), p. 78.

[73] Nozick, *Anarchy, State, and Utopia*, p. 161.

[74] Specifically, Barbara Fried argues that "Lockean theory has been plagued from the start by the difficulty of justifying a private right to that portion of market price that reflects scarcity rents." ("Wilt Chamberlain Revisited: Nozick's 'Justice in Transfer' and the Problem of Market-Based Distribution," *Philosophy and Public Affairs*, 24 (1995), p. 230) See also Thomas Nagel, "Libertarianism without Foundations" [1975] in *Reading Nozick: Essays on "Anarchy, State, and Utopia,"* Jeffrey Paul, ed. (Blackwell, 1981), esp. pp. 200–2; and Lawrence Becker, "Against the Supposed Difference between Historical and End-State Theories," *Philosophical Studies*, 41 (1982). It is also worth noting that both Locke and Kant, whom Nozick sometimes cites as inspiration, rejected anything like Nozick's libertarian conception of property rights. See, for example, John Locke, *Two Treatises of Government* [1690], Peter Laslett, ed. (Cambridge University Press, 1960), p. 170 [I.42], and Immanuel Kant, *The Metaphysics of Morals* [1797], Mary Gregor, trans. (Cambridge University Press, 1996), p. 101 [Ak.6:326].

individuals in the society. If that were the case, each time 25 cents was dropped into Chamberlain's box, Chamberlain would only be entitled to 20 cents with the balance rightfully belonging to the poor. The crucial point is that this scheme would not involve violating the principle of just transfer. On the contrary, taxing Chamberlain's gross income would be required in order to follow the principle. To be sure, some transactions that were permissible under Nozick's libertarian scheme would be prohibited. This would be necessary in order to enforce the property rights of the poor under this alternative scheme. Furthermore, under this scheme all exchanges would be completely voluntary, and nobody's liberty (as Nozick conceives it) would be restricted. This is because Nozick holds that whether a restriction limits liberty depends on whether an individual had a right to perform the action in the first place.[75] But according to this principle of just transfer, fans do not have a right to transfer money to Chamberlain without also giving some to the least advantaged. It may be tempting to say with Nozick that "[p]atterned principles of distributive justice necessitate *re*distributive activities."[76] The thought is something like this: first, Chamberlain gets the full 25 cents, and then some of it is taken from him and given to someone else. But this is misleading. Although the 5 cents may be sitting in his box, under our revised transfer principle, he has no right to it. It belongs to the poor. If he were to fail to pay the tax that he owes, he would be stealing money from its rightful owners and engaging in an objectionable and unjust form of redistribution of goods from their rightful owners. It is no restriction on his liberty to prevent him from doing this.

The point of the previous paragraph was not to argue that a transfer principle that included a 20 percent tax would be superior to one without it. The point, rather, was that either principle could be part of an entitlement theory, and Nozick gives us no reason to prefer one over the other. He simply assumes that it is obvious which principles of acquisition and transfer (and perhaps of rectification) we should rely on. But it is not at all obvious. It is not even clear on what grounds we should declare one set of principles superior to another. As we have seen, the declaration cannot be based on the

[75] See, for example, Nozick, *Anarchy, State, and Utopia*, p. 262.

[76] *Ibid.*, p. 168, his emphasis.

claim that only one preserves our liberties while the other involves restrictions on our rights. We can only make such a determination after we know what our rights and liberties are – that is, after we know which principles should govern our acquisition and transfer of property.

By now it should be clear that Rawls is interested in answering the question that Nozick hardly even recognizes – what are the grounds on which we can declare one scheme of property rights more or less just than another? The principles of justice are to be used to evaluate rival institutional schemes, including economic institutions that specify the principles of just acquisition, transfer, and rectification of property. The principles of justice, including the difference principle, are not to be used to evaluate the distribution of goods directly. Rawls makes the point this way: "If it is asked in the abstract whether one distribution of a given stock of things to definite individuals with known desires and preferences is better than another, then there is simply no answer to this question." (*TJ*, 88/76) Once a just institutional scheme is in place, we rely on pure procedural justice to allocate specific shares to particular individuals: "the distribution that results will be just (or at least not unjust) whatever it is." (*TJ*, 304/267) Assuming the procedures are not violated, a large inequality would be unjust only if it undermined the fair value of the political liberties or interfered with fair equality of opportunity. Beyond this, a large inequality may be evidence that the basic structure is unjust if it seems likely that the least advantaged would do better under some other scheme. Although the difference principle makes reference to a pattern, justice as fairness is a historical theory according to Nozick's definition: "whether a distribution is just depends upon how it came about."[77] The disagreement between Rawls and Nozick is not about whether equality or liberty is more fundamental. Rather, it concerns which are the just institutions and procedures within which individuals and associations pursue their goals and acquire their specific entitlements. As Rawls puts it: "We have a right to our natural abilities and a right to whatever we become entitled to by taking part in a fair social process. The problem is to characterize this process."[78]

[77] *Ibid.*, p. 153.

[78] John Rawls, "A Kantian Conception of Equality" [1975] in Freeman, *Collected Papers*, p. 263, footnote excluded.

COHEN AND LUCK EGALITARIANISM

In recent years this focus on the basic structure and on pure procedural justice has led some critics to charge justice as fairness with being too timid and insufficiently egalitarian. The most prominent of these critics is G. A. Cohen. For Cohen, "justice cannot be a matter only of the state-legislated structure in which people act but is also a matter of the acts they choose within that structure, the personal choices of their daily lives."[79] Now from one point of view it may seem as though there is no real disagreement with Rawls here. Although he does not explore them much detail, Rawls agrees that principles for the evaluation of individual conduct "are an essential part of any theory of justice." (*TJ*, 108/93) But Rawls also holds that the principles appropriate to evaluating individual conduct are not necessarily the same principles that we use to evaluate the basic structure itself: "The principles of justice for institutions must not be confused with the principles which apply to individuals and their actions in particular circumstances. These two kinds of principles apply to different subjects and must be discussed separately." (*TJ*, 54–5/47) Cohen, in contrast, insists that principles of justice are those that concern the "just distribution of benefits and burdens in society" and that these apply "to the choices that people make *within* the legally coercive structures to which . . . [the] principles of justice (also) apply."[80] Furthermore, Cohen holds that when the difference principle is properly applied to both the basic structure and to individual conduct, it will sanction far less inequality than it would when applied to the basic structure alone. The effect of Rawls's limited application of his principles to the basic structure is to make his conception insufficiently egalitarian.

To see why this might be so, recall which inequalities the difference principle permits when it is applied only to the basic structure. The difference principle permits a structural inequality only when the least advantaged position has a higher expected share of primary goods than the least advantaged position would have under a scheme

[79] G. A. Cohen, *If You're an Egalitarian, How Come You're So Rich?* (Harvard University Press, 2000), p. 122.

[80] *Ibid.*

without the inequality. This will only be possible when the inequality generates a net increase in available primary goods and when everyone shares in this gain (although not equally). In *A Theory of Justice* Rawls mentions that this might be possible in some circumstances when the "better prospects act as incentives so that the economic process is more efficient, innovation proceeds at a faster pace, and so on." (*TJ*, 78/68) The point is not only, or even primarily, that people will work harder and produce more when there is an incentive. It is also possible for inequalities to promote social efficiency by putting "resources in the hands of those who can make the best social use of them."[81]

The problem, as Cohen sees it, is that whether an inequality works to everyone's advantage depends in part on the attitudes and preferences of the individuals in the society. For example, a society might consider providing an incentive to its most talented or efficient producers in an effort to induce them to work more (or harder) and thereby to increase the aggregate level of wealth in the society. If this increased the aggregate sufficiently, it might also be possible for everyone to share in the benefit even though the talented would gain more than others. The difference principle would endorse this inequality (at least in comparison with the baseline of equality without that incentive). But Cohen points out that this inequality is necessary only on the assumption that the talented would not do the additional (or harder) work without the greater reward. They could do the work without the incentive. And if they did so, the least advantaged would do even better, since they could share in the resources that would have been used as incentives to the talented. So it is only if we take the preferences of the talented as given that the incentive is necessary. Cohen holds that "an anti-egalitarian selfishness must be attributed to the more productive, as part of the explanation for why inequality is necessary, to the extent that it is indeed necessary."[82] The difference principle, when applied only to the basic structure, allows such objectionable selfishness to generate structural inequalities. In effect, a society that accepts the difference principle allows the talented to extort resources from the society by threatening to withhold their productive assets. If the talented were motivated by the difference

[81] Rawls, "A Kantian Conception of Equality," p. 257. See the discussion by Philippe Van Parijs, "Difference Principles" in Freeman, *The Cambridge Companion to Rawls*, especially pp. 203–4.

[82] Cohen, *If You're an Egalitarian . . .*, p. 121.

principle in their individual conduct, they would forgo the additional incentive, thereby maximally benefiting the least advantaged and maintaining a fully egalitarian distribution of goods. Only by applying egalitarian principles to individual choices as well as to the basic structure can we achieve a stronger and more consistent egalitarianism not held hostage to the unjust selfishness of the talented.

There are several things that can be said in reply, and the secondary literature contains many rich discussions of the issues.[83] My discussion will be brief and aim to bring out what I take to be the deeper contrast between Cohen and Rawls. First of all, nothing that Rawls says precludes us from making moral assessments of individual conduct. On the contrary, as I emphasized above, he holds that "[i]t is clear" that in addition to principles of justice that apply to the basic structure "a complete theory of right includes principles for individuals as well." (*TJ*, 108/93) If individuals are motivated to pursue their narrow self-interest to the exclusion of others, we can properly call them selfish and greedy. And if individuals trick or otherwise take advantage of others, by exploiting their ignorance, for example, we can properly say that they are unjust even if they do so within the limits of the law and the rules of a just basic structure. The question is whether the same principles that apply to the basic structure must also apply to individual conduct.

Second, the design of the basic structure is likely to have a significant effect on the ethos that guides individual conduct in the society. As Rawls points out, "the social system shapes the wants and aspirations that its citizens come to have. It determines in part the sort of persons they want to be as well as the sort of persons they are." (*TJ*, 259/229) The design of the basic structure must be sensitive to this role. Institutions "must be not only just but framed so as to encourage the virtue of justice in those who take part in them." (*TJ*, 261/231) In

[83] In addition to the works cited below, see Andrew Williams, "Incentives, Inequality, and Publicity," *Philosophy and Public Affairs*, 27 (1998); Jonathan Wolff, "Fairness, Respect, and the Egalitarian Ethos," *Philosophy and Public Affairs*, 27 (1998); Paul Smith, 'Incentives and Justice: G. A. Cohen's Egalitarian Critique of Rawls," *Social Theory and Practice*, 24 (1998); Thomas Pogge, "On the Site of Distributive Justice: Reflections on Cohen and Murphy," *Philosophy and Public Affairs*, 29 (2000); Samuel Scheffler, "What Is Egalitarianism?" Samuel Scheffler, "Is the Basic Structure Basic?" in *The Egalitarian Conscience: Essays in Honour of G. A. Cohen*, Christine Sypnowich, ed. (Oxford University Press, 2006); Kenneth Baynes, "Ethos and Institutions: On the Site of Distributive Justice," *Journal of Social Philosophy*, 37 (2006); Freeman, "Rawls and Luck Egalitarianism" in *Justice and the Social Contract*.

a well-ordered society, the kinds of objectionable extortion-like cases that Cohen criticizes are likely to be relatively infrequent.[84] This does not refute the critique, but it does somewhat blunt its force.

A more fundamental reply, however, emphasizes that incentives are required not only because of selfishness but simply because of the diversity of reasonable conceptions of the good. Consider a talented individual who demands an extra incentive to exercise his talent in a way that makes a greater than average contribution to the aggregate wealth of society. Now if that individual would be willing to work for less, but demands the incentive only because he knows that the society accepts the difference principle and would be willing to pay him, this looks like a kind of extortion. This is the image of individual selfishness that Cohen emphasizes. But suppose the individual demands the incentive because without it he would genuinely prefer a different career that was less productive. Suppose that he faces a choice between an emotionally bland but financially productive career as an investment advisor and an emotionally satisfying but economically less productive career as an artist. If the levels of pay were equal, he would genuinely prefer to be an artist. He would only be willing to pursue the more economically productive career if he received additional compensation. It would be misleading at best to say he was being selfish. The difference principle responds not only to selfishness but also to the wide variety of reasonable conceptions of the good. And if the considerations in the previous paragraph are correct, in a well-ordered society cases of selfishness will be relatively rare compared to reasonable preferences.

Cohen believes that once the objectionable cases of incentive inequalities are eliminated, "hardly any serious inequality"[85] would remain. Still, he thinks that some inequalities would remain because "each person has a right to pursue her own self-interest to some reasonable extent."[86] Such personal prerogatives make it morally permissible for individuals to pursue their own self-interest at the cost of the broader goals of social justice. Without a more complete account of these prerogatives, it is hard to assess Cohen's optimism that they

[84] See the discussion in Joshua Cohen, "Taking People as They Are?" *Philosophy and Public Affairs*, 30 (2001).

[85] Cohen, *If You're an Egalitarian . . .* , p. 124.

[86] *Ibid.*, p. 206, n. 24.

will not significantly interfere with his egalitarianism, although David Estlund has argued convincingly that these prerogatives should properly be wider than Cohen suggests.[87] But whatever the extent of permissible inequalities, the important point is that for Cohen such prerogatives are external constraints on the requirements of justice, imposed in deference to values other than justice itself. As Estlund explains, these prerogatives are "permissible deviation[s] in individual deliberation from what social justice would require considered alone."[88] Cohen has long held that it is appropriate to compromise justice when it competes with other important values.[89]

It is here that the fundamental contrast between Rawls and Cohen becomes clear. For Rawls, although the principles of justice are regulative, they are not "all controlling." (*TJ*, 565/495) There are many actions that, from the point of view of justice, "we are at liberty both to do and not to do." (*TJ*, 117/100) For Cohen, in contrast, justice will give individuals no discretion concerning any action that affects the distribution of goods in society. Such discretion can only come from external considerations that override and limit the demands of justice. The reason that justice cannot be indifferent to any individual action is because distributive justice, as Cohen conceives it, is a matter of bringing about an equal distribution of some good: "I take for granted that there is something which justice requires people to have equal amounts of, not no matter what, but to whatever extent is allowed by values which compete with distributive justice."[90] Any action that produces an inequality in this good is unjust. The injustice might not be terribly significant, and we may have good reasons based on other values to grant the individual a prerogative to engage in that injustice. But even small injustices are unjust. No action which

[87] See *ibid.*, p. 124; G. A. Cohen, "Incentives, Inequality, and Community," *The Tanner Lectures on Human Values*, 13, Grethe Peterson, ed. (University of Utah Press, 1992), pp. 302–3; David Estlund, "Liberalism, Equality, and Fraternity in Cohen's Critique of Rawls," *Journal of Political Philosophy*, 6 (1998).

[88] Estlund, "Liberalism, Equality, and Fraternity in Cohen's Critique of Rawls," p. 102.

[89] See, for example, G. A. Cohen "Robert Nozick and Wilt Chamberlain: How Patterns Preserve Liberty" [1977] in *Self-Ownership, Freedom and Equality* (Cambridge University Press, 1995), pp. 25, 31.

[90] G. A. Cohen, "On the Currency of Egalitarian Justice," *Ethics*, 99 (1989), p. 906. Compare his earlier statement that he is "persuaded that distributive justice, roughly speaking, *is* equality." ("Robert Nozick and Wilt Chamberlain," p. 25, n. 12)

affects the distribution of goods can be indifferent from the point of view of justice.

We need not be concerned with the precise formulation of this good, which Cohen calls "access to advantage."[91] It is enough to see that his basic orientation is a form of luck egalitarianism: "My root belief is that there is injustice in distribution when inequality of goods reflects not such things as differences in the arduousness of different people's labors, or people's different preferences and choices with respect to income and leisure, but myriad forms of lucky and unlucky circumstance."[92] Justice requires an equal distribution of goods, except where an individual's greater or lesser share can be traced to choices for which that individual is responsible. An individual "suffers from (bad) *brute luck* when his bad luck is not the result of a gamble or risk which he could have avoided."[93] Justice requires that we restore equality when an inequality is generated by brute luck. But it does not require that we correct inequalities that are the product of deliberate choice: "Brute luck is an enemy of just equality, and, since effects of genuine choice contrast with brute luck, genuine choice excuses otherwise unacceptable inequalities."[94]

I argued in the introduction that Rawls is not a luck egalitarian. He explicitly rejects the principle of redress, according to which all undeserved inequalities, such as unequal natural talents, must be compensated for. We can now see that this is connected to his reliance on pure procedural justice and his belief that justice is not a matter of bringing about any particular pattern of distribution that can be known in advance. This takes us to the heart of Rawls's understanding of justice. For Cohen, we first identify the allocation of goods that would be perfectly just and then determine the extent to which the state and other agents can effectively achieve it without jeopardizing other values.[95] For Rawls, in contrast, social justice is primarily a matter of how citizens should mediate their relations through the institutions of the basic structure. The application of the difference principle to the basic structure alone is not a half-hearted

91 Cohen, "On the Currency of Egalitarian Justice," p. 907.

92 Cohen, *If You're an Egalitarian . . .*, p. 130.

93 Cohen, "On the Currency of Egalitarian Justice," p. 908.

94 *Ibid.*, p. 931.

95 See, for example, G.A. Cohen, "Expensive Taste Rides Again" in *Dworkin and His Critics*, Justine Burley, ed. (Blackwell, 2004), pp. 4, 6–7, 17.

or compromised effort to achieve some goal that could possibly be achieved more efficiently or more completely by other means. It is not motivated by the end of eliminating the influence of luck or of bringing about any particular allocation of goods. The basic structure must satisfy the principles of justice in order to ensure that individuals are able to interact on the basis of reciprocity without domination or subordination. As Christine Korsgaard has pointed out, "[t]he subject matter of morality is not what we should bring about, but how we should relate to one another. If only Rawls has succeeded in escaping utilitarianism, it is because only Rawls has fully grasped this point."[96]

The principles of justice apply to the basic structure of society because that is what citizens collectively create, share, and impose on themselves to mediate their interactions. The virtue of justice is not a response to the arbitrariness of the world but rather to the need for fairness in the interactions among people with different and conflicting conceptions of the good. A just basic structure establishes fair terms of cooperation. Here it is useful to be reminded of Rawls's model of a property-owning democracy. The idea is that property is kept widely distributed in the society to allow individuals to pursue their various goals without being dependent on or subordinated to anyone else. This emphasis on fair terms of interaction informs not only the interpretation of the difference principle but all of justice as fairness. At its core, justice as fairness is about establishing and maintaining relations of reciprocity among the members of a society.

The virtue of social justice would not have a point if people did not have goals and ends that they took to be valuable and pursued individually and in groups. The problem of justice arises when these values diverge yet individuals want to establish fair terms of interaction with one another. The principles of justice cannot be all controlling without denying the independent value of the different conceptions of the good. Yet, a society can only have one basic structure – one set of basic institutions to mediate the interactions among citizens. Therefore, its design cannot be predicated on any single comprehensive doctrine but must be based on principles that all can recognize to be

[96] Christine Korsgaard, "The Reasons We Can Share" [1993] in *Creating the Kingdom of Ends* (Cambridge University Press, 1996), p. 275.

fair. A well-ordered society does not eliminate the influence of luck or achieve any particular pattern of the distribution of goods. Rather, it establishes terms of interaction that do not deny or undermine the diversity of reasonable doctrines, but achieves fairness that all can recognize. The lasting legacy of *A Theory of Justice* is that it helps us to see that fair terms of interaction are compatible with diverse values. Once we see that a just society is possible in conditions of pluralism, we can also see that it is worth struggling to achieve.

Bibliography

WORKS BY JOHN RAWLS

A Study in the Grounds of Ethical Knowledge (PhD Dissertation, Princeton University, 1950).

A Theory of Justice (Harvard University Press, 1971; rev. edn, 1999) (text citations to *TJ*).

"John Rawls: For the Record," *The Harvard Review of Philosophy* (spring, 1991).

Political Liberalism (Columbia University Press, 1993; expanded edn, 2005) (text citations to *PL*).

Collected Papers, Samuel Freeman, ed. (Harvard University Press, 1999).

The Law of Peoples (Harvard University Press, 1999).

Lectures on the History of Moral Philosophy, Barbara Herman, ed. (Harvard University Press, 2000).

Justice as Fairness: A Restatement, Erin Kelly, ed. (Harvard University Press, 2001).

"Afterword: A Reminiscence" in *Future Pasts: The Analytic Tradition in Twentieth-Century Philosophy*, Juliet Floyd and Sanford Shieh, eds. (Oxford University Press, 2001).

Lectures on the History of Political Philosophy, Samuel Freeman, ed. (Harvard University Press, 2007).

A Brief Inquiry into the Meaning of Sin and Faith: With "On My Religion," Thomas Nagel, ed. (Harvard University Press, 2009).

BOOKS AND COLLECTIONS ON RAWLS AND *A THEORY OF JUSTICE*

"Symposium on the Reception of Rawls in Europe," *European Journal of Political Theory*, 1 (2002).

Barry, Brian, *The Liberal Theory of Justice* (Oxford University Press, 1973).

Blocker, H. Gene and Elizabeth H. Smith, eds., *John Rawls's Theory of Social Justice* (Ohio University Press, 1980).

Daniels, Norman, ed., *Reading Rawls: Critical Studies on Rawls' 'A Theory of Justice'* (Stanford University Press, 1989).

Freeman, Samuel, *Justice and the Social Contract: Essays on Rawlsian Political Philosophy* (Oxford University Press, 2007).

Rawls (Routledge, 2007).

Freeman, Samuel, ed., *The Cambridge Companion to Rawls* (Cambridge University Press, 2003).

Kukathas, Chandran and Philip Pettit, *Rawls: "A Theory of Justice" and its Critics* (Stanford University Press, 1990).

Mandle, Jon, *What's Left of Liberalism? An Interpretation and Defense of Justice as Fairness* (Lexington Books, 2000).

Martin, Rex, *Rawls and Rights* (Kansas University Press, 1985).

Pogge, Thomas, *Realizing Rawls* (Cornell University Press, 1989).

John Rawls: His Life and Theory of Justice (Oxford University Press, 2007).

Richardson, Henry and Paul Weithman, eds., *The Philosophy of Rawls: A Collection of Essays*, 5 vols. (Garland, 1999).

Talisse, Robert, *On Rawls* (Wadsworth, 2001).

Wolff, Robert Paul, *Understanding Rawls: A Reconciliation and Critique of "A Theory of Justice"* (Princeton University Press, 1977).

OTHER WORKS CITED

"The Good of Justice as Fairness," *Times Literary Supplement*, May 5, 1972.

"Rawls is Given Two Awards for Book on Justice Theory," *The Harvard Crimson*, December 7, 1972, www.thecrimson.com/article.aspx?ref=245388.

Ackerman, Bruce, "Political Liberalisms," *The Journal of Philosophy*, 91 (1994).

Anderson, Elizabeth, "What is the Point of Equality?" *Ethics*, 109 (1999).

Arneson, Richard, "Against 'Complex Equality'" in *Pluralism, Justice, and Equality*, David Miller and Michael Walzer, eds. (Oxford University Press, 1995).

Barber, Benjamin, *The Conquest of Politics* (Princeton University Press, 1988).

Barry, Brian, "*Political Argument* after Twenty-Five Years: An Introduction to the Reissue" in *Political Argument: A Reissue with a New Introduction* (University of California Press, 1990).

Baynes, Kenneth, "Ethos and Institutions: On the Site of Distributive Justice," *Journal of Social Philosophy*, 37 (2006).

Becker, Lawrence, "Against the Supposed Difference between Historical and End-State Theories," *Philosophical Studies*, 41 (1982).

Berlin, Isaiah, "Does Political Theory Still Exist?" in Laslett and Runciman, *Philosophy, Politics and Society* (second series).

Brandt, Richard, *A Theory of the Good and the Right* (Oxford University Press, 1979).

Clark, Barry and Herbert Gintis, "Rawlsian Justice and Economic Systems," *Philosophy and Public Affairs*, 7 (1978).

Cohen, G. A., "Robert Nozick and Wilt Chamberlain: How Patterns Preserve Liberty" [1977] in *Self-Ownership, Freedom and Equality* (Cambridge University Press, 1995).

"On the Currency of Egalitarian Justice," *Ethics*, 99 (1989).

"Incentives, Inequality, and Community," *The Tanner Lectures on Human Values*, 13, Grethe Peterson, ed. (University of Utah Press, 1992).

If You're an Egalitarian, How Come You're So Rich? (Harvard University Press, 2000).

"Expensive Taste Rides Again" in *Dworkin and His Critics*, Justine Burley, ed. (Blackwell, 2004).

Cohen, Joshua, "Book Review of *Spheres of Justice*," *The Journal of Philosophy*, 83 (1986).

"Democratic Equality," *Ethics*, 99 (1989).

"Taking People as They Are?" *Philosophy and Public Affairs*, 30 (2001).

"For a Democratic Society" in Freeman, *The Cambridge Companion to Rawls*.

"The Importance of Philosophy: Reflections on John Rawls," *South African Journal of Philosophy*, 32 (2004).

Cohen, Marshall, "Review of *A Theory of Justice*," *New York Times Book Review*, July 16, 1972.

Dewey, John, "The Need for a Recovery of Philosophy" [1917] in *The Essential Dewey*, vol. 1, Larry Hickman and Thomas Alexander, eds. (Indiana University Press, 1998).

"Experience, Knowledge and Value: A Rejoinder" [1939] in *The Philosophy of John Dewey*, Paul Schilpp and Lewis Hahn, eds., 3rd edn. (Open Court, 1989).

Dworkin, Ronald, "John Rawls," *The Harvard Review of Philosophy*, 11 (2003).

Eberle, Christopher, *Religious Conviction in Liberal Politics* (Cambridge University Press, 2002).

Elster, Jon, *Local Justice: How Institutions Allocate Scarce Goods and Necessary Burdens* (Russell Sage Foundation, 1992).

English, Jane, "Justice between Generations," *Philosophical Studies*, 31 (1977).

Estlund, David, "Liberalism, Equality, and Fraternity in Cohen's Critique of Rawls," *Journal of Political Philosophy*, 6 (1998).

Freeman, Samuel, "Congruence and the Good of Justice" in Freeman, *Justice and the Social Contract*.

"Rawls and Luck Egalitarianism" in Freeman, *Justice and the Social Contract*.

"Frontiers of Justice: The Capabilities Approach vs. Contractarianism," *Texas Law Review*, 85 (2006).

Fried, Barbara, "Wilt Chamberlain Revisited: Nozick's 'Justice in Transfer' and the Problem of Market-Based Distribution," *Philosophy and Public Affairs*, 24 (1995).

Galston, William, *Liberal Purposes: Goods, Virtues, and Diversity in the Liberal State* (Cambridge University Press, 1991).

Gauthier, David, *Moral by Agreement* (Oxford University Press, 1986).

Gray, John, "Contractarian Method, Private Property and the Market Economy" in *Liberalisms: Essays in Political Philosophy* (Routledge, 1989).

Gregory, Eric, "Before the Original Position: The Neo-Orthodox Theology of the Young John Rawls," *Journal of Religious Ethics*, 35 (2007).

Habermas, Jürgen, "Life-Forms, Morality and the Task of the Philosopher" [1984] in *Autonomy and Solidarity*, rev. edn., Peter Dews, ed. (Verso, 1992).

Moral Consciousness and Communicative Action, Christian Lenhardt and Shierry Weber Nicholsen, trans. (MIT Press, 1990).

Hampton, Jean, "Contracts and Choices: Does Rawls Have a Social Contract Theory?" *Journal of Philosophy*, 77 (1980).

Hare, R. M., "Rawls' Theory of Justice" [1973] in Daniels, *Reading Rawls*.

"Ethical Theory and Utilitarianism" in *Utilitarianism and Beyond*, Amartya Sen and Bernard Williams, eds. (Cambridge University Press, 1982).

Harsanyi, John, "Can the Maximin Principle Serve as a Basis for Morality? A Critique of John Rawls's Theory" [1975] in *Essays on Ethics, Social Behavior, and Scientific Explanation* (D. Reidel, 1976).

Hart, H. L. A., "Rawls on Liberty and Its Priority" [1973] in Daniels, *Reading Rawls*.

"Between Utility and Rights" [1979] in *Essays in Jurisprudence and Philosophy* (Oxford University Press, 1983).

Kant, Immanuel, *The Metaphysics of Morals* [1797], Mary Gregor, trans. (Cambridge University Press, 1996).

Kearns, Deborah, "A Theory of Justice and Love – Rawls on the Family," *Politics*, 16 (1987).

Korsgaard, Christine, "The Reasons We Can Share" [1993] in *Creating the Kingdom of Ends* (Cambridge University Press, 1996).

Krouse, Richard and Michael McPherson, "Capitalism, 'Property-Owning Democracy,' and the Welfare State" in *Democracy and the Welfare State*, Amy Gutmann, ed. (Princeton University Press, 1988).

Larmore, Charles, *The Morals of Modernity* (Cambridge University Press, 1996).

Laslett, Peter, Introduction in Laslett, *Philosophy, Politics and Society*.

Laslett, Peter, ed., *Philosophy, Politics and Society* (Blackwell, 1956).

Laslett, Peter and W. G. Runciman, eds., *Philosophy, Politics and Society* (second series), (Blackwell, 1964).

Locke, John, *Two Treatises of Government* [1690], Peter Laslett, ed. (Cambridge University Press, 1960).

MacIntyre, Alasdair, *After Virtue*, 2nd edn (Notre Dame, 1984).

Mandle, Jon, "Having It Both Ways: Justification and Application in Justice as Fairness," *Pacific Philosophical Quarterly*, 75 (1994).

"Justice, Desert, and Ideal Theory," *Social Theory and Practice*, 23 (1997).

"The Reasonable in Justice as Fairness," *Canadian Journal of Philosophy*, 29 (1999).

Meade, J. E., *Liberty, Equality and Efficiency* (New York University Press, 1993).

Mill, J. S., *Considerations on Representative Government* in *On Liberty and Other Essays*, John Gray, ed. (Oxford University Press, 1991).

Millgram, Elijah, *Ethics Done Right: Practical Reasoning as a Foundation for Moral Theory* (Cambridge University Press, 2005).

Mulhall, Stephen and Adam Smith, *Liberals and Communitarians*, 2nd edn. (Blackwell, 1996).

Nagel, Thomas, "Rawls on Justice" [1973] in Daniels, *Reading Rawls*.

"Libertarianism without Foundations" [1975] in *Reading Nozick: Essays on "Anarchy, State, and Utopia,"* Jeffrey Paul, ed. (Blackwell, 1981).

Mortal Questions (Cambridge University Press, 1979).

"Rawls and Liberalism" in Freeman, *The Cambridge Companion to Rawls*.

Nozick, Robert, *Anarchy, State, and Utopia* (Basic Books, 1974).

Okin, Susan, *Justice, Gender and the Family* (Basic Books, 1989).

Parekh, B., "Reflections on Rawls's Theory of Justice," *Political Studies*, 20 (1972).

Partridge, P. H., "Politics, Philosophy, Ideology," *Political Studies*, 9 (1961).

Pogge, Thomas, "On the Site of Distributive Justice: Reflections on Cohen and Murphy," *Philosophy and Public Affairs*, 29 (2000).

Posner, Richard, *The Problematics of Moral and Legal Theory* (Harvard University Press, 1999).

Ron, Amit, "Visions of Democracy in 'Property-Owning Democracy': Skelton to Rawls and Beyond," *History of Political Thought*, 29 (2008).

Rorty, Richard, "The Priority of Democracy to Philosophy" [1988] in *Objectivity, Relativism, and Truth: Philosophical Papers*, vol. I (Cambridge University Press, 1991).

"Human Rights, Rationality, and Sentimentality" [1993] in *Truth and Progress: Philosophical Papers*, vol. III (Cambridge University Press, 1998).

Sachs, David, "How to Distinguish Self-Respect from Self-Esteem," *Philosophy and Public Affairs*, 10 (1981).

Samuelson, Robert, "Faculty Shelves Draft Resolution after Debating for Hour and Half," *The Harvard Crimson*, January 11, 1967, www.thecrimson.com/article.aspx?ref=270764.

Sandel, Michael, "The Procedural Republic and the Unencumbered Self," *Political Theory*, 12 (1984).

Democracy's Discontent (Harvard University Press, 1996).

Liberalism and the Limits of Justice, 2nd edn. (Cambridge University Press, 1998).

Schaller, Walter, "Rawls, the Difference Principle, and Economic Inequality," *Pacific Philosophical Quarterly*, 79 (1998).

Scheffler, Samuel, "What is Egalitarianism?" *Philosophy and Public Affairs*, 31 (2003).

"Is the Basic Structure Basic?" in *The Egalitarian Conscience: Essays in Honour of G. A. Cohen*, Christine Sypnowich, ed. (Oxford University Press, 2006).

Schwartz, Adina, "Moral Neutrality and Primary Goods," *Ethics*, 83 (1973).

Singer, Peter, "Sidgwick and Reflective Equilibrium," *The Monist*, 58 (1974).

Smith, Michael, *The Moral Problem* (Blackwell, 1994).

Smith, Paul, "Incentives and Justice: G. A. Cohen's Egalitarian Critique of Rawls," *Social Theory and Practice*, 24 (1998).

Sobel, David, "Full Information Accounts of Well-Being," *Ethics*, 104 (1994).

Van Parijs, Philippe, "Difference Principles" in Freeman, *The Cambridge Companion to Rawls*.

Walzer, Michael, "Philosophy and Democracy," *Political Theory*, 9 (1981).

Spheres of Justice (Basic Books, 1983).

"'Spheres of Justice': An Exchange," *New York Review of Books*, July 21, 1983.

Weldon, T. D., "Political Principles" in Laslett, *Philosophy, Politics and Society*.

Williams, Andrew, "Incentives, Inequality, and Publicity," *Philosophy and Public Affairs*, 27 (1998).

Williams, Bernard, "A Fair State," *London Review of Books*, May 13, 1993.

Wolff, Jonathan, *Robert Nozick: Property, Justice and the Minimal State* (Stanford University Press, 1991).

"John Rawls: Liberal Democracy Restated" in *Liberal Democracy and Its Critics*, April Carter and Geoffrey Stokes, eds. (Polity, 1998).

"Fairness, Respect, and the Egalitarian Ethos," *Philosophy and Public Affairs*, 27 (1998).

Wolterstorff, Nicholas, "The Role of Religion in Decision and Discussion of Political Issues" in *Religion in the Public Square: The Place of Religious Convictions in Political Debate*, Robert Audi and Nicholas Wolterstorff, eds. (Rowman and Littlefield, 1997).

Index